The Family Snitch

The Family Snitch

A Daughter's Memoir of Truth and Lies

Francesca Fontana

STEERFORTH PRESS
LEBANON, NEW HAMPSHIRE

For information about permission to reproduce
selections from this book, write to:
Steerforth Press, #1063, 254 Plainfield Rd Unit 11
West Lebanon, NH 03784

Cataloging-in-Publication Data is available from the Library of Congress

ISBN 978-1-58642-422-0

Printed in the United States of America

The authorised representative in the EEA is eucomply OÜ, Pärnu mnt. 139b-14,
11317, Tallinn, Estonia, hello@eucompliancepartner.com, +33757690241

1 3 5 7 9 10 8 6 4 2

For Mia,
the greatest love of my life

CONTENTS

You, little ones, if you were old enough
to understand, there is much I'd tell you.

. . .

Pray god you find a better life than mine,
the father who begot you.

Sophocles, *Oedipus the King*

(translated by Robert Fagles)

1

_____

Where I Started

Autumn in Oregon was hopeless. The gray skies were one thing, the rain was another — a few Midwestern thunderstorms worth of rainfall doled out over months of torturous drizzle. There wasn't a more lush time for all the Doug firs, I'd give you that. But I don't remember all that beauty. I remember the chill that set in and stayed, the interminable dampness, the stench of a wet dog.

I don't know if that is how it would feel to me now, if I were to go back. But that's how it felt to me then, so that's how it was. Hopeless.

I haven't gone back to Eugene since the day I graduated. My beat-up Honda was packed by the time crowds of green robes and tassels lined the streets outside the campus bars. I took my diploma and ran.

My years in Eugene were defined by a fixation upon fact. I was there to study journalism, to earn the degree that cost me thousands of dollars a term, to become the first in my family to go to college. I didn't grow up with some great passion for the Fourth Estate — I wanted a job with health insurance.

But journalism grew on me, quickly and naturally. What appealed to me was the clear-cut nature of journalistic truth: You wrote only what you knew beyond a shadow of a doubt to be true. This truth was an assembly of fact that, while not absolute, was verifiable, objective, and unimpeachable. All I had to be was a fly on the wall of the world.

Even matters of gray area had black-and-white solutions. Say that, in your reporting, you discovered discrepancies between the accounts of two reliable parties, two versions of some detail of some event. If it was an important detail, you presented the reader with both versions, side by side. If it was not, you threw it out.

My mind thrived in dealing solely with concrete facts and tossing any bias, opinion, or unsubstantiated claim. If ever too many questions floated up — *Can a story be factual and not true? Or true and not factual, like a memory? What if your honest-to-God memory deviates from someone else's, or from any verifiable facts, and the meaning of the rest of your life is piled up on top of it? Does that just mean you're wrong?* — I shoved them down.

Only now, removed by time and distance, can I see my own blind spots — the facts I chose to ignore.

Let's take one autumn in particular, the fall of my junior year. Here's a fact: Every day of those months was not dismal and rainy. There were days when the clouds parted and the sun lit up the fallen leaves. But those days never stuck in my memory; I don't recall them, so they never happened. All I have of those months is the cold, the wet, and the fear.

I had no name for the fear. I knocked on wood each time I thought of my mother dying, or my brother dying, or me dying. At first the knocks came in sets of three. Then it was six, then twelve. Then three sets of twelve, then six sets, then twelve sets. In class, I tried to avoid attracting attention as I drummed my fingers on the table. I learned to improvise. I kept a few pencils for exams in the front pouch of my backpack; they were always within reach and would work in a pinch. They were wood, weren't they? Otherwise, if I had to, I'd find a reason to wander over near a tree or wooden sign pole and get close enough to brush my knuckles against it, casually, as if it were natural.

When I wasn't knocking, I picked at calluses real and imagined. I peeled back hangnails. I dug into the skin under my sleeves or at the nape of my neck. Sometimes, when I snuck my hand back to my lecture notes, I saw blood pooled under my fingernails. I wiped them on my jeans. No one ever seemed to notice.

There were other rituals. Each night I spent an hour at my desk, using scratch paper to draw out the same calculations over and over. I added up how many scholarship dollars I received for the term, how many of those dollars were left in my bank account after class registration, and how many more months of rent and textbooks and the occasional meal those dollars would cover. Then I flipped the page over and recorded up-to-the-minute balances of my bank accounts, which I checked a minimum of five times between morning and night. It wasn't the numbers that comforted me so much as the act of checking again and again, conjuring up the sums that told me I was safe.

I had no practical excuse for all the bookkeeping, or the picking, or the knocking. The fear had no basis in fact. But tension filled my bones like static until I gave it a release.

One night during that miserable autumn, I was blindsided. My boyfriend had come home to our shared apartment, washed the dishes, and left for the final time. *I was blindsided* — that's what I told myself and the few friends I had to confide in. That's what I chose to believe. But now, I check the facts.

Justin asked me out when we were in high school, back home in Portland. We met in choir class. Everyone said we made an attractive couple. We contrasted each other in a way that many find visually compelling: his blue eyes and light hair, mine all dark. I liked that he had all the traits I lacked. I told him I loved him far too soon, but he was the one who said it first.

We followed each other to the University of Oregon. During our sophomore year, we decided to ditch the campus dorms and leased a small apartment in an old complex called Eugene Manor. It was not, in fact, majestic. The building boasted threadbare carpet and an antique gated elevator that lurched and squealed at every stop. I chose to romanticize its quaintness and its age. Really, its sole selling point was its distance from noisy Greek row, and from all of the newly constructed apartments that my classmates' parents shelled out for. I hated all of it; I hated any reminder of where I was and how I fit into my surroundings; I hated everything I didn't have.

The summer before our junior year, everyone was talking about the Big One: the super earthquake scientists expected to ravage the Northwest at any moment. I'd read about it, like everyone else, in *The New Yorker*. Our postwar complex was built to stand a fighting chance against atomic bombs, not earthquakes. The dread consumed me. I cried in quick gasps at least once a week at the thought of debris burying me alive in a five-hundred-square-foot tomb.

Justin knew our relationship was over by the end of that summer. I made us move into a wooden town house on the outskirts of Eugene, the kind of structure that would be less likely to kill us when — not if — the Big One hit. He'd tried to break up with me as we packed up the bedroom at Eugene Manor. I didn't let him. I told him the feeling would pass. I told him I would get better.

To make good on my promise, I went to a therapist at the university's health center, where each student was entitled to ten free sessions. She thought I sounded depressed. She thought I was showing some obsessive-compulsive tendencies. She emailed me a couple of MP3 files: guided meditations.

Then I got a physical. The doctor put me on fifty milligrams of Zoloft. My panic attacks eased in physical severity — my hands stopped going numb every time — but they never went away.

Then I took a hard look at myself and at the relationship I was so desperate to save. What was I bringing to the table here? And for that matter, what was he? During that summer, I had started to resent our contrasts, the differences between us. Justin was naive, privileged, unfocused, at risk of becoming stunted. I was self-righteous in my poverty and my suffering, and I wasn't shy anymore in telling him exactly what I thought of his defects. I was encouraging him to grow, I told myself, but I knew deep down I was just being mean. His immaturity embarrassed me in public; my anger scared him in private.

That October, after we'd unpacked the last of our moving boxes, just as the rain began and never let up, Justin handed me a key. It was a copy, for a studio apartment next to campus. *His* new apartment. We weren't breaking up, he insisted; he was just moving out for a while. I'd have the spare key, and we'd each get some much-needed distance. I took the key, put it on my lanyard, and believed him. He dumped me days later, sometime between my twenty-first birthday and Halloween. That night, when he came home and did the dishes and left, I was stupid enough to be surprised. *Blindsided.* Now I see it differently. I shake my head. Where, then, was my reporter's eye?

It's a fact that I lost weight rapidly in the days that followed. I stopped trusting fresh produce not to make me sick with some foodborne illness. I ate what I could of cheap canned food. I struggled to clean the plates Justin and I had bought together, just like I struggled to do anything that required standing up. They piled up in the sink, and the ants came in swarms until I threw the whole set away. I explained away my absent appetite and loosening jeans before anyone had a chance to ask questions I didn't want to answer. When I went home to Portland for a visit, I noticed the crease in my mother's brow. I ignored its meaning. While she was busy in another room, I dug her scale out of its old hiding place and stepped on.

I still remember the number I saw that day, even as the years accumulate between that cold, wet autumn and the one I find myself in now. I saw that number not too long ago, on my own scale, in my own home. I wasn't surprised to see it again. I knew I'd been losing weight. My husband watched me cry over a plate of pasta I didn't prepare myself and its uncertain contents. For weeks at a time, I ate only protein bars, string cheese, and bananas, each protected from the world's contaminants by its wrapper. When he approached me with concern, I didn't know what to say. I had no words for the fear, no more than I'd had back in Eugene, all those years ago.

But back in Eugene, I lived alone. I answered to no one, and the fear flourished.

After the breakup, sometime around Halloween, I read online that smiling could help reverse-engineer a good mood. I never interrogated the science behind the phenomenon. Each time I stepped out into the unforgiving wet, I yanked up the corners of my mouth like a marionette. I kept them taut on my long walk to campus until eventually, however many blocks later, I forgot about the experiment. The smiles never stuck, and I never felt much better. But I did it anyway.

I managed to keep up appearances in my classes for a while, and I found some small sources of hope. For one, my reporting class that term was taught by the journalism school's newest professor. Brent — never Professor Walth; he refused the honorific — had once worked at *The Oregonian*. He had won a Pulitzer. My friends at the school newspaper sang his praises; he'd been their editor during their summer internships in Portland. When I found out he was joining the faculty, I set three alarms for the minute fall registration opened. I *had* to be in his class.

Brent recognized me on the first day. I still don't quite know how he managed that — the only widely accessible photo of myself that I could think of was on a looping slideshow on the journalism building's first floor, celebrating the year's scholarship recipients. It was a little embarrassing, whenever I came face-to-face with my own goofy, forced grin on my way to class.

I, of course, recognized him from the J-school's press release about his arrival, and from his new faculty page. It was a faithful portrait: He still sported a beard, flecked with gray, and wore a brown blazer and tie. Students were filing into the computer lab and rolling their chairs into a semicircle as he made small talk. He stepped over to me.

"Are you Francesca Fontana?"

For a moment, I was mortified. I thought I knew what was coming next. He was going to ask me, softly but sternly, to leave. There had been some administrative error — I was not, in fact, registered for his class, and one of his actual students needed to take my seat.

That wasn't what he said. Brent told me he'd seen my byline in the local paper over the summer; I did good work. I was buzzing for the rest of the day.

My admiration of Brent wasn't just born from a bit of flattery or out of professional awe. It became apparent to me after only a couple of classes that he truly gave a shit — about our craft and our industry, and about us. He wasn't like some of the professors I knew who coasted on their dazzling CVs and left students hanging during office hours they never bothered to keep. Nor was he like the ones who seemed *too* accessible to their students, who seemed to keep a clique of favorites eating out of their hands.

Brent didn't give us busywork or demand hours of reading from some expensive textbook he authored himself. He had us read Orwell's "Why I Write." He spoke deliberately, with a quiet humor. And it was in his class that, for once, I let myself think of my future. I rarely considered it except in vague abstractions: *Once I'm done with school, once I get a job, once I'm out of this shithole, I will find a way to be happy.* In fleeting moments, I hoped that one day, my miserable present would be reduced to mere exposition — if, of course, it ever ended.

I didn't recognize myself anymore. That hopeless autumn was where I started. All that came before — stretching back to when I was small, when everyone called me Frankie, not Francesca — that was someone else. A fault line had ruptured, and I was set adrift from that long stretch of life that came before. It didn't belong to me now. I watched it grow smaller in the distance, and I couldn't get it back.

"Okay, who else should we look up?"

"Jared Fogle."

"The Subway guy? All right, let's see."

There were a few laughs as Brent typed the suggestion into the search bar. He read out the results from PACER, the federal court record database. We sat in our usual semicircle in the computer lab, watching Brent's cursor move along the list projected on the screen.

"Here it is. Fogle, Jared S. That *DFT* stands for 'defendant.' *USA v. Fogle*, filed on August 19, 2015."

Beside me, a girl took notes. We were preparing for an upcoming class project that required us to research Oregon politicians using public records. I wrote nothing. I had closed my notebook the second I heard Brent introduce the lesson. The public database contained federal court cases from all over the United States. You could find any file on anyone who was in there, so long as you knew how to spell their name.

In a few clicks, he showed us the docket for Fogle's case. We read the first filing that laid out the charges against the former sandwich spokesman, including distribution and receipt of child pornography and traveling to engage in illicit sexual conduct with a minor. I clocked the price displayed on the screen: $1.20 for access to a twelve-page document. I wondered how quickly those fees added up.

A few days later, I went to Brent's office. He asked what he could do for me. It came out in a stutter: Could I use his PACER account to look up a criminal case I was interested in?

Of course, he said. He couldn't give me his login, but we could look it up right now. All he needed was the case number, which I didn't know, or the defendant's name, which I did.

"Great. Who is it?"

"Albert Fontana."

I never called him Albert. I never called him Dad, either. In my head, he was always Al. If I needed his attention, I didn't know what to call him. I tapped him on the shoulder instead.

Al remembered everything. If he's telling you a story, he knows every detail: dates, ages, what people were wearing. I only really noticed it after that day in Brent's office, when I called my dad for the first time in years. He still lived in Chicago, where I was from. We'd been semi-estranged. It was complicated. I'll explain later.

The phone call was awkward at first, but Al made no mention of the silence that had grown between us. He answered the phone like he always did. *"Hey baby girl, how's it goin'. You good?"* It wasn't long before he launched into stories about the past. I was surprised by the details he tossed out with such ease, as if my baptism or his sister's first wedding had only just happened.

"Yeah, I'll tell you anything you want," he repeated between retellings of tee-ball games and afternoons spent by my grandmother's pool. I asked if I could call him again sometime soon, to hear about his life, his memories, for a project I was working on. He agreed.

He said he'd tell me anything I wanted, but could I believe any of the things he said? I thought his impeccable recall could be a sign that his stories were credible. I knew some of the facts, like my mom's birth date, were correct. But what about all the rest?

Maybe he's making it all up, I thought. *Or maybe he* thinks *it's true. Maybe his "memory" is all just the stories he tells himself.* I waved the doubt away and tried to keep an open mind, despite all I knew of him.

In flipping through my recollections of my father, the same themes turned up again and again. Al wasn't a fixture in my daily life as a kid. He was more like a special guest. Even during the brief years that Mia and I lived with him, until we left him when I was five, I have two or three memories of him. The rest is all Mia: fixing us dinner in our kitchen; reading *Sleep Book* by Dr. Seuss to me as I dozed on her shoulder; combing my hair into a ponytail before school; making me laugh in the grocery store parking lot, the sun setting behind her. My mother was the grounding center of my world.

What I do remember of Al reads like standard fare for a deadbeat dad. He was unreliable. He always left me waiting. I'd be standing in the goalie box at a soccer game, scanning the crowd for his giant frame, or sitting at the front window at home — the house in the suburbs where Mia and I lived together — waiting to be picked up for one of his weekly visits. If he showed up, he was late. Sometimes he didn't show at all. Mia was the one who came to school performances, read my report card, knew what I liked for breakfast, kissed me good night.

There's a photograph of Mia and me on a swing set — after one of my soccer games, I think it was. She and I are smiling, squinting under the sun. In the background, over my shoulder, is a man on a bench. I'd seen this photo dozens of times, going through the family photos, yet I never noticed him before. It was Al, unaware of the camera, squinting but not smiling, part of the image but not part of the scene. Peripheral.

Yup, *peripheral*. That was my dad, all right. He wasn't totally checked out; he had some of the basics down. He knew our address, the house I lived in with Mia. He knew my birthday.

He knew I wouldn't eat meat on pizza. That was pretty much it.

But I was a kid. I didn't know any different, so I just assumed that was how it went when you had divorced parents. Though Al and Mia were never married, so they were never actually divorced. When I was little, I thought *divorce* was what you called it when your parents broke up. Eventually I learned the difference.

Mia married Keith when I was seven, a year or so after she and I had left my dad. Keith was nothing like Al: tall, fair, bald, with a soft voice and a goatee.

Al got to see me on Wednesdays after school and every other weekend. Sometimes Mia would come outside when the truck pulled up. My parents would make conversation. My dad would pull out a wad of cash held together with a rubber band, peel off a few bills, and hand them over to my mom. She called it child support. Sometimes he gave her an envelope instead of cash. Sometimes he gave her excuses. Al's payments, it seemed to me, were never on time, never in full.

Keith came outside to meet my dad only once, at least that I can remember. He tried to smile and introduce himself. Al leaned against his truck and muttered before kissing me good-bye. I felt bad for both of them. After that, Keith stayed inside.

Here, fact and truth clash in my mind again. My calling Al a deadbeat dad would certainly be accurate, but I'd never use that term. It didn't quite match up. There was a warmth to him in my memory. I could never be sure of its source. Maybe it was the love I felt from my father, when I wasn't feeling disappointed or let down, when he called me *baby girl* and kissed my cheek. Or maybe it was the love I had for him, making him more than what he was.

But love goes only so far. When my dad said he'd buy me a laptop for Christmas, or he was on his way to pick me up, or he'd make it to my next game, I knew better than to believe him. All the evidence showed me that my father said one thing and did another. Al's word meant little, like the proverbial stopped clock, right on rare occasion and only by mere circumstance. Most of the time, it meant nothing.

Did that mean that each false promise was a *lie*? I couldn't say. But I knew that Al lied. I knew it before I knew my times tables. I was still a kid when I learned that Al was *unfaithful* in his relationship with my mother. *Unfaithful* meant he had a baby with someone else when I was two years old, when he and Mia and I still lived together as a family. Easy arithmetic told me that Al did a lot of lying in his life. Did that make him a *liar*? As a child, I wouldn't call him one. As a resentful teenager, I changed my tune.

I knew better than to trust my father's word, but I believed him when he called me from prison every couple of weeks and said he'd be back soon. "*I'll be home by next Christmas.*" I turned ten; next Christmas came and went. "*I'll be home by the summer.*" I finished fourth grade; summer came and went. "*I'll be home by next Christmas.*" Before I turned eleven, I'd had enough. I made my own ruling. I decided that his inconsistencies meant he didn't know when he was coming home. He was lying to bring me some comfort, to make me feel better. This rationalization made it easier. The next time he lied to me, I didn't feel so stupid. It didn't hurt so bad.

My life started when you were born.

That's the refrain that echoed through my childhood. I'd ask Mia about what she was like when she was my age. "Did you go to dance classes like me? Did you always have curly hair? Do you think you would've liked me? Do you think we'd be friends?"

She always answered simply and cheerfully. If I pried for more, she'd shrug and smile and shake her head.

"I can't remember," she'd say. "My life *really* started when you were born. *That's* what I remember."

I didn't think of it as getting blown off. It went straight to my head, actually — that there was something so glorious about *me*, about *us*, that the years she spent without me were so easy to forget. I had no reason to think there was anything she didn't want to tell me.

Mia always told me the truth, even when she didn't want to. One summer afternoon when I was seven or so, I came home from a friend's house and asked her to *please* tell me what the F-word was. I can't recall where the fixation came from, but I remember the hours I spent between lunch and dinner following her from room to room, spouting off reason after reason that supported my campaign.

"I'm only asking for *one* swear word, not *all* of them. I already know the H-word and the D-word and the S-word and the C-word —" I had recently learned that *crap* was considered by more delicate families to be a curse. "— so it's not even like you have to tell me those. *Just* the F-word. Please."

Mia wasn't responding. She wasn't angry, but an hour into my pleas she gave me fair warning that she'd already told me no and wouldn't talk about it anymore. She went along with her chores, tidying the entryway and walking out to the front yard to collect our sidewalk chalk. I ran after her, barefoot, circling her.

"What if I hear some other kid say it, but I don't know that it's the F-word so I don't know they said a bad word? Or what if *I* accidentally say it because I don't know what it is, and then I get in trouble? I won't say it if you tell me. *Promise.* I just wanna know what it is so I *don't* say it. Mom. *Mom!* Are you listening?"

Deep down, I was self-aware enough to know that this was a game of endurance more than persuasion. Mia was endlessly patient with me, so I felt bad about wanting to wear her down. But I really, *really* wanted to know. I hated not knowing something that other people knew. I was drawing another breath when she stopped suddenly and turned to me. Her smile was gone.

"Fuck." She said it quietly, like a sigh.

"What? *Oh.*" I tried to look contrite and grateful, repeating the word in my head to commit it to memory. *Fuck. Fuck fuck fuck fuck fuck.* She blinked long and hard, and went inside.

I always wondered why Mia's openness and honesty didn't extend to her own life. Like, how did she meet my dad? I loved both of my parents without question, back when I was a kid, but I wasn't blind. Al was a tough guy, distant and rough; Mia was soft and glowing, like Julie Andrews and Mr. Rogers wrapped into one. As a couple, my parents made no sense. How did they ever find each other? But I never knew. I guess I never asked, or at least I don't remember asking.

My life started when you were born. I questioned Mia's refrain as I got older. Sure, sure, but what came *before* me? Where did *I* come from?

In all the time I spent with Mia, up until that autumn in Eugene, there were only two strange incidents, two times I got a sense that Mia had been through things I could never imagine. Each event — if you could even call them that — remained well within the bounds of normality, bordering on wholly unremarkable. Only the barest hint of not-quite-right-ness hung around it, and even that could be explained away. That's what I tried to do to these strange vignettes: explain them away, forget them. But they stuck out in my memory, and I could never smooth them down.

Justin and I were in Portland, home from college during the summer between our freshman and sophomore years. We had been out, it was getting late, and we were watching TV in my mom's town house. My little brother was away for the night, at a sleepover or something. Mia slept upstairs.

I felt the thud as I heard it, through the hardwood. Then heavy, rushed footfall. My mom was running, racing, to the landing, down the stairs. I was afraid; something must be wrong.

"Mom? You okay?"

She came to a halt and stood uneasy in her pajamas and socks. She blinked hard at the light. Her eyes were glassy, her face still flushed with sleep.

"Yeah, I'm sorry, I was — I was having a dream." I knew Mia had been a sleepwalker when she was little. My grandparents had told me about it. But I'd never seen her do it. I didn't know it still happened.

"Are you okay?" Justin rose to his feet, looking worried. "Do you wanna watch with us?" She didn't look at either of us, only back to the stairs.

"No, no, it's okay, I'm gonna go back to sleep."

I wished her good night. Justin settled back into the couch, resumed the episode. But my mind stayed in that moment before she had appeared at the top of the stairs, when I heard her running and when I felt afraid. I'd had plenty of night-mares; I'd been stalked, chased, hunted; but even in those dreams I had never been driven out of my own bed. *What could she be running from?* I couldn't let it go, but I knew I could never ask her.

It was dark outside. I was a teenager, still living in our old house — the one where my brother and I had lived with Mia and Keith, together, before their split. I was in the living room after dinner, packing up my school bag for the next morning, when I heard a soft, high-pitched sob.

Through the open doorway leading into the kitchen, I saw one silhouette. Keith was holding Mia to his chest — a rare embrace that I saw between them. That cry had been from her. I never heard my mom cry, ever. Not that she wasn't open with her emotions. She was. I'd seen her well up at the movies, or wipe away some happy tears from time to time. But that was pretty much it.

I don't remember when or how I learned the full meaning of what I'd witnessed. I only recall the information itself: Mia had just found our neighbor's cat, Cowboy Dan, lying in the street, struck by a car. She loved Cowboy Dan. But I was a little surprised at how distraught she seemed. Our family had our own cat, Esme; at least she wasn't the one dead in the road.

I watched Mia and Keith in silence. I don't think either of them noticed me. Once I realized what I was seeing, I knew I shouldn't be seeing it. I left my backpack lying open on an armchair and made my way upstairs. I could still hear her.

A glimpse behind a veil. That's how each memory feels to me; it's the only way I can describe it. In revisiting them now, the same sensation returns to me: a deep unease. That feeling — it's not guilt, not necessarily. I hadn't gone out stealing glances, looking for secrets. It wasn't even an accident; it was simply a matter of circumstance, each *glimpse behind a veil* — a soft breeze picking up the fabric before it fluttered back into place. Even so, those two moments had revealed to me something that wasn't meant for my eyes. In their wake, they left a glimmer of the unknown, suggesting to me that there was much more that lived beyond my sight.

When I started looking for the truth about Al's life, I had to ask my mother to do what she always avoided: to try to remember what came before *me*, before *us*. And I had to ask her to sacrifice the one thing she held closest: her privacy. It was always so important to her, and I never understood why. I saw it play out only in action. When she wrote anything down — a doctor's phone number, a grocery list — she ripped the paper into little pieces and threw them all away.

———

That day in his office, I sat next to Brent at his desk as we scrolled through the results for "Albert Fontana, defendant." I tried to tell him that I would pay him back the fees I saw accumulating on the screen. Brent just shook his head at me as he continued to read.

"So this is him." The resulting case, *USA v. Fontana*, led into a larger overarching one. Brent read aloud. "*USA v. Hicks et al.* Looks like there were five guys who got charged. In 2001 — does that sound right?"

"Yeah, that's it." I tried to steady the tremor in my voice. "He went away in 2003, so the timeline adds up." Brent emailed me the docket and complaint.

"And what's that?" I pointed to the screen. There was another *USA v. Fontana*. Only this case was earlier, from 1992.

"Looks like he had another federal case back in the '90s." Brent looked at me. "Did you know about that?" I shook my head.

As we sat in his office, Brent asked me about how willing or unwilling Al might be to answer my questions about the past. It was a reasonable question: Al and I had a complicated relationship, and not all ex-cons were keen to talk about their crimes — certainly not ones they'd kept secret for years, and certainly not to their estranged children.

I only noticed when I revisited the scene in my memory, weeks later, that he never asked me the same question about Mia — and I sure wasn't going to bring it up. I didn't want to think about it yet.

December arrived, ushering in the fall term's final exams. The campus crowds dwindled; the rain remained. When I drove back to Portland for the holidays, my jeans were still too loose. My face was still drawn. But I had more energy; I had momentum; I had a purpose. I told Mia about my revelations in Brent's office, my first phone call with Al in years, my idea for a reporting project about my family's past. And I asked her for a favor.

While my brother was at Keith's place for the weekend, Mia and I went out for dinner. It was our first informal interview. I brought my tape recorder. I waited to take it out until our iced teas had arrived.

Mia was tense. When they weren't moving, her lips pursed into a flat line. I felt that old guilt; I had worn her down to get what I wanted.

"Ten minutes," she said. "Then we'll talk about something else."

2

Secrets

Chicago, 2000

Frankie always slept in Al's bed, on the side closest to his
dresser. She never slept in her bedroom, the one across the
hall, not since she and her mother moved out of the apartment. She didn't think of that room as hers anymore, just
like she didn't think of the apartment as home. Her real room
was in Mia's new house in the suburbs, where all her toys
and blankets and books were. That was her real home. The
apartment was Al's apartment now, and she didn't live there.
She visited.

The apartment was different without Mia around. Frankie
felt shy, like she was a guest at a friend's house. Al let her stay
up late, watching TV in his big bed. He drank milk straight
from the plastic jug. She never knew you could do that. Mia
never did.

That morning, when Al went off to shower, she took the
moment alone to wander around his room. The dresser was
covered in little mementos of Al's other life, the life he led
when she wasn't around: piles of loose change, stray tooth-
picks, a small box of liquor-filled chocolates. A paperweight
caught her eye. It stuck out compared with all the other things,

compared with Al. The sphere held two red roses suspended in resin, one large, one small. She smiled. She imagined the big rose was Al and the tiny one was her.

When she lifted the paperweight, a trifolded letter fell open. Frankie recognized the name signed at the bottom. It was the landlady, who lived with her son in the downstairs apartment. The words jumped out at her in a jumbled order. UNPAID RENT. FINAL WARNING. EVICTION. This was private, the sinking feeling in her belly told her. She shouldn't be reading this. She pressed the letter closed and returned the paperweight to its place.

That afternoon, as they wandered the aisles of a toy store, she didn't let Al out of her sight. She listened for his foot-steps behind her and waited for his cell phone to ring. He was always on the phone. When it rang, Al answered and lowered his voice; Frankie listened but couldn't make anything of his murmurs. The music overhead was too loud. She closed her eyes and listened hard. Nothing.

The next stop was a small business park on the Southwest Side of Chicago, home to her dad's bodybuilding gym: Al's Gym. Frankie spent many afternoons working the counter. Even before she started kindergarten, Al would let her sit on the worn red stool and exchange dollar bills for Gatorades. Sometimes they took a nap on the old recliner in his office. With the lights off, she couldn't see the bikini-clad women on the glossy calendars and magazine clippings that covered the walls. She didn't like to look at them. Their chests looked like beach balls had been inflated under their skin. It looked like it hurt.

Once, Frankie asked her mom if she could go to the Gym for Take Your Daughter to Work Day. She thought it was cool. Her Daddy, as the Family called Al, was the boss. That made her the boss's daughter; that made her special. But Mia said no.

She only ever saw a couple of members of the Family at the Gym. Al was one of ten children, five brothers and five sisters.

Two of Frankie's uncles had died, and her dad said they were in heaven. Her uncle Marco, Al's youngest brother, worked at the Gym. He showed her how to use the PC in the office to play Pong.

Her aunt Connie swung by, too, from time to time. She was the baby of the Family. She wore glossy brown sunglasses and drove a silver car. She smelled like perfume and cigarettes. Frankie thought she was fancy.

Connie didn't like the way Al decorated, either. Every time her aunt flipped on the office lights and looked around, she sighed and shook her head. "Oh, your Daddy," she'd say.

After the Gym, Al cranked the truck window down and got on the highway. The wind roared in Frankie's ears. They were going to see her grandparents, her dad's parents. They had moved out of the South Side when Al's dad retired. Now they lived in a ranch house on a quarter acre of land out in the sticks. The path to the front door was lined with garden gnomes, cherubs with their hands clasped in prayer, and Virgin Mary statues. Inside, she and Al made their way down the usual receiving line of aunts, uncles, and cousins, ending in the kitchen where Grandma Sonia held court, chain-smoking Pall Malls and watching TV.

Sometimes Frankie felt like she was playacting when she was with the Family, only she didn't have the script like everyone else did. On her way out of the kitchen to play with her cousins, an aunt stopped her. "Frankie! When's your Communion?"

Frankie shrugged. She didn't know her line. She didn't know what to say. This happened a lot when she was with the Family. That's why everyone always said she was so shy. She wasn't shy at home with Mia, or with Mia's family. This place was different.

Frankie knew she was Catholic because Al told her so. She thought it was an inherited trait, like freckles or brown eyes. But she knew she was different from her cousins, who went to church and knew how to pray the rosary and other things she didn't know. Once out of earshot of the adults, she asked her cousin what a Communion was.

"It's like graduation from Sunday school," he said.

"I don't go to Sunday school."

"Oh," he said, before going back to his Batman figures.

After dinner came the invitation from her cousins, the one Frankie dreaded: "Do you want to sleep over?" "Yeah! Sleep over!" She hated sleepovers at Sonia's house. She could never sleep. The austere portraits of Jesus and Mary in their gilded frames kept her awake. They watched her, and she watched them back. She didn't know whether Al stayed or left during those nights. She was too afraid to notice. Sometimes she thought about all the things she didn't know.

"Let me ask my mom."

Frankie stood alone by the kitchen's wall phone, dialed the number she knew by heart, and waited, clutching the phone's receiver to her ear like a life preserver. Each ring seemed to spell out her fate: *No one was home — No one would save her — She would have to sleep over —*

"*Hello?*" The warmth of her mother's voice dissolved the fear.

"Hi. Can I sleep over?"

"*Of course you can!*"

Frankie held her breath, letting the silence speak for her.

"*Is that what you wanna do?*"

She held on.

"*Do you wanna come home?*"

"I don't know. Maybe." That was all she had to say.

"*Okay. Then you can just tell everybody that I said Frankie's gotta come home tonight.*"

"Okay." Relief washed over her.

"*Are you okay? Are you having fun?*"

"Yeah. I'm okay."

Frankie heard the kids playing in the living room. It was time: her big performance, the small price of getting what she wanted. She fixed her face in the big mirrored wall next to the dining table. Brows furrowed, lips pursed. She had to look bummed, annoyed, disappointed. She practiced the words in her head. *My mom said I have to go home.* Through the reflection, her eyes fell on the room's centerpiece: a white statue of Jesus dying in his mother's arms. *My mom said I have to go home.* She glanced back to the mask she wore to make sure it was still there. *My mom said I have to go home.* Then she ran off to deliver the bad news.

Al kept the radio low on the drive back to the suburbs. Frankie laid her temple against the cool window and watched the sky. The leaves were turning. She closed her eyes and pretended to fall asleep. Whether she actually nodded off, she never knew, but the stop at the toll always jolted her awake. She listened to Al dig for change. The words returned to her suddenly — UNPAID EVICTION WARNING EVICTION. She squinted her eyes shut. Frankie would never tell Al what she saw. She wouldn't tell Mia, either. She knew this was a secret.

She'd all but forgotten about the letter by the time December rolled around. She was busy thinking about Christmas. Al took her to the Chicago Ridge Mall to buy presents for the Family. Frankie loved the colorful lights strung up along the concourse, the smell of warm cookies outside the Mrs. Fields store, the rustle of their shopping bags as they crossed the snowy parking lot.

She was excited for the holidays this year. What would Santa bring her? Last year, she had gotten everything she wanted: Connect Four, plenty of books, a Barbie keyboard — that Barbie keyboard —

A sadness was sweeping over her. Frankie tried to push the memory away as she buckled herself into the passenger seat. She tried, but it was too strong —

It had been last year, on Christmas Day, that she and Mia left Al. Her parents had that horrible fight after she'd opened all of her presents under the tree. She couldn't stop it now, the flood of memory: Al rushing down the hal, Mia's cries, her own tears that fell onto the white keys of that Barbie keyboard, the stubble on Al's cheek as he kissed her good-bye —

Frankie blinked hard. She looked out the truck window. She focused on the snowflakes that floated past her. She didn't want to remember right now.

Al switched on the heat, and Frankie reached for the radio dial. The Charlie Brown Christmas song was just starting.

Christmas time is here . . .

Al sang along in an earnest falsetto. Frankie giggled as his voice cracked and strained for the high notes. If his phone rang on that car ride, Frankie didn't hear it. Her guard was down. Back at the Gym that afternoon, she and her dad wrapped presents in the office. They used the extra wrapping paper to fold airplanes. She watched them glide out of her father's hand, sailing past the shiny ladies on the wall.

They flew pretty good, Al thought. Frankie thought so, too.

Chicago, January 2001

With one more push, the lock snapped. A man burst into the living room, a crowbar swinging at his side. A baseball cap obscured his face, save for a thick mustache and a heavy jaw. The guy looked like a cop, badged and armed, leather gloves. Probably DEA, or the narcotics division of the Chicago Police Department.

Two more men followed the Officer, same brimmed caps, same leather gloves, same gun belts. One of them held a pair of handcuffs at the ready, but there was no one home to restrain. Someone had left the lights on, but the apartment was empty. Just like the Officer had hoped. They weren't there to make arrests.

The crew communicated in silent nods and pointed glances, resorting to hushed murmurs when absolutely necessary. They kept each other anonymous; they used no names; their CPD stars bore only badge numbers.

They all scattered, searching. They rifled through drawers, checked behind the stove. One of their police radios chattered in the background. The place was pretty bare even for a stash house, with hardly any furniture beyond the sofa and TV. And it was clean. When the Officer opened the fridge, a small package fell to his feet. Cash, bundled, wrapped in cellophane. He tucked it into his jacket and kept moving. He found another one taped to a cabinet under the kitchen sink. Altogether, it was maybe ten grand. He looked around the room. *Where was it all? Where was the dope? Where was all the fucking money?*

The Officer widened his search: the porch out back, the building's basement. The others retraced their steps. They walked circles through the apartment. There was supposed to be more. *Way* more. For fuck's sake, the Kid — a young dealer, their informant — said this guy had five keys of coke stashed at his place. So where *was* it all?

The Officer shook his head. This had happened last time, at the raid a few weeks before; they'd left empty-handed. The Kid insisted the money had been in there; the men had just missed it. The fixer, another dealer, vouched for the Kid; the crew trusted the Fixer. The crew wouldn't make the same mistake again.

At the Officer's direction, the men did another round, inside and out. They worked slower this time; they knew they weren't finding anything more tonight. One of the men went to take a leak.

A cell phone rang out. It was the Sergeant, the leader of the crew. He was parked outside in a red Chevrolet, keeping an eye on the street, wondering what the fuck was taking so long in there. The Officer filled his boss in. They had looked everywhere — yes, *everywhere*. There was nothing left to find. And yes, he was sure. And yes, they checked the fridge. He snapped his cell shut. The other guys knew what that look meant. The three men left the apartment the way they came. Single file, back through the living room, out the front door. There were pry marks on the doorjamb, some cracks around the lock, but it closed shut just the same.

The unmarked car rolled up to the precinct at 51st and Wentworth, followed by the Cadillac. The Officer stayed behind the wheel while the other two cleared out, the man with the handcuffs lugging an old electric typewriter under his arm. They followed the silhouette of the Sergeant inside.

The Officer killed the headlights and swung around the block, pulling into the motor pool lot. He parked the unmarked car in its assigned spot, grabbed a stack of blank warrant forms from under the passenger seat, popped the trunk. Out in the dark, he ripped open a black duffel bag, shoved the papers inside, and rooted around for a screwdriver. The license plates came off; another set from the bag replaced them. He worked quickly and quietly, then joined the crew inside.

The table was littered with torn plastic and bills of various denominations. The other men had counted the cash and divvied it up. It was barely better than nothing at all. The Sergeant sucked his teeth. Something had gone wrong. They had never been this unlucky. But there was nothing they could do about it now.

Each man took his share and disappeared into the night. They'd regroup and try again soon. Their luck would turn.

The next morning, on the first of February, the Officer was arrested on his front porch. His name was Larry Knitter. He wasn't a real officer. The star he'd worn didn't belong to him. And the previous night's raid? It was no raid at all. It was a robbery.

In reality, Knitter worked for the police department's motor pool as an electrical mechanic. The man with the handcuffs and the typewriter — Matthew Moran — was a civilian, too. He'd worked for the Illinois Department of Professional Regulation.

Only the Sergeant was an actual cop. Eddie Hicks had joined the Chicago Police Department as an officer in 1970, working his way up the ranks. He spent most of the '90s in the narcotics unit, before retiring from the force in the year 2000. During that last decade of his esteemed career in law enforcement, Hicks had another job keeping him busy. More of a side hustle, really. In the early '90s, he and fellow CPD sergeant Larry Hargrove recruited Knitter and Moran, forming this tight-knit crew.

Hargrove retired from the police department the same year as Hicks. Unlike his partner, Hargrove also quit the crew. He moved out West with plans to enjoy his golden years — and his promised cut of the crew's future proceeds.

Not Hicks. He left the force, but he kept working his dealer sources and planning future raids. Hargrove's retirement meant that Hicks's crew was approaching the twenty-first century short by one man. They had always been four. So they found a replacement and took him along for a ride on that last night of January.

That fourth man was nobody special. The feds didn't know who he was; the complaint that led to the arrest of the original crew referred to him as an unidentified male. But it didn't take long for them to figure it out. The guy was no cop; he had no ties to law enforcement or any governmental agency. He was just a guy who knew a guy: in this case, Larry Knitter. That was all Albert Fontana was. Just some South Side bodybuilder who wanted some easy money, a guy who was big and who knew how to keep his mouth shut.

Soon enough, the whole story made the papers:

> Two veteran Chicago police sergeants allegedly teamed up with two police civilian employees to steal cash and cocaine from drug dealers for nearly a decade.

That about summed it up. The crew would impersonate on-duty officers with forged warrants to steal money and drugs from dealers around the city. They'd confiscate cocaine and gallon-sized plastic bags stuffed with tens of thousands of dollars. If a dealer wanted to hurt a competitor or avoid getting ripped off himself, he might give Hicks a tip for a cut of the profit.

The operation wasn't unique. This was Chicago, after all. Corruption and crime ran deep in its DNA. You could trace it to its beginnings, long before Blagojevich or Capone, before the turn of the century. In the 1800s, the city was built on a swamp that turned streets to mud and collected sewage, poisoning the water. Architects jacked up the buildings and streets, raising Chicago out of its filth. While the feat was successful, it created tunnels below, where the city's criminals and their various trades could remain out of sight. The city's health thrived; so did its degeneracy. From these rotted roots sprang generations of duplicity and greed, upheld by Chicago's finest.

The remaining members of the original group — Hicks, Moran, Knitter — were arrested on the day after the day gone wrong. Soon, Hargrove was, too. In hindsight, it was obvious that the drug house was a fake. There was no Kid; he didn't exist. The Fixer, the dealer they trusted, had worn a wire. Concealed cameras caught them in the act. Hicks's crew lasted longer than other rings of corrupt Chicago cops at that time. You had to give them that. But after nearly a decade, it was over.

The replacement, Fontana, stayed free for a while longer, until the feds identified the "unidentified male." Knitter's friend sure had some luck, didn't he? The one time he goes on a ride, it ends up being a fucking sting.

Chicago, 2003

The trial of USA v. Hicks was supposed to begin on June 3, 2003, at 9:30 A.M., in Judge Andersen's courtroom — but it didn't.

In attendance that morning, along with their respective counsel, were four codefendants: Hargrove, Moran, Knitter, Fontana. The fifth — Eddie Hicks — never arrived. They waited. And waited.

"Let's go on the record for a second," Judge Andersen said. The court reporter typed along. "Let the record reflect that it is now ten twenty-five, and who has not shown up?"

"My client," answered Hicks's attorney.

"So, Mr. Hicks has not materialized today. And have you been able to locate him?"

No, the attorney had not. He called his client's house — no answer. He called his job — he wasn't there. Hicks was swiftly declared a fugitive; a warrant was issued for his arrest. On his WANTED poster, the FBI noted his aliases and that he was known to travel to Brazil.

Over the coming months that turned to years, each of the remaining four men pleaded guilty or were found guilty by a jury of their peers and sentenced to federal prison to serve their time. But Hicks was gone.

Al, for one, chose to admit his guilt rather than go to trial.

The Family helped him pay his legal costs. He emptied out his apartment, and his parents let him store everything he owned in a shipping container on their property. But the raid, the charges, the coming sentence — Al kept it all a secret from Mia and Frankie for as long as he could.

Later that year, on an overcast November afternoon, Frankie came leaping up the porch steps and waved to Mia through the window. She had a *great* time with her dad, she told her mother as she bounded inside, swinging a shopping bag. Her dad took her and a cousin to Portillo's for cheese fries and bought her a PlayStation.

After dinner, Frankie was in her room when her mom knocked on the open door.

"Can I talk to you for a sec?"

Something was wrong. Frankie knew it. Mia's smile didn't reach her eyes.

Her mother told her that Al was going away for a while, to South Dakota. He was going for work. Like a business trip.

"Oh. Okay." Frankie's brow creased. "When is he leaving?"

"I don't know. He didn't say."

He must've called her after I got home, Frankie thought. She recalled her dad's face from that afternoon, grinning under the neon light at the restaurant. They'd spent the whole day together. Why didn't he tell her himself?

Her first letter from Al arrived on December 4, three days after he left Chicago. By then, Mia had told her the truth: Her dad was in prison. Frankie noticed a long number — his inmate ID — next to his name on the envelope, along with the address for Yankton Federal Prison Camp in South Dakota. Inside, a college-ruled sheet that bore both her names:

Dear Francesca, (Frankie Girl) . . .

Al had printed each word carefully in pen:

> The place I live looks like a college campus in the middle
> of a park with houses around it. Across the street you
> can see houses with their Christmas lights on. If you can,
> send me a picture of you, and one of you and your mom
> in front of your live tree.

Frankie squinted her eyes shut, trying to conjure up an image of his new home. She didn't know what a college looked like, so she imagined the nearby middle school instead. Old, big, lots of brick. He said he did all the same stuff there that he did at home: go to work, work out, eat.

In his next letter, she couldn't help but pay attention to his spelling mistakes. In school, her class was practicing proofreading. She learned all of the different notations — three lines under a letter to capitalize it, stuff like that. There were other errors, too; she noticed that Al liked to capitalize the *D* in *Daddy* when he referred to himself in the third person — *Your Daddy loves you* — even though it was a common noun. She imagined marking up his work.

> How are you. I'm doin fine. How's everybody. I hope their
> all doin fine. Christmas is coming soon. I hope your ready
> for it. I'm sure you'll get a lot of gifts from everybody. When
> you see both your grandparents give them a kiss from me.
> Hope your doing good in school. I'm sure you are.
>
> I hope you like your PS2. We'll have to get you some
> games.

She did like her PlayStation, but she didn't like thinking about the day that she got it. She still wondered why her dad hadn't told her that he was leaving.

Christmas came and went. Al sent his usual letter, with his usual requests:

Send another one soon with a couple pictures. Your Daddy misses you so much little girl. Sorry I can't be there for the things you have at school. Take pictures and videos and I'll see everything when I get home. Time's going by and soon all this will be behind us. I think about you and look at your picture every day.

He gave his usual compliments:

Hope everything's going good in school. You sound very smart, keep reading your books and doing what you've been doing it will pay off when your older. Your very smart and beautiful like your Mama.

And he made his promises:

Wish I could be there with all that snow, it would be fun. But I'll be there next winter and we'll make some stuff at your grandparents' house, like some snowboard hills and a hockey rink on the pond. Maybe I'll get some skates, too. Don't laugh yet.

All of this was a secret. Frankie knew this, even though Mia never said so outright. Her mother told her that what happened to her dad was *private*, and it wasn't something to talk about at school or to her friends. *Private* didn't mean "secret," but that's how it felt.

After Al went away, Frankie spent most of her time reading and rereading her new favorite book, *From the Mixed-Up Files of Mrs. Basil E. Frankweiler.* She loved all the planning that the twelve-year-old protagonist, Claudia, did as she ran away from home with her brother to go live in the Metropolitan Museum of Art. She imagined her own adventure; she knew just where she'd go. Using the atlas from the living room bookshelf, she plotted the long way from Chicago to South Dakota, tracing a path across the page with her finger.

One night, Mia got a call. It was one of the moms from school, passing along *something concerning* that Frankie had told her daughter, *something about running away to see her dad?*

Frankie was mortified when Mia sat her down. She'd completely forgotten about her made-up plans. She didn't even remember telling her friends — tons of stuff came up on the playground — and she hadn't really meant it. *Of course* she hadn't meant it! She wasn't even allowed to cross the street without permission; she knew she'd never make it to a highway.

Frankie felt rotten. She had just been playing pretend. Now look where it got her. Maybe this was a warning sign, that she was too old for pretend now. After all, she and her cousin had mostly abandoned their Barbie houses. Now they played Sims or sang along with her karaoke machine. *Maybe,* she thought, *this is what happens when you play pretend for too long. It gets you into trouble.*

The guilt hung around for weeks. The worn copy of *From the Mixed-Up Files* gathered dust on her bookshelf. Frankie couldn't look at it without feeling ashamed.

Chicago, 2004

Third grade came and went. Fourth grade was exciting, and different. Frankie liked her homeroom teacher, Ms. Fox. She liked her new advanced math class, which she took with some of her closest friends from the accelerated reading and writing program. But Frankie wasn't as good with numbers as she was with words, so it wasn't as fun. In her social studies class, the mean old teacher was making them write in cursive, always in erasable pen. After school, she played clarinet in the school band. And she had started shaving her legs. Mia taught her one afternoon, as Frankie sat on the countertop, her legs in the kitchen sink. She told her dad all about it, and he mentioned it in his next letter:

> Talk to you soon and be careful, even when you shave your legs, ok?

Oregon, 2005

The summer before fifth grade, Mia and Keith sold their house. The family was moving to Portland, Oregon. Frankie was worried about telling Al. She hoped that her leaving Chicago wouldn't hurt his feelings. Mia and Frankie packed up her baby brother's room while he played with a plastic bowl from the kitchen. He was two years old, and he had grown a layer of reddish hair on his head — more like down than hair, soft and almost translucent. She was a little worried that he would be bald forever, but she didn't tell anybody.

Her brother had Keith's blue eyes, and you could see an echo of Mia's soft face in his. Frankie loved him fiercely, even though now she was outnumbered. She was the only one in the family with a different last name. Before, it was equal. Keith had one name, Mia had another, and Frankie had a third. But then Mia and Keith got married, and the baby was born, all the while Frankie kept Fontana. There was never any question about that; she'd never change her name. But sometimes she felt left out.

Al sent his letters to their new address. He started using cursive instead of writing in print. She guessed it was because he knew she was growing up. And she was — she saw things differently now. She knew better than to believe everything that her dad told her. Like all the stuff he said about when he would be coming home from prison. At the beginning, he said he'd be home by Christmas. That first Christmas came and

went. Then it was next summer. Then it was the following
Christmas. She knew he was lying. And she knew it made her
feel stupid.

Even in cursive, Al ended his letters as he always did:

— Love, Your Daddy

3

———

Need to Know

What is the purpose of memory?

That was the question on my mind each morning when, in the early light before my classes began, I turned up the corners of my mouth and trekked down to the University of Oregon's sprawling library.

On the Collegiate Gothic facade of the Knight Library were two imposing sets of double doors decorated in bronze. Above each was an inscription in stone.

Over the east entrance:

YE SHALL KNOW THE TRUTH.

Over the west:

AND THE TRUTH SHALL MAKE YOU FREE.

I always came in on the western side, my forced smile long gone by the time I approached, and I'd slow my pace to read the words. (I thought the saying was "the truth will *set* you free," but according to King James, it wasn't.)

I wanted to know the truth about Al. That afternoon in Brent's office, when we found the records of the raid gone wrong, had cracked open the dam inside me. All I refused to remember about my father flooded in, the old confusion and hurt. I thought I had left it way back in the angst of my adolescence. I didn't know it could follow me. But it had. There was no forcing it back; I was stuck sitting in the wreckage, and all I could do was puzzle my way through it.

It seemed to me then that the only way through was to assemble the facts and work it all up. In the end, the real Al would be revealed to me. I wondered what I would make of him.

But I stopped myself before I thought too much about the man himself. I found it best to think in abstractions: lists of possible sources and relevant literature and the like. To justify to myself the hours of work, I submitted a proposal to make a journalistic examination of my father's criminal past the subject of my honors thesis. To my surprise, it was accepted. I received grants from the journalism school and the honors college, money I could use to fly back to Chicago, do on-the-ground reporting and research, and reunite with Al. Brent graciously agreed to be my thesis adviser. Now I had support.

But deep in the stacks of the Knight Library, I was alone. I knew nothing, so I read everything. I was looking for a directive. I knew I could no longer be a fly on the wall of the world. I had to contend with my memory and, soon, the memories of others. I needed to know what to trust, what I could accept as fact or truth or the next closest thing.

I cast a wide net. I read about Proust's madeleines and Augustine's visions. I read abstracts of epistemology, of what constitutes knowledge and how we know that we know anything, but I didn't make it too far before it gave me a panic attack. I moved on, shifting to psychology and neurology — to the anatomy, function, and phenomenology of our memory.

What is the purpose of memory? To learn, and to survive.

Humans can be distinguished from much of the rest of the animal kingdom in part by the way we remember, according to the literature. Researchers say our advanced capabilities allow us to reason and communicate and plan. We recollect the past so as to learn from it.

In strictly mechanical terms, the system of our memory has three primary tasks: *encoding*, or acquiring information; *storage*, or retaining that information for various amounts of time; and *retrieval*, or being able to recall that information when we need it. There were plenty of analogies to choose from to bring the concept to life. In my mind, I kept coming back to one in particular: the file cabinet. I'll run you through it.

My mind is an office; my memory is a file cabinet; I am a clerk. I'm assigned a desk, a Smith-Corona, and a set of small keys, one for each drawer. I type up my experiences, what I see and learn and feel, and wait for the ink to dry. I place the pages into a folder, the pieces of a memory assembled and made whole. I file it away into the cabinet where the records are kept cool and dry and out of direct sunlight, lest they degrade. I keep every drawer locked, so nothing can be stolen. There is complete order. When I return for one folder or another, I can find them with ease. Each recollection is right where I left it. Then back it goes into its proper place. I close the drawer and lock it. And repeat, on and on and on.

It gave me a strange amount of satisfaction to imagine, to walk through that process, again and again. I was playing pretend, like a kid. I could feel the keys in my hand.

That's the model of our memory, the theory of a perfect process. I wanted that to be the end of my research, to pack it up and call it a day. I wanted the perfect system.

But I couldn't have it. The model is simplistic, assuming everything will go right every time. That's never how it goes.

Take long-term memory, for example. The place we keep important information for the long haul has nearly unlimited capacity, scholars say. That impressive feature seems to be linked to the way we move memories into long-term storage: We compress them down, stripping them of any nonessential detail we can spare. This compression process focuses on retaining meaning, the gist of it all. The flip side is that by losing those extra pixels, our memory becomes vulnerable to error.

What's more, the experts have come to believe that memory itself isn't so focused on being a carbon copy of past events. The concept of constructive memory started with Sir Frederic Bartlett, who wrote the book on remembering. He literally wrote it — *Remembering*, published in 1932, I was pretty broke when I stumbled upon it, so I downloaded a copy online: a free PDF file with a questionable provenance. I felt guilty about not buying an actual print copy until I did the math and realized, of course, that Bartlett was long dead.

Bartlett argued that our recollection process was more imaginative than reproductive, and remembering was less of a reliving and more of a reconstructing. Scholars differed on whether constructive memory was a net virtue or vice; I worried about what constructive memory meant about my memory's trustworthiness, about all the possible inaccuracies. All of this filled me with an anticipatory dread, the prospect of doubt.

Let's talk about some of those inaccuracies of memory while we're at it. There's no shortage of synonyms the literature uses to describe them: malfunctions, errors, distortions, failures, illusions.

Some of them involve one form or another of forgetting, of the inability to remember. A common one: the tip-of-the-tongue phenomenon. That's an example of *blocking*, in that the information isn't missing. It's on the right page, in the right folder. What's gone awry is the retrieval. A jammed drawer or a lost key.

Others involve the ways our mind skews our memories and erodes their truthfulness. Like *misattribution*, when an event from one memory is misplaced into another. Or *hindsight bias*: the knew-it-all-along effect.

As I read about all of the ways my mind could betray me, I became especially preoccupied with *confabulation*, the creation of false or distorted memories without the intention to deceive.

Let me give you an example of confabulation. On a winter day some years ago, far removed from the days I spent in the Knight Library, I returned home from running errands. I was twenty-five. My husband was making dinner. As I stood in the doorway of our Brooklyn apartment, stomping snow from my boots and shedding my layers, I rattled off all that I had accomplished: I walked around the park across the street, stopped by a bookstore in the neighborhood, took the L train into the city to do some window-shopping —

My husband stopped me mid-sentence. His brow was furrowed.

"You took the L?"

"Yeah." I always took the L into the city.

"Are you sure?"

"Yeah. I took the L."

My husband shook his head. "But you couldn't have taken the L."

"But I did — I got on right by the bookstore." Now I was annoyed. "I'm pretty sure I know what train I took." I could see it in my mind's eye: the usual stairs, the usual turnstile, the dark platform.

He shook his head again.

"You couldn't have. The L isn't running 'cause of all the snow. The MTA sent out an alert about it." His brow sank deeper — from confusion to suspicion.

"Well, that's what I took," I said, more curt, less certain. The words hardly left my mouth before the images flooded in with humiliating clarity: I *had* taken the usual stairs down to the usual turnstile, but I hadn't boarded the L train. I'd stopped when I saw the trains weren't running, sighed, trudged back up into the snow, and walked over to one of the elevated lines. The M, or maybe the F.

Only in that moment did I remember: When I was on the train, I had looked out the window and watched the sky turn dark. I felt my face redden. Of *course* I hadn't taken the L — I couldn't have seen the sky from a car *underground*.

"You're right. I took the M."

"Did you really go into the city?"

"Yes!"

"Then why didn't you know the L wasn't running?"

"I did, I just forgot — I went to the L *first*, but — really, I forgot I took a different train — but of course I went into the city — I got coffee, and then I went to the Strand —"

I went on, stumbling to describe my misremembrance. I wanted to reach into my purse and find the crinkled receipt from the café, bearing the time stamp of my order and the shop's Manhattan zip code, but the damage was done. He didn't say so, but I knew he didn't believe me.

I was frustrated, with myself more than with him. I replayed the entire scene, from my key turning in our front door to his skeptical face. The rest of the night was tense; I hadn't lied, but I felt like a liar. I couldn't stand it. I knew how it felt to be lied to.

This misremembrance was a confabulation: a false memory that I believed was true, even in the face of evidence of its falsity. In its lagging search for the answer to a simple question — *How did I get to the city today?* — my brain supplied a composite memory of my usual routine in its stead. And, ever trusting of my fallible mind, I passed it along without question.

We are driven to make meaning of the things that happen to us. Our inborn need to know *why* outweighs our ability to verify. Gaps in our understanding are filled with conspiracy theories and creation myths, religions and horoscopes. Randomness is intolerable. We make meaning so we can continue to live.

A scholar in psychology might say my confabulation was a momentary lapse in *epistemic vigilance* — the true explanation was there to find, if only I thought about it for a few more seconds. The phrase delighted me when I read it in some journal article. I circled it three times.

The literature proved to me what I already knew by instinct: that our memory is fallible. It's not a photo album or a reel of film. We can never see things exactly as they were. This idea has always troubled me, and it especially troubled me as I began to plumb the past for answers. In memory, the past is inherently ambiguous. I wanted black and white.

I wanted to know: Could my memories be trusted overall? For all of the weaknesses in memory and remembering, was there enough truth there for me to find? Enough to outweigh my doubt?

I waded through decades of debate among memory scholars — much of it seemed to support "overall" reliability. I encountered the work of one such scholar, Daniel Schacter, while buying a stack of psychology books on credit at Powell's Books in Portland. I used my student library portal to read his articles. In one, Schacter wrote that, on the whole, the systems of our memory manage to do a "remarkably good job" when it comes to accurately recording important events and storing the "general contours of our pasts."

"We could not have evolved as a species otherwise," he wrote.

What's more, he argues that these troublesome flaws in our memory aren't inherently bad. They aren't proof that our cognitive design is defective or prone to dangerous error. They're simply the costs of doing business, the consequences of our minds' "adaptive construction processes." Our memory adapted to strategically ease our cognitive load. We learned to travel light by default: to hold on to the info we'd likely need the most and leave the rest behind. This generalization, the experts say, is what begot key aspects of our intelligence — our abilities of categorization and comprehension.

So that was the good news: I had nothing to fear. Our memory's features outweighed its bugs. I asked my mind if I could call it a day. I was thirsty. The library was closing soon. Could I *please* go home and think about something else?

Nope.

I knew I had done my due diligence in interrogating my brain's abilities. But at the end of the tunnel, I felt no comfort. Maybe I hadn't dug deep enough. So deeper I went, into all the ways our memories deceived us. I took my work home with me. I took it everywhere. Didn't matter where I was — sitting in the library or in a lecture, lying in my bed or in someone else's. If I was conscious, I was ruminating on all the ways it could go wrong.

This wasn't a new trait of mine, these mental obsessions. But I didn't see this research as *obsessive* back then, back in 2016. It was the start of my senior year. I was leaving for Chicago on Halloween: my first thesis research trip. I counted down the days until my flight. A year had passed from where I started: sad and desperate and sick of all the fucking rain.

I thought I had gotten better, thanks to that day in Brent's office and all that had come after. After long nights of research and planning at the library, I'd get home and find that I hadn't once done any of my obsessive calculations or triple-checked my bank balances.

Forget that I was still sad, still bitter, and still knocking on wood from time to time. *Look at where I was a year ago!* I told myself. *Compared with that, I'm on top of the fucking world.*

But before we go forward, let's go back to "where I was a year ago," in the fall of 2015. That was when I first learned what *rumination* meant, at least in a clinical sense. My therapist at the university's health center had filled me in during one of those ten free sessions, as she listened to my fears about the Big One and watched me tap and knock and pick. She made some allusions to obsessive-compulsive disorder. She asked me about my ruminating and my compulsions. Were they making me unhappy? Were they disrupting my daily life?

I don't know if I lied to her or not. The truth was that I was losing my ability to keep my shit together. I had trouble leaving my apartment. Something horrible was going to happen, I knew it. I felt it coming.

During our sophomore year, Justin had given me a silver ring — a kind of promise ring, as stupid as it sounded in my head. I'd worn it on the middle finger of my right hand every day, without fail. After he dumped me, I knew I couldn't wear it anymore — and not only because that would be pathetic. I also had the sense that would bring some kind of biblical misfortune down upon my head, to wear the ring of a loved one when the love itself was dead.

But the minute I took it off, another fear set in. Every day that I had worn that ring, I had stayed alive. So had Mia, and my brother. These were facts. I couldn't prove beyond a shadow of a doubt that this small, constant variable — a ring on the middle finger of my right hand — was not the cosmic glue holding my world together, that it wasn't the common thread that kept us all safe. There was a sliver of space large enough for doubt to creep in. The doubt put down its roots; it bred fear. And the fear was stronger; it pried open the space, wider and wider, until it became a chasm.

The fear was certain. It knew: If I went out into the world without that ring on, I might knock over some unseen domino and set off a chain reaction, cascading north up I-5 from Eugene to Portland, that would send a car careening into my mother's living room or a school shooter into my brother's classroom.

Do you want to take that chance? the fear asked me.

Some days I managed to fight the fear; on other days, I stayed home and emailed excuses to my professors, stewing in my own panic and shame. I was mortified when I missed one of Brent's classes. That day's session was one I'd been looking forward to. The fifteen or so of us students were going downtown to the Lane County Courthouse, to learn how to find search records and look through the microfilm archives. I drafted out a lie to send to Brent that morning. I erased it; I couldn't stomach it. I told the truth instead. Later, I dry-heaved into my dingy bathroom sink.

I managed to make it to the next class, back in our usual computer lab. I arrived long before anyone else, to catch up on my coursework. I was falling behind.

Brent showed up before the other students. We greeted each other; I avoided eye contact. My stomach dropped when I felt him walk down the aisle and pull up a chair next to mine. He thanked me for telling him. In his experience, people in our line of work seemed fairly prone to various forms of anxiety and neuroticism.

"Some of the best reporters I've ever known have OCD," he said. I looked at him for the first time, scanning his face for signs that he was just being nice or feeding me bullshit. He looked like he meant it. He assured me that the absence wouldn't count against me — and neither would my disclosure. "Just let me know what you need."

Other professors I knew — the ones who required printed obituaries in order to excuse bereavement-related absences — would've failed me for the day. Not Brent. The next week, we met at a Starbucks downtown and walked over to the courthouse, where he let me make up the lesson. My gratitude couldn't be teased out from the shame that was twisted and knotted around it.

But that was then. This was now: the fall of 2016. I was better, in my eyes. And out of anyone, I'd be the one to know. I was nothing if not *epistemically vigilant*.

That vigilance took root in my reporting project. I collected every Cook County record I could find of Al's criminal past: mostly petty stuff from the '80s and '90s. Selling bottles of Old Style beer to guys at the Gym without any kind of license, marijuana possession, something about a stolen bicycle — and these cases seemed to have gotten tossed out at one stage or another, so no time served. I was relieved that I didn't find anything worse. I let my hope reach a little further: Maybe I'd find that Al was on the straight and narrow now.

Still, one of those petty Cook County cases stood out. It was recent, from just the past year: 2015. Al was stopped by some cops on the South Side for a broken taillight. They'd been keeping tabs on a nearby chop shop and saw him leaving the garage. In the back of the truck were the stolen motorcycle parts they'd expected to find. My dad spent a weekend in jail and ended up with two years of probation and a few grand in fines.

His mugshot from that day in 2015 came up in a Google search. *He looks like shit*, I thought. I cursed myself for being so unkind. But it was true. His face was puffy and worn. His expression wasn't defiant or angry — he looked resigned. I wondered if that stupid chop-shop case was a sign of more to come, a sign that my father was back to the hustling ways that had landed him in prison with Hicks's crew all those years ago.

Before reuniting with Al, I needed to be prepared. I wanted to know what he might say before he said it, to know the facts so I could prove or disprove anything he told me. But I found myself making excuses before I'd even boarded my flight to O'Hare. I reminded myself that memory wasn't perfect, making sure to put all my fancy new words and concepts to use. If Al's stories didn't add up, he could be *confabulating* rather than lying. Or he could be referring to a false memory that he believed to be true, the veracity of which had never been tested before. Or what about a true memory that made its way into the wrong file? I reminded myself: None of us are immune to flaws in our cognitive machines.

As much as I wanted to think I was being cool and rational, giving fair play to both sides, that wasn't what I was doing. Deep down, I knew that.

You see, when I was still taking notes in the library, lost in the stacks — long before I began this story — I knew the ending I wanted to write. But I never let it take a complete form in my mind, and I never wrote it down. I didn't want to jinx it. That means I can't tell you what it was — at least, not yet.

But I *can* tell you that during those months of reading and planning and steeling myself, I thought about the Al I knew as a child, as a teenager. I hoped he wouldn't lie to me.

This time will be different, I told myself. I almost believed it.

4

—

The Family

Al looked like he did in that mugshot I found online. His hair was buzzed and thinning, more gray than black. He still had a hulking frame, but gone was the impossibly defined physique of his bodybuilding days. His eyes were wet and red when he hugged me for the first time in years — like the day he left for prison, the only other time I saw him cry, really saw it. I heard his voice grow thick with emotion on that night when I was four or five, when Al got the call that his brother was dead from a heart attack and Mia had to pick me up from the apartment. But I didn't get a good look at his face that time. I think I avoided it; I think I was afraid.

I told you earlier that Al and I had been estranged; that it was complicated; I'd explain later. Let me fill you in.

I hadn't seen my dad since the last of my annual visits to Chicago, the summer after my junior year of high school. After Mia, Keith, and I moved to Oregon, I returned to my hometown during the long break. I stayed with Mia's parents, my grandparents: Cal and Ellen. Al would come by a few times, pick me up to grab lunch and then drive out to visit his parents. Sometimes he'd take me and one of my cousins to the mall or a movie theater. Al would listen to me rattle off everything I'd done in the past year: I'd gotten a starring role in our spring play; I'd aced advanced Spanish; I was reading Victor Hugo. Then I'd fly back to Oregon, where my real life was.

During that last summer visit, things had gone awry. He'd promised to take me and my cousin to the latest Harry Potter movie. A few hours before, he called me up and said he wouldn't make it. For once, I let him have it. I'd kept it all bottled up: all my anger, my disappointment in him. It had fermented into vitriol. It made my voice shake. I told him I didn't respect him. He was a shitty father. He was a bad man. The cheating on Mia, the lies, the prison sentence, all of his selfishness. I was done with it, with him. I told him I should've hated him.

I don't remember a single thing he said. Any of his interjections, apologies, attempts at reconciliation — they made no imprint on my memory.

Eventually, I hung up on him. I stood and sobbed, forgetting where I was and how thin the walls of Cal and Ellen's house could be. I gathered myself back up, wiping my eyes and nose on my sleeve. I wandered past my grandparents' bedroom. The door was open, and Ellen greeted me, lying on the bedspread with her sandals on, her legs crossed. I thought she'd been napping. I thought she wouldn't hear me. But she told me that she was proud of me. It was so hard for her to hear me so angry. At one point, she said, she'd put her head under her pillow.

I didn't cut myself off from him during that call — not exactly. I'd insisted that I deserved better treatment from him, that he should actually pick up the phone from time to time and pretend he gave a shit about me and my life. After I got back to Oregon, he called a couple of times. Then he stopped. And the silence grew longer.

On my nineteenth birthday, two weeks into my freshman year of college, I was working. I finished my shift in the dorm cafeteria and took the elevator back up to my room, smelling like dishwater, looking like shit. I saw a missed call from Al, and a text. It was a birth announcement for Andrea Marie Fontana, weighing some pounds and some ounces, born today. On my birthday. I'd known Al had a longtime girlfriend who was ten or so years younger than he was. He'd never told me she was pregnant.

After that, he had sent me a second text, wishing me a happy birthday. The day I now shared with his new daughter. I turned off my phone.

I didn't really drink; I never found it much fun. But I knocked on a friend's door down the hall. I poured myself a tall glass of his vodka. It looked like water. Then I blacked out.

That was pretty much it for Al and me until that day in Brent's office, until I called him for the first time in years. I was pretending that all that came before had been just as much my fault as his. I had been immature, adolescent. Now I was grown up. I was a rational adult, an impartial journalist, and that meant leaving all that old hurt behind.

My aunt Rosie had picked me up from the airport and brought me back to the two-flat my uncle Marco owned on the North Side. He was loyal to the Family; he always gave back. He lived on the top floor, while Rosie and other members of the Family took over the first floor and the basement apartments. I was given a hero's homecoming, with more aunts and cousins waiting for me in Rosie's living room. I excused myself; I was overwhelmed. I laid out my stuff in the spare guest room: my old purse, my cheap IKEA suitcase, and my tote bag of binders holding all the records I had gathered.

"Your dad's on his way," one of my aunts called to me from the kitchen. "Traffic. He should be here soon, though." I didn't want to see him yet; I wasn't ready. I didn't know that anyone had called him. How could I have expected anything different? Al was my dad. Of *course* one of his sisters would invite him over to see his own daughter. But I felt myself losing control. I emerged with a smile that felt like a grimace and braced myself for his arrival. I placed myself by the front door, but he came in from the backyard.

After our teary embrace, he sniffled and made small talk with his sisters. "You got any food? I want pizza." He looked at me. "You hungry?"

I talked too much in the truck en route to Aldi. It was a different truck than I remembered him driving when I was a kid. But back then, he was always driving different models — always a loan from a different buddy of his. In the side mirror, I noticed a booster seat in the back. My appetite dissolved.

We wandered the aisles, Al manning the cart. I walked off to the side, taking my father in. He grabbed a box of granola bars with one hand, held it up to me. "You eat these?" I nodded. He tossed them in the cart.

I knew better than to trust a quick survey of my imperfect memory, but I couldn't think of another time he and I had ever been grocery shopping together. Stopped into a gas station for chips, maybe. But in my mind, this was the first and only time.

. In the checkout line, he pulled out a wad of cash. Same old rubber band. Then he withdrew a pair of drugstore cheaters. He caught my glance as he put them on. He smiled and shrugged. "What? I'm old."

On the way back, the glasses pushed up and resting on his head, Al told me about how Marco chose this neighborhood when he decided to move back home a couple years back. He'd been living out West for years, one of the few in the Family to leave Chicago.

"This neighborhood used to be real different," he said. "It's all yuppies now."

Yuppie. Man, that word took me back. I was seven, and Al took me out for pizza in the suburbs where Mia and I had lived. He shook his head while we ate: "This place is all yuppies."

When I got home, I asked my mom what the word meant. I thought it sounded like guppies, the fish. She sighed and closed her eyes and said it wasn't nice to call people that. Years later, once I was older and had a computer in my room, I looked it up. *Yuppie: Young Urban Professional.*

As we drove along Milwaukee Avenue, I noticed a group that looked about my age, smoking outside a tattoo shop.

"You know, I think *I'm* technically a yuppie now."

"Nah." My dad smiled. "Nah, you're not."

I pointed at myself. "Young. Urban. Soon-to-be Professional."

He shook his head. "Nah. It's different." He grasped for the right words. "You're from *us.*"

I didn't press him on it.

Before I left Eugene, Brent and I had gone over my plans for the trip, the agenda that was coming together. I would gather records at the Cook County courthouses, interview attorneys involved in the case, meet some *Chicago Tribune* reporters who'd covered Hicks and his crew back in the day, maybe find some local academics who could put it all into perspective — the crew's place in the larger puzzle of Chicago and its ever-lasting corruption.

I also planned to spend time with Al and the Family, to talk to them about the past and everything I never knew, to get to know who they were now, and to observe.

I wanted to know how Al *survived* — how he made his way in the world, day by day. It was a mystery to me in the years after his imprisonment, and the mystery remained when I arrived. I knew he was living with his girlfriend, his daughter's mother. But I had no idea how he made money. Al's gym was no more. He clearly didn't have a regular job: He came and went from Marco's building seemingly without a schedule.

I remembered that years earlier, he told me he was working at a convention center, moving and breaking down sets, part of some program that hired felons. It was a good gig; one of his sisters found it for him.

I asked him about it while we made pizza from scratch in Rosie's kitchen.

"Oh yeah, McCormick Center," he said. "I didn't do that for too long."

"Why?"

"Didn't like it. The work was fine, but —" He kneaded the dough into a ball, a slight scowl on his face. "The guy in charge was a real dick."

Dick or no, I was pretty sure of the real reason he bailed on the job. Al always worked for himself. I knew that's how he liked it. That's how it was when I was growing up: running the Gym and selling motorcycles he built himself.

"I'm tryna get that going again, you know," he told me as he carried the sheet pans over to the oven. He was hustling, going to swap meets to buy and sell parts, building custom bikes for friends of friends. I knew his girlfriend worked in a salon part-time, but could all that be enough? I kept asking myself, *How is he getting by?*

Then I reunited with the Family — not just the motley crew that greeted me when I first arrived, but a full and proper reunion at my grandparents' house, the ranch house out in the sticks. Ever since Al's parents sold their house on the Southwest Side, that property had become the Family's home base, the center that everyone orbited. At that center was its matriarch, my Mexican grandmother Sonia. She and my Italian grandfather shared a deep Roman Catholic faith. They imparted unto their ten children a fierce and abiding fear of the Lord and an equally strong commitment to the Family. As in: No matter what anybody did or said, you were part of the Family; you had to look out for the Family; you never went against the Family. Between all the talk of the Family and the constant procession of Italian meals made by my grandmother, even into her old age, I always felt like I was in a shitty knockoff of *The Godfather*.

It became obvious to me that when my father was in need, the Family provided. A brother gave him gas money; a sister found him free health services; everyone pitched in babysitting Andie; he always had a rent-free place to crash when his girlfriend kicked him out. He showed up and left whenever he wanted.

One night, Al swung by Rosie's place after dinner. He saw the remains on a plate and flagged down his sister. "Get me some of that." She did what he said, brought him his meal. He grabbed his fork from her and dug in. I was the one who thanked her. He didn't notice.

I knew that Al was their brother, their son, but Jesus Christ. I couldn't help feeling like they were all being taken for a ride, like his charisma had put them under a spell. I couldn't really blame them; I fell prey to it myself.

When he was telling a story, something came to life in Al. Whatever it was, this quality about him was unpolished, unrefined. He wasn't eloquent, but he always spoke in a way that was quick and excited, almost urgent. In setting the scene, he stumbled over his words in his rush to get them out. Still, there was something almost rehearsed in the rhythm of his chattering. He knew which beats to hit and when to pull back for an effective pause. His voice was rough, and so were his words — he swore gratuitously — but you wanted to listen to him, almost more than you wanted to know what happened.

The content of his stories, too, had a particular quality. It was as though he was climbing a set of stairs as he was building them. Even when Al had recounted the same memory to me four times before, the fifth time would be different. Those other versions? They never existed, as if even Al didn't know how his story would end until he finished telling it.

He had a knack for making any coincidence seem fantastical and turning a mundane response into a punch line, and this ease of his aroused as much suspicion as it did entertainment. No matter what he was telling you, something about the way Al said it made you think he was selling you a bill of goods.

One afternoon at the Family's house, I finally met Al's daughter Andrea — Andie, for short. She was three years old. Al insisted she call me Sissy. I played with her dolls and let her serve me imaginary tea. She looked at me intently, as I'm sure I did to her. We were fascinated with each other.

Everyone adored her. "Now, tell me that girl isn't smart!" was the refrain of one of my aunts as Andie showed off for me, rattling off every single thing she knew.

"Yeah, she's real smart," Al said. "She's always listening. She listens to everything."

There was a surprise after lunch. We were drinking our coffee around the kitchen table when someone brought out a giant cake, white frosting, black icing: It was the front page of a newspaper, wishing me a happy birthday. My twenty-second birthday had passed weeks ago, but when they heard I was coming into town, the Family wanted to celebrate.

"We're so proud of you," my grandfather said, tugging at my heartstrings. My grandmother kissed my cheek; I breathed in the smoke. Why, as a child, had I found the smell so awful? It didn't seem so bad to me now.

In talking about my project, reporting out my family history, Sonia got to talking. In her slow, deliberate voice — deepened and textured by the decades of cigarettes — she told me about her parents, who came to Chicago from Jalisco, Mexico, to start a family. But when Sonia was a little girl, she and her brother were sent back to Mexico to live with other family members, without their parents. They didn't come back to Chicago until 1945, when Sonia was eight years old.

I asked her why she had been sent back to Mexico in the first place. Well — Sonia took a drag of her cigarette — her mother was too busy, working long hours as a switchboard operator, and her father was in prison.

"Really?" I had never known. But when I thought about my late great-grandpa Jesse and the tattoos that covered his arms, it made some sense. "What for?"

"Robbery and murder."

"*Murder?*" I looked around the table. No one else was surprised. How was I always the last to know everything?

Everyone chimed in to tell the story. Jesse and a couple of guys were robbing a tavern. There was a lot of argument over the details, but from what I gathered *somebody* had pistol-whipped a guy. Jesse was blamed for it, and he got three years. But no one could remember whether the pistol-whipping victim actually died, so we amended his charge to *attempted* murder.

"Why were they robbing the place?"

"Money!" Sonia laughed. My grandfather finished the answer: Jesse hung out with no-good guys, and the lot of them would do small jobs for the mob — break into places, steal things. He had wanted to be a soldier for them, but he was Mexican. The Outfit didn't let Mexicans get made.

"Yeah, he told me he would steal cars and sell parts for the mob," my dad said. I thought of the chop shop.

Sonia wrested back control of the narrative. After all, this kitchen table was her domain and hers alone. "My father's partner was a Jew," she said. "The Jew pissed off this young mobster. My father goes to meet with his partner out at a tavern — his partner's not there but there's all these police. Know what happened? That young mobster had come back for the Jew. The police had found him outside that tavern with his *heart ripped out.*" She relished each word. Maybe I knew where Al got his storytelling chops from.

Before the Jew met his gruesome end, he and Jesse had worked for Tony Accardo, the legendary mob boss. Sonia claimed that Accardo liked to eat sparrows, so her father and his partner would go out to fields and pack up crates of the birds, delivering them to the mobster's North Side home for his chef to prepare. But Jesse's relationship with the mob began to sour.

"My father was doing landscaping work for the mob's lawyer, along with the Jew and their friends, and somebody stole a ring from the house. And they blamed my father."

Again, the overlapping chorus. "And that's why they never brought him back." "One of his friends must've taken it." "You *don't* do that. You don't steal from the mob."

"It was probably that Jew boy," Sonia said, ashing her cigarette.

That was just the neighborhood back then, the Family explained. It was all organized crime. My grandfather piped up. "But not *everybody* went out stealing. And the ones who go out stealing, you know why they do it? It's not the money. They like the excitement."

Some mumbled in vague agreement. My grandfather was serious now. Sonia used his interruption to light a new cigarette. He continued. "You want to make money, you're better off doing something that's *honest*." I didn't dare look over at Al; I wondered if he was listening to his father.

"Is the Italian mob still a thing?" I asked to fill the silence. Everyone shook their heads. No, not in Chicago.

"They're all dead," Sonia said.

My dad nodded. "It's done. Most of those mob guys? Their kids are writing books."

One of my aunts looked at me with an earnest, solemn stare. "Frankie, *never* write about the Mafia."

Even if he didn't have a job, my dad had places to go and people to see, so there were some days that I managed to get alone time with members of the Family's "second generation" — Al's siblings. Two of the five brothers had died back in the '90s; I don't remember them very well.

Of the living brothers, I saw the most similarity between Al and Marco, the youngest, who took after Al in some ways — mostly looks and build. He was tan, big, muscular, just like Al, and they had similar smiles. Marco loved his older brother, and started working for him at the Gym as a teen. But, as I'd gathered from stories I picked up over the years, their paths diverged. Al loved being his own boss, but he was no good with business. He burned through cash. He was selfish, cut corners, got others caught up in his own petty crimes. Marco didn't want to follow in Al's footsteps. He left the Gym and made a career of his own, eventually moving out West, making himself something of a black sheep. I saw that Marco took care of his older brother. He loved him deeply. Still, sometimes love has limits.

Rosie was her own brand of black sheep, the only one of the five Fontana daughters to never marry. She had her own career but remained in Chicago, in the orbit of the Family.

When I tried to talk to my other aunts, I found that they tended to fawn over Al. But Rosie seemed to sympathize with me in a way the others didn't. She and I talked about our interior lives, about politics, about art.

All those days I spent in Marco's building, in Rosie's apartment, I felt like I was casing the place. I was a thief hiding in plain sight. They had let a stranger into their home, and they didn't even know it. The guilt chased me into my room after dinner while everyone else stayed up and watched TV. I kept myself secluded until the cracks of kitchen light that shone through under my door went out.

Looking back, I can see more clearly. I was always forthcoming about my trip, about what I was searching for, about why I had come home. I never lied or hid the truth. The choice of what to tell me was up to the Family. Maybe they didn't want to think about what those conversations would turn into — or maybe they didn't care. The second possibility didn't occur to me right away: that maybe, for some of them, it was nice to be off the hook for once, to put down their familial duty. They didn't have to bullshit around; they could address the elephant in the room for a little while.

One night, we went out for Chinese food. Rosie drove, and I told her about my mom, how she'd been doing.

"Everybody always loved your Ma," she said. "She was so *different*, you know? She dressed so nice. And she was so sweet. Not like one of those barroom broads your dad was always hanging out with before her." She flashed a smile. "That's what I call 'em: *barroom broads*. You know, loud . . . trashy . . ." She checked her rearview. "But no, no, your Ma was different."

Mention of Mia usually led to the retelling of my birth. In October 1994, I was born three months premature. In the Family's eyes, my survival was nothing short of a miracle.

Here, I knew I had to tread lightly. I didn't want to scare Rosie off. I tried to sound spontaneous, asking the question I had been rehearsing since I left Eugene.

"You know, as part of this project, I've been looking through all the old court records, including this federal case from 1992 — I guess he'd originally gotten probation, but he broke it a couple years later?"

"Mm-hmm." Rosie nodded with pursed lips, as everyone always did when I raised the subject of Al's record.

"So that means he served that first sentence in 1994, and — I never put this together before, but I was doing the math, and I realized — Al must've *just* gotten out of prison before I was born. Right? When I did the math, I think it was like three days before my mom gave birth. I never knew that before."

Rosie was a few beats behind me. She seemed to be in a slight haze.

"You said '94? That one was for — what was it?"

"Selling steroids." I recalled the charges from the criminal complaint that Brent and I had found on PACER. "So there was that raid in 1992, then he spent a couple of years on probation. But he ended up —" I looked back over at Rosie. I trailed off.

It was the look on her face. She was still sitting behind the wheel, of course, but I could see it: She wasn't all there. She was somewhere else now, too. She nodded to herself, silently. She was remembering.

"I couldn't believe it. I just couldn't believe it." We pulled up to a red light. She looked out the window. "How he could go against the Family like that."

5

USA v. Fontana

Chicago, 1992

Rosie wasn't home when the feds showed up that morning. It wasn't until after work that she got the whole story. As she walked up the sidewalk that evening, she could see the front door was ajar. In the doorway, her mother, Sonia, was talking to a cop.

She hustled up the porch steps, slipped past her mother and the officer, and took in the sight of her first-floor apartment. It was wrecked: Her mattress was upturned, leaning against a wall. Drawers were open and askew, cabinets emptied, their contents scattered.

Some of her siblings were at the building when it happened. It was the de facto home base for all of her brothers and sister, now that they were all grown; at least four of them were living in the three-story building at any given time back then. Her parents owned the house, which sat in the McKinley Park neighborhood on the Southwest Side, and had split it up into apartments. Al lived on the top floor. Rosie looked around. Where was Al?

Her siblings filled her in. That morning, while Rosie was at work, a FedEx truck showed up with four packages for Al. He came down, signed for them, and disappeared back up the stairs, balancing them in his arms. Someone said, "See? He had to sign for them — he *must've* known what was in there." Another innocently wondered if their brother had been none the wiser — maybe he didn't know that the boxes were filled with so many small glass vials.

Rosie shook her head. *No way. He knew.* It was no secret Al used steroids — all you had to do was look at him to know that. But she didn't know her brother sold them, too. And how could he bring that into their home? The Family's home?

The story wasn't over. Someone had ratted Al out. The FedEx truck driver was an undercover fed. Al had barely made it back into his apartment when, downstairs, the front door burst open. A pack of DEA agents searched the building floor by floor — shouting commands, guns drawn.

Those guys, the feds, they scared the shit out of everyone. One of Rosie's sisters was downstairs with a handful of their young nieces and nephews. When the men broke down the front door, she hurried the kids out the back. She led them away down the alley and kept them at the corner store. She let them buy whatever candy they wanted, making sure the kids wouldn't see their uncle Al getting pushed out of the house in handcuffs.

Mia had been up there, too, someone told Rosie. She had just gotten out of the shower, or finished washing her face, or something. She was drying her eyes with a towel, and when she looked up — there were the feds, like something out of a movie, all their giant weapons pointed her way.

The rest of the Family didn't sit in their shock or disappointment for long. Someone went to bail Al out of jail; others started tidying up the place. But Rosie couldn't do anything for a few minutes but stand there in the doorway. She was just so *mad*. She didn't understand how her brother could be so selfish, how he could do that to the Family.

Tom liked Al from the moment they met.

Al was the kind of client Tom preferred. He didn't try to

feed him bullshit. As a trial attorney, Tom got more than his fair share of bullshitters. It came with the territory — to a lot of criminals, their attorney was the first test of their cover-up stories. If they could lie to you and get away with it, they thought they could get away with anything. But Al did not play that game. No, Al was sincere and straightforward from the beginning, from that first meeting when he sat down in Tom's office — struggling to fit his giant body into the small chair across from the desk. Al told him the whole story: how he was using and selling steroids, how the DEA raid had gone down. Tom noticed his new client's leather jacket, the Catholic scapular hanging from his neck, and the logo on his T-shirt: AL'S GYM.

Tom considered himself a good judge of character from his days as a beat cop. He would tell anybody: He knew the difference between a *good* guy making *bad* choices and a *bad guy*. Al was not a bad guy.

The feds alleged that in those packages Al had received were 1,850 cubic centimeters of steroids. And upon searching his bedroom, DEA agents found plastic bags of weed: 921 grams — dealer quantities — worth around three grand. All told, the charges could run him up to ten years' imprisonment and a five-hundred-thousand-dollar fine.

But Tom had a plan to get Al out of doing time. One day Al had mentioned to Tom some trouble he was having with his hip. A big lump, like a goiter, had swelled up on his hip, where he typically injected the nandrolone. Tom could work with that.

At the next hearing, Tom told Judge Hart that his client, Mr. Fontana, was in poor health. *Very poor health.* At his counsel's request, Al stood and lifted his untucked dress shirt enough to show the court the *growth* that Tom was referring to, the one he said was *very, very serious.* Now, Tom never said the word *cancer*, but he heavily implied it.

It paid off. After Al pleaded guilty, Judge Hart determined that he was a good candidate for probation. He sentenced Al to four years of it, along with 120 days in a work release program.

Al's girlfriend had shown up to support him in court that day. Mia shook Tom's hand and smiled. She was very attractive — *way* out of Al's league. He knew Al's history, but he didn't hold the infidelities against his client. He wasn't Al's priest; that wasn't part of his job.

But *God*, Tom thought as he watched the couple walk out of the courthouse, how could anyone stray from a woman like her?

One day, Tom decided to seek counsel of his own from Al. Tom was short and stocky, true to his Irish blood, and he wanted to get in shape. Could Al advise him? Al grinned, grabbed one of Tom's legal pads and a pen off his desk. He concentrated, writing out a detailed workout regimen, and told Tom to swing by the Gym anytime. Tom never did end up going by the Gym, but he held on to the list.

Yeah, he thought, *Al's a good guy.*

Chicago, 1994

Tom didn't hear from Al for months. He hadn't been concerned. He usually figured that no news was good news when it came to his clients.

He discovered that he'd been wrong at the end of 1993. A few weeks before the New Year, the federal prosecutor filed a motion in Al's case. The government had reason to believe that Al had been using steroids despite the terms of his probation. Judge Hart had ordered Al to undergo urinalysis testing throughout the four-year probationary period. A "specimen" of Al's was selected to be analyzed by an expert witness. Then, in the summer, came the affidavit: *nandrolone.* Al's urine came back positive.

Tom did what he could. He got his own expert witness to prepare his own affidavit, poking holes in the government's allegations. But he and Al both knew that wasn't gonna hold water with the judge. Al would have to do some time, no two ways about it.

Sure, Al wasn't pleased, but he didn't hold it against Tom. He told him so — that he was a real good lawyer, and he knew it wasn't his fault.

The whole thing was just too bad, Tom thought, what with the baby on the way. Al mentioned that Mia was due after the holidays, in January. It would be their first child.

But hey — Al was lucky that Judge Hart only gave him sixty days in the Metropolitan Correctional Center, the MCC, the prison just around the corner, over at Clark and Van Buren. Tom tried to put the outcome into perspective for him: "August, you go in — October, you're out. Two months? That's *nothing.*"

The time would fly by, Tom assured Al. He'd be home by Halloween, long before the baby came.

6

The Red Light

Al told me again and again, before I flew out to Chicago, that he would tell me whatever I wanted to hear. *Whatever you want, baby girl. Whatever you want.* He told me this many times. No question was off limits; he would be an open book.

I didn't waste any time in taking him up on that offer. I knew that, before I started pounding the pavement downtown, talking to prosecutors and attorneys and all the other players, I needed Al to tell me about the night he impersonated a cop with that crew, about that fake-raid-gone-wrong. The case of *USA v. Hicks*. We agreed to talk it over with a coffee and doughnuts.

My father's eyes glinted as he told me the story of how he ended up on that ride with his buddy Larry Knitter, and those guys Hicks and Moran. That was always how he would talk about that kind of thing, whenever he did something wrong: He just *ended up* doing it, as though it happened *to* him. The Family had the same habit. They referred to Knitter and the others as "those guys who wouldn't stop messing with your dad." I don't think any of them were conscious of the way that their language pardoned Al, but that didn't make it less so. Every time I heard someone say it, I felt a pinprick of rage. I wanted to feed it some oxygen and let it grow, but I couldn't afford to lose focus.

"So," I told Al, "why don't we start with the first raid —"

"That I *didn't go on,* 'cause I told Larry — I *told* him, when he called me that first time, I said —"

"No, I know, I just mean — let's start at the beginning. When was that? December 2000, right?"

Yes, that was right. Christmas was approaching. Knitter — Al always called him Larry — had been pestering him nonstop about this "opportunity." A chance for Al to make some money. This crew needed another guy to go on a ride with them. It's easy. Al said no. His friend backed off.

Until New Year's, at least. Then Knitter was at it again, my dad said, calling him nonstop, badgering him at the Gym. It was relentless. The way Al told it, his sin was not a matter of choice; he wouldn't say he chose to go on that ride. His sin was his submission; he was overcome, he was worn down, he gave in. The next raid was set for the end of January. That night, Larry picked up Al and drove him to his fate.

The second he stepped through the door of that apartment, Al knew: It was a fucking setup. The rooms were too neat, too bare of the characteristic clutter of a stash house — where were the stacks of empty pizza boxes? Chip bags, napkins, receipts? But he went along as the three men, per Hicks's orders, searched the place from top to bottom. Al took the living room. He knelt down, craning his neck and running his hands along the drawers of the TV stand, looking and feeling for any parcels of coke or cash taped to one side or another. Nothing. He paused for a moment and raised his head, face-to-face with his own reflection in the television set. That's when he saw it.

The red light. Faint but unmistakable, shining out through his reflection from behind the darkened screen.

"There was a fuckin' hidden camera in there — and *that's* when I knew it was the feds," Al said, chewing on a toothpick. "I was like, *It's over. We're fucked.* I fuckin' knew it."

I hadn't realized how far he had leaned over the table between us during the story until he sat back and paused for effect, to really let it land that *they were fucked*. He shook his head, too, for good measure.

"Then, sure enough, months later the cops picked me up and showed me the tape, and —" This time I noticed him ramping up, leaning in. "You can *see* it. If you watch the tape — I swear to fuckin' God — you can see me looking right at the TV, where the camera is. And that was it, man. The *second* I knew."

For a moment, I had the thought: *He sounds possessed.* His eyes were wide, intense, as he stared in my direction. I knew this look. Whenever Al and I talked in person, face-to-face, I always knew that he was speaking *to* me: As I reacted, his eyebrows would shoot up or knit together in emphasis; when I laughed, he smiled. But as he spoke, his gaze was always slightly unfixed, as though his eyes were focused on something right behind me, like there was someone sitting in my shadow. He wasn't looking *at* me, but past me, through me. Once I saw this, I could never unsee it. It gave me the creeps, that ghostly feeling: like someone walked over your grave.

"And —" He let out a wry laugh. "You won't fuckin' *believe* this."

I'm sure I won't, I thought.

"The charge they got me on, it was, uh, it was, uh, uh —"

"Unlawful possession —" I offered. My voice was hoarse; I hadn't spoken for a long time.

"Right, right, gun possession. So listen to *this* — me and my attorney, Tom, we're in a room with the prosecutors and they're telling me I'm done for, I'm going away for years, this and that, unless I plead guilty — unless I say I had a gun."

"But you *did* have a gun on you," I said. For a moment, my eyes were clear; the spell was broken. "Right? I mean, the court records say Knitter gave you a gun, a Ruger — what was it, a nine-millimeter?"

"Yeah, but I didn't have no fuckin' gun. I never fucked with guns. *Never.* Never had a gun, and Larry never gave me no fuckin' gun. I mean, I don't know if *he* had one, but I know *I* didn't. And so I looked at Tom, and he just kinda did this —" Here Al pantomimed: a shrug, a limp nod. "— and I was like, *Okay, fine. I guess I had the fuckin' gun.*"

He paused, as if for applause. He was almost grinning, half nodding — *possessed*, I thought again — his wide eyes looking through me. I wondered if he was seeing me at all.

"What do you think of that, huh? Didn't even *have* a fuckin' gun."

What did I think? I thought his story was all bullshit — no, I *knew* it was bullshit. I read the records. I could see the type-written charges in my mind's eye. But I didn't correct him. I was quiet. I was remembering.

Before I left for Chicago, Brent had given me some advice. He was no stranger to difficult sources, who were reticent to open up or who did nothing but lie once they did.

I remember our conversation well. At least, I think I do. We were wrapping up one of our regular meetings about my thesis. I was headed to the library for a long afternoon of research; he was off to his next class. I gathered my notes as we rose from the table.

"Sometimes," he said, "the best thing you can do is just let 'em talk, tell the story that they want to tell. And if it's not true, your reporting will show that."

Brent pushed the door open, out into one of the journalism building's noisier thoroughfares. He held the door; I stepped through.

"Sometimes, once it's all out of their system, that's when they'll start answering the harder questions. And then . . ." He shrugged. "Then you just have to figure out who you can trust."

It was the same thing with Al. I just needed to get the evidence to prove his lies to be lies. *That's* why I kept my mouth shut, I told myself, even though pretending to believe him made me feel stupid. I couldn't admit the other reason I let him talk uninterrupted: I just wanted to hang out with my dad. I didn't want to make things hard.

Before I arrived in Chicago, I had no idea the World Series was even happening, or that the Cubs had made it to game seven. The night of that last game, my dad joined us at Rosie's to watch them face off against the Cleveland Indians. Despite being from the South Side, home of the White Sox, the Family was a Cubs family.

The Cubs won, making history, their first championship in more than a hundred years. Rosie cried tears of pure joy, and as the commotion died down, Al returned, as always, to stories of the past. He started retelling one that I had heard over the phone, back when I was still in Oregon: the genesis of his relationship with Mia. My attention waned as he walked through the familiar details: It was Saturday night, he was at this body-building competition, Mia was there with her sister Jackie and Jackie's piece-of-shit boyfriend Rick, and —

"Wait." I sat up. "Who's Rick?" I was close to my aunt Jackie growing up. She picked me up from school while my mom worked. We spent nearly every weekend together, the four of us: me and Mia, Jackie and her daughter. I was certain of it — I'd met all of Jackie's boyfriends — I'd never heard of —

"Rick. Rick Stratton." Al's eyes widened. "What, your Ma never told you about Rick?"

I drew breath to defend myself, to tell my dad that he was wrong, that he must've been confused. Then Brent's words returned to me. Instead, I shut up. I let Al talk.

7

What Al Tells Me

Chicago, 1980s

Rick Stratton was a fucking maniac.

It wasn't long after high school that Al started running with tough crowds. But that was just how it was around McKinley Park. The gangs were everywhere. Once he was out of school, Al set up a bodybuilding gym in a storefront on the neighborhood's main street, Archer Avenue. His brother helped him design T-shirts, satin varsity jackets, keychains and magnets, all bearing the logo AL'S GYM. His friends from high school hung around the Gym and helped spread the word. All his buddies had a nickname that spoke for itself. There was Dago Dave, who inexplicably chose the slur himself. Fossil, at forty-two years old, was the group's senior citizen; Plate had a metal plate in his head from a motorcycle accident; Hee-Haw was from Kentucky. Al, fittingly, was Jagoff.

Sure, Al was a jagoff. He was nineteen. But he was just like any other jagoff in the neighborhood. He ran his business and hustled on the side, selling weed or Valium or steroids. Al wasn't a made man or a gangbanger. Nothing like that. In fact, his sketchy dealings made him an outlier in his family. His parents were straight: His dad worked at the Wrigley factory; his mom reared ten children, took care of her immigrant parents, and kept the household running. Maybe a couple of his brothers sold weed, but so did everybody their age.

Al didn't need to get made or roll with a crew to get what he needed. He had his stature and his reputation. He was tough, and everybody knew it. Whatever it was, respect or fear, they gave it to him.

But Rick Stratton wasn't like Al. He wasn't just tough. He ran the McKinley Park street gang, the South Side Popes. *POPES* was an acronym: "Protecting Our People, Eliminating Spics." If the name wasn't enough to send the message about their values, you just had to look at the members' tags, spray-painted on cars and windows: a hooded ghost, a cross, the occasional swastika — you get the picture. Skinhead shit.

Al and Rick were good friends, close friends. They worked out together at the Gym, hitting up the local bodybuilding competition circuits. Rick knew Al was Mexican, and sometimes he'd get in a mood and call him a spic. It hurt, but Al never took it personally. He kept his own mouth shut and counted himself lucky that it was the worst he ever got from Rick fuckin' Stratton.

There were three Stratton brothers: Rick; Matt, the youngest; and Darrell, the eldest. Their dad was a cop, a lieutenant patrolling the North Side. He was the one who raised them. From what Al heard, Rick's dad was straight as an arrow. He was a prick, but he wasn't a crooked cop like so many of the others. *Straight*, though, didn't always mean *good*. Some said the patriarch ran the house like a military commander; others likened the treatment to torture. Inside their corner house on Hoyt Avenue, Mr. Stratton tied his sons to kitchen chairs. He threatened them with knives. Then he put on his badge and cap and went out to serve and protect the city of Chicago.

At one point there had been a Mrs. Stratton. There had been a fourth brother, too: a baby. But when the boys were still young, their mother saw her chance and ran. She took the baby with her, leaving the other three behind: Rick, Matt, and Darrell.

Al and his family didn't live too far from the Strattons' place, just a five-minute drive down Western. Right across the street from Rick was the Huffman house. Cal and Ellen Huffman came from some coal-mining town — you could hear it in their accents. They came to the city to work in the factories, and they had two daughters: Jackie and Mia. Rick had been dating the older one, Jackie, for a while now. Al liked her; he knew her pretty well. They were in the same graduating class, and she hung out with a couple of his sisters.

Al felt bad for Jackie. Everyone knew Rick beat the living shit out of her. For a while, Al let the couple live in a back room at the Gym. They didn't have nowhere else to go. It was always the same story: Jackie would find them an apartment with a trusting landlord. She'd fix it up real nice. Then Rick would go ballistic and wreck the place — and he'd knock Jackie around for good measure. Anything or anyone he got his hands on, he destroyed one way or another.

Once in a while, Jackie tried to leave him. It took guts for her to try. But it was never long before Rick found her again. There was one night, after Jackie tried to break it off and run, where Al's friend Joey got caught in the crossfire. Everyone knew Joey was a sweet guy. Al remembered, back when they were all still kids, that Joey had gone out with Jackie. It seemed like they always had a soft spot for each other.

Al would be the first to tell anybody that he didn't know fuckin' shit about what went down at the time. *Nothing*. It was only after the fact that the story got back to Al. And that story was all he knew.

Jackie had left Rick again, and Rick was busy hunting her down. No one knew if it was just dumb luck, or if somebody ratted her out, but one night Rick caught Jackie in an alley, walking with Joey. And they probably were just walking — not even holding hands — but it didn't take anything more for Rick to do what he always did. He lost his shit. He snapped Jackie's arm bone in half, landing her back in the ER. He started waving one of his guns around — might've taken a shot or two, might've jammed the muzzle up against Joey's temple. All Al could get out of Joey about that night was one sentence: *I don't know how I got out of that alley alive.*

Rick wasn't an outlier in the Stratton family. Darrell and Matt were Popes, too, working under their untouchable brother. Al knew Darrell was a fucking nut case, and he'd heard Matt was going out with Jackie's little sister. Matt put hands on her, too. Al hadn't met Mia yet, but he felt sorry for her. Those two sisters, man. They sure had some kinda luck.

It was the first weekend of May, a few days before his twenty-third birthday. Al and Rick were at a bodybuilding competition held in some high school gymnasium. Rick invited Jackie; Jackie brought her little sister. Everybody was right about those two: They looked just like each other. You'd be more likely to mistake them for twins than think they were sisters six years apart. Al saw only two big differences between the Huffman girls. One: Jackie's expression was severe, where Mia's was open and friendly. Two: Mia — not Jackie — was the one with all the freckles.

After the competition, Al offered Mia a ride home. He pulled into her parents' driveway, and they talked all night. He only realized what time it was when Mia said she *really* had to go: It was nearly 3:00 A.M., and her dad would be leaving for his shift in an hour.

The next day, he took her to coffee at the diner on Archer where Jackie worked. Mia's big sister served him cup after cup of black coffee and kept a close eye on the two of them from behind the counter. Al didn't mind. He understood. He had younger sisters, after all. He'd do the same thing for them.

Mia was eighteen or so — some five years younger than Al — but her face looked even more youthful. She wasn't like the other girls in the neighborhood — barroom broads, his sister called them. She wasn't loud or crass or tough. She was sweet and spoke softly.

No one ever asked to hear the story of how they met, but Al remembered it anyway. If they did ask, he wouldn't use movie terms: no *She was the one*; no *Love at first sight*. There was only *Before* and *After*. After they met, they were together. Simple as that. Within a few days, she was living at his place. He let her borrow his truck while he was at the Gym. When they went out to eat, she kept a running tally of how much she owed him. She would write it down, cents and all.

"So I don't forget," she'd say. Al would grin, reach over to her side of the table, and flip her memo book closed.

"You know what? Forget it."

When he dropped off Mia at her parents' house or at the tanning salon where she worked, she always turned around to wave to him. He waved back before he drove away.

Back on the road, on his way back to the Gym, Al chewed on a toothpick, lost in thought. He knew Mia had a fucked-up past. So what? She wouldn't have to worry about any of that shit anymore, not now that she was with him.

Sure, Al knew he wasn't perfect. But at least he wasn't Rick fuckin' Stratton.

8

On Myth

We watch Al, at twenty-two years old, driving down Archer Avenue, lost in thought. We watch the same man, decades older, as he tells that same story to his twenty-two-year-old daughter. Then those moving images flicker out. We see nothing but a darkened screen. The theater is quiet. You can stay in your seats, but we'll step out of time all the same. There isn't much else to do for these moments as we wait, while the projectionists change the reels.

There was a practical purpose served by intermissions — or as the Brits apparently call them, intervals — back in the early days of cinema, when giant spools of thirty-five-millimeter film were mounted on towers and fed through the projectors. Before that, somewhere between the Renaissance and the Kinetoscope, actors left the stage and swapped their costumes as staff replaced and relit candles. And, of course, if you go all the way back to the Greeks, there they are: the breaks embedded into the classical five-act structure.

For me, growing up has been one big slow-drip process of understanding how all our modern roads lead us back there, back to the Greeks — psychology and philosophy, democracy and law, drama and myth.

As a kid, I loved all the ancient Greek myths. I tried to give the Catholic mythology a fair shot at my heart, but the illustrated book of all the angels and saints, gifted by the Family, failed to inspire in me the same enthrallment. In fact, they really creeped me out. I think Mia could tell. One day, that book quietly disappeared from my bookshelf, never to be seen again.

I loved Greek myth; I was also obsessed with it. These were two different things. My obsession arose from the same aspect of Greek mythology that troubled me. For every single myth contained its multitudes, all of its different versions that had been passed down through time; any given god or goddess had his or her own conflicting biographies; there was no agreed-upon canon, no final say of exactly which story was *the* story. And that was a hard pill to swallow for ten-year-old me, when I spent a summer glued to our desktop computer, trying to compile from scratch my own family tree of all of the Greek gods and goddesses. I tried to make my best guesses at which single version of each story to let stand. Out of all the different birth stories, who would I choose to be the one true mother of So-and-So? Or of all the different ways that Such-and-Such battle was said to have ended, which one would I allow to endure? It was a lot of pressure for a ten-year-old to take on. I started getting headaches. I tried to work through them. Eventually, I gave up.

I've been revisiting the subject, some twenty years removed from that humbling defeat. Recently I read about Claude Levi-Strauss and his suggestion that a myth consists of all of its versions. (I'll admit that before this recent instance, the only Levi-Strauss I knew was the one that makes jeans.) The trouble I had with myth as a kid is the same trouble I had when I started searching for where I came from. It's the same trouble I have now. This story that I am telling you, that we bear witness to in this theater, consists of all of its versions, all the gaps that form between them, all of their contradictions. Anything less than that, and the story ceases to be.

We can return our focus to the darkened screen that sits before us — only let's change things up, mix our metaphors. Now it's a darkened stage.

What we just saw play out before the curtain fell: This is what Al *says* he believes; this is his construction of the past. He wants to say it's a memory? Fine, we'll call it a memory. After all, memory is inherently constructive — an imaginative process. In telling this story, I have made rules for myself, bound myself to certain standards. I have to let the past stand for itself, no matter whose version it is.

I've done my duty. I let my father's memory play out for you, allowing it to unfold without any intervention, just as I let it play out when he first told me the story all those years ago. I have to stay quiet during the acts. I can only observe.

But — *here I bend the rules, I take liberties; here I lower my voice to a whisper* — if I could have, I would have warned you. I would have told you the things I knew. Because in this intervening period, this brief step out of time, I'm not bound to chronology. I can see the future. I know what's coming.

For instance, we saw Al's good old friend Rick and the gang he led, that McKinley Park street gang, the South Side Popes, *Eliminating Spics*. In the years to come, the hood will diversify. The Popes will have to move with the changing demographics. They'll set aside their white-supremacist origins, at least on paper, by replacing the S in *Popes*: "Spics" will become "Scum."

Then there were Rick's brothers. Al thought Darrell was the craziest of the three. If only he knew how right he would turn out to be. In the '90s, the eldest Stratton will be picked up by the cops. Darrell and another Pope will be charged with solicitation to commit murder and murder for hire; a third Pope will catch a misdemeanor weapons charge. Al will hear that Darrell was trying to order a hit on his own brother Rick. At Darrell's house, police will find twenty-seven guns — handguns, rifles, shotguns, assault weapons, all stolen from the homes of

Chicago police officers — along with thirty-one grams of coke and more than seven thousand dollars in cash. All three of the men, the newspapers will report, are sons of Chicago cops.

By the time the news hits the papers, Al will have already heard it for himself, from one of his buddies, maybe even from Rick himself. My father will think to himself, *Who the fuck tries to murder his own brother? Like something out of a Greek fuckin' tragedy.*

Decades later, Al will try to explain and defend his friendship with Rick. He'll tell me that the only reason he kept Rick close to him for all those years was to protect Mia and her sister, to keep them safe.

I should've just shot him. I would've saved a lotta people. A lotta people. He was the fuckin' devil, man. That's what he will say.

But I'm talking out of school here, aren't I? That young Al didn't know about any of this back in the '80s, back when he was working at the Gym or lifting with Rick or driving Mia home. I didn't know any of this, either, on that November night in 2016, as the postgame celebrations roared outside and I listened to a story that my father called a memory. I have to remember the rules. The actors can only know the scene they're in, as if experiencing it all for the first and only time.

You know what? Forget I said anything. Put it out of your mind. All that matters is that I did my job. I let Al say his piece. I let his story stand. The actors and I put in the work, we got it up on its feet, so you could take it all in. But — *and lean in, listen closely, I can only say this once, I can't say it too loud* — knowing what I know now? About Al and all of the stories he tells me? I'm not inclined to do it again.

The stage is gone. The screen is back, and the projector hums back to life.

9

What Kind of Man

Al was my chauffeur while I was in town, driving me around to visit aunts and cousins. No matter where we were — stuck at a train crossing; in the drive-through at Dunkin'; sitting double-parked, waiting for an open spot — I observed him like he was a captive animal at the zoo. I wanted to understand him and how he interacted with the world. I wanted to know: What kind of a man was Al?

I started with the superficial and worked my way down from there. For my father, being a man meant being big. Most of his life revolved around achieving and maintaining a tanned, muscular physique to show off in his Al's Gym–branded stringer tanks. When I was little, the Family always joked that my boyfriends better be careful not to mess with me.

"Otherwise, your Daddy will have to come over and beat 'em up!" someone would call out. Al would grin and flex an arm; his sisters would laugh. I'd wrinkle my nose: *Yuck.* I was only five, what'd I need a boyfriend for? But Al's giant frame was fun for me. He could do push-ups while I sat in a laundry basket on his back. He could throw me into the pool like a bag of flour. When I sat on his shoulders, I felt like I was on top of the world. To me, he seemed invincible.

To Al, being a man meant being tough. Imposing tattoos — crosses, daggers, thorns. Biker jackets, custom Harleys, the works. When he took me out for pizza, other customers looked at him twice. I was just a kid, so I didn't think too hard about it. I was proud of the stares. I thought it meant I had a cool, tough dad.

When he went to prison, his tattoos and muscles took on a different connotation in my young mind. They were clues that I had been too dumb, too much of a baby, to understand. If I'd known what they meant, I wouldn't have been surprised that he got locked up. I would've expected it from a guy who looked like that.

In his absence, I grew resentful of the kind of man Al was. My friends' dads didn't wear leather jackets or ride motorcycles, but they were *around*. They lived in the same house, ate dinner as a family, helped with homework. These guys took care of their kids when they were sick. They really knew their kids.

I remember being eleven years old, talking to Al on the phone at the first house we rented in Oregon. We had just moved, and he was still in prison. But it was only some months now until he was getting out — *actually* getting out.

As usual, before he hung up: "*Love you, baby girl. Love you so much.*" I looked down at the phone. *Love me? You don't even know me.* It was the first time I ever had a thought like that. I shook it out of my head, feeling ashamed. I wanted to forget it, but I never did.

When Al left, I was a nine-year-old tomboy who wore knee-length basketball shorts and oversized T-shirts. The first time I saw him after he got out, I had just turned twelve, I was nearly as tall as my mother, and — to my absolute horror — I was entering puberty.

I was also finding new and exciting ways to resent my father. Thanks to his Mexican-Italian genes, I had thick, dark brows I was begging my mom to pluck. Every other day I shaved my arms and legs, yearning for the near-translucent body hair of my blonde friends. When we all went to the mall and surveyed our reflections in the mirrors at Claire's, they would say they wished they looked "exotic" like me. I thought they were being nice, trying to make me feel better for my droopy eyelids, my strong nose, and all my fucking hair.

To make things worse, small breasts had sprouted on my chest that year. Though I hardly would have called them breasts — *tiny inconveniences*, that's what they were. They forced me to cave my shoulders when I hugged Al and the rest of the Family. My favorite oversized T-shirts no longer draped the way I liked. They billowed out beyond the widest point of my chest. I thought they made me look pregnant. So I abandoned boys' apparel for formfitting shirts that ended at my hip, not the middle of my thigh.

"Oh wow, Frankie's got boobies!" my aunt Connie exclaimed during that first visit after Al's return. My face burned. I wanted to tell her to shut the fuck up. Instead, I buried the feeling. That year I stopped eating. I stopped getting my period a few months after I first bled. I spent seventh grade hiding food I'd "eaten," walking circles in our backyard that wore away the grass, and weighing myself on our bathroom scale. Mia kept trying to hide the scale from me, but I always found it. I didn't even bother putting it back in whatever secret spot she'd tried that week. I left it out on the floor, to show her she'd been bested. I watched the number sink lower in the double digits. I felt invincible.

I thought that one day I'd grow out of all of my discomfort, but some parts of myself never changed. I never became comfortable with my femininity. I felt less like I was born a woman, and more like I was shaped into one against my will. I didn't like it; I tolerated it.

My childhood with Al painted a pretty clear picture of the way Al viewed and treated women. There were, of course, the ripped, nearly nude models gleaming and glowering all over his old office at the Gym. Then there was the matter of Al's infidelities. He was someone who cheated on his girlfriends and knocked up one or two while he was at it. When I was a kid, after my mom and I left Al, I met a rotating cast of female "friends" that my dad would bring out to my grandparents' house. I never put together that they were his girlfriends — and because of that, I never found it suspicious when we saw Adriana one weekend and Brittany the next. When I was older, I pieced together the puzzle.

Rosie was right when she told me that Mia was different from all of the other women Al dated. I could tell even as a kid. Of all Al's "friends," I spent the most time around Brittany. She had red hair and a tan. She wore lots of eyeliner. She had a daughter my age, Leila, and sometimes Al would drop me off at their house and say he was going back to work for a while. Brittany would curl our hair and give us makeovers for fun, including mascara. I couldn't stand it. I was pretty sure kids weren't even *allowed* to wear makeup, and I hated the way it made my eyes itch.

The last weekend I spent with Al before he left for prison, he took me, Brittany, and Leila to a Holiday Inn. It was supposed to be like a vacation. We brought our swimsuits and played in the indoor pool. I brought a book to read, but abandoned it when everyone else got in the water. I didn't want to be a party-pooper. But that didn't stop me from protesting when Al and Brittany took us to the sauna.

I pointed at the sign on the door. "Guys. *Guys.* It says ADULTS ONLY. See? NO MINORS. Leila, c'mon, we're not allowed in there."

Leila just sat there, her wet hair dripping onto the wooden bench. Al laughed and watched. Brittany told me that it was okay if we had grown-ups with us. That wasn't what the sign said; I wasn't buying it.

"But — but it's the *rules* —"

"Come here, sweetie." Brittany patted the empty space next to her. Resistance would get me nowhere. I gave up and joined the group, letting the door close behind me. But I had to have the last word. "If we get in trouble, it's *not* my fault."

I never knew what happened to any of these women Al dated, the ones I spent weekends with here and there throughout my childhood. I don't think I ever saw any of them again after I moved away to Oregon and Al returned to Chicago from prison. As far as I could tell, he had been more careful after getting a woman from the Gym pregnant when I was two years old — I never heard of any other secret children he'd fathered.

But at some point in high school or college, I did get one glimpse at where Al's girlfriends might end up when a cousin forwarded me a YouTube video. It was a bunch of clips from a reality show, *Rock of Love*. I recognized the red-haired contestant immediately: Brittany. I couldn't believe it. She was sent home in one of the first episodes, but in her short time on the show she became something of a fan favorite. She was a fucking mess. I watched in awe as Brittany got absolutely tanked on national television, started teary fights with the other women, and shouted the N-word — twice.

So *that's* what Rosie had meant, I guessed, when she talked about *barroom broads*.

I hoped time had softened Al, or given him some greater perspective, some newfound resolve to be a man that I could respect. After all, he had a young daughter now. *Remember*, I told myself. *Keep an open mind.*

One afternoon, he did surprise me. We were hanging out with the Family, as his sisters debated whether to vote for Clinton or Trump in the upcoming election. One said she'd vote for Trump; her husband was voting for him.

"Hillary wants abortions," she said.

Al piped up. "Trump is full of shit, you can't believe a friggin' word he says. C'mon, he says he hates Mexicans. *You're* Mexican." He leaned in toward me. It made me feel special; his commentary was only for me to hear. "You know, I'm Catholic, I don't believe in abortions, but I ain't gonna tell a woman what to do with her body." I realized that I was impressed; then I realized how low my expectations of Al had been.

Later, my dad and I sat at the kitchen table, comparing our tattoos, holding up our arms to each other. When I was a teenager, I was convinced I'd never want to get any tattoos. They had reminded me too much of Al. I wanted to be nothing like him. Once I'd grown up a little more, I changed my mind.

"You remember this one?" he asked, showing me the inside of his forearm. Of course I did. Two hearts, surrounded by flowers, with curved scrolls bearing our names: MIA. FRANCESCA MARIE.

I wanted to ask him how he felt to see Mia's name on his skin all these years later — or had the tattoo been reduced to a mundane and familiar feature, like any old freckle or scar? — but I didn't.

I noticed a tattoo on my dad's forearm that I didn't recognize. He lifted his elbow higher so I could see. A chiseled devil-woman with long, tall wings, horns, and a sour expression stared at me. She was lifting her top to expose her small waist and a generous portion of the underside of her breasts. She was also flipping me off.

"Got it right after your Ma and I split up. When I was thinking that all women were evil, you know." He smiled sheepishly. Now, *there* was the Al I remembered. There was the father I knew.

"How's your Ma been? Good?"

I came to in the passenger seat. I had been dozing off on our way back to Rosie's place, like I used to when I was a kid.

"Yeah." I rubbed my eyes. "Yeah, she's good."

"How that guy?"

"*That guy*? What, you mean Keith?"

"Yeah. That guy. How's he?"

I laughed to myself; Al could be so goddamn petty. It was funny, I didn't remember Al ever having a problem with Mia marrying Keith. They tied the knot when I was seven. I never called him Dad or anything like that. I already had a dad. There was a certain emotional distance to Keith, inherited from his WASP-ish parents, I gathered. I only remember him saying "I love you" to me one time. But I knew he genuinely cared about me. At the very least, Keith was the one who stuck around.

Al and Mia didn't talk anymore, so anything Al knew about her life he learned directly through me or from stalking my aunt Jackie on Facebook.

Yeah. That guy. How's he? I tried to keep it brief, but I got carried away in the story. Mia and Keith got divorced the summer before I went to college. I was relieved when they told me the news; it was clear they weren't happy, and I dreaded the thought of them staying together for the rest of their lives.

The breakup turned out fine. Keith and Mia shared custody of their son, my brother. But — and in my retellings I always stumbled here; I never knew quite how to say it — Keith ended our relationship about a year after the split. I was nineteen; I had just finished my freshman year of college.

We hadn't been getting along since the divorce — truthfully, we hadn't been getting along since I turned fourteen. I thought my stepfather was immature and passive-aggressive; he thought I was disrespectful and difficult. On top of that unsteady foundation, we had new issues, new sources of tension crop up as his marriage to Mia ended. I was paying my way through college myself, totally financially independent. Before I started my first term, Keith had made a kind offer, promising to buy one of my textbooks that year. He had several advanced degrees; he commiserated with me, saying he knew firsthand how pricey those things were. But months later, when I asked to redeem his gift, he balked. I made it work, factoring the extra $150 into my nightly bookkeeping calculations. I bought the book myself.

I don't know what brought the fight on that day, the last day I ever really spoke to him. I don't recall what exactly the fight was about. I just remember crying, listening to his voice on the phone. He was exasperated. "*Why don't we just call this what it is?*" And I never saw Keith again.

I hid all of this from my brother, Keith's son. He was a young kid, dealing with the divorce on his own with me away at school. I couldn't live with myself if his relationship with his father became colored or tainted in any way by me.

At least one of us should get to have a dad, I thought.

Every so often, my brother would mention his dad in passing, giving me little updates. Last I had heard, he was in AA and finding a lot of meaning in the 12-step process. I was glad; whatever he needed to do to be a good dad to my brother, that was all I cared about.

That's what I told Al, pretending the old hurt was buried, forgotten. I wondered how he would react: The father figure who had once usurped him was now out of the picture; his daughter had suffered another paternal loss. I dared to hope for a sympathetic ear.

I regretted telling Al as soon as the words left my mouth. He never showed me any sympathy. He never asked how it made me feel. He started grinning, like he'd won a long-held bet.

"I *knew* it. I always *knew* something was off between him and your Ma. Knew before you guys even moved to Oregon." Al pronounced it wrong, the way everyone in Chicago pronounced it: Ore-*gahn*, instead of Ore-*gun*. "No wonder. What a piece of shit, man. A fuckin' drunk." He spoke with an air of condescension, as if he looked much better than Keith in comparison — who, for the record, was never a "drunk." But I didn't correct Al's pronunciation or his insults. I just tried to change the subject, repeatedly.

He didn't notice my discomfort. Or maybe he just didn't care. He harped on the topic for days, retelling the same stories over and over again to hammer his point home. There was one that he took particular pride in, that he especially relished retelling.

The story goes: Al drove over to Mia's house in the suburbs after they broke up; by then she was dating Keith. My parents got into an argument on the front lawn, in front of her sister, my aunt Jackie. And boy, was Jackie pissed, "probably more pissed than your Ma"; one of them threatened to call the cops on him. No matter how hard he tried, Al couldn't remember what the fight was about, how it had started. But he remembered what he said to Mia before he jumped back into his truck: *If I ever see that boyfriend of yours, I'll cut his fucking hands off.*

"I don't know why I said that," Al said. That sheepish smile. I could never put my finger on it but there was something about his unassuming expressions that made him likable, even when he was saying horrible things. I resented this about him; it felt like a cheap trick.

I didn't know what to say. I couldn't force a laugh if I tried. Was that supposed to impress me, if it were even true? What kind of person did he think I was?

"Yeah, I don't know why," my dad repeated, with a low laugh. "But that's what I said."

One day, after lunch, Andie ran off to watch TV. When she was out of earshot, I asked Al in a low voice, "Is it weird for you at all? You know, to have a little kid again?"

He laughed. "Yeah. 'Cause I'm old. When she's your age, I'll be in my seventies."

That seemed to remind him of something. He called Andie back into the room and pulled her onto his lap. He handed his phone off to one of his sisters. "Get a picture," he said. The three of us smiled at the lens: my father, his daughter, and me. When I saw the photo, I couldn't deny that Andie looked more like Al than I ever did.

If Al went on for too long about the similarities between little Frankie and little Andie, he ended up going to the same place. At first, I thought it was introspection, but I soon saw he was just rationalizing his mistakes. Either way, it went like this:

"I wish you could've had a normal father, you know? A normal childhood, and all that. And I wish I never went on that friggin' ride — wish I never stepped out on your Ma neither. You know, maybe if she and I hadn't broken up, you might've stayed in Chicago. Who knows, you might've gone to high school in Brookfield and I would've seen you all the time and —"

Here, Al interrupted himself and seemed to shake himself awake. But if he hadn't cheated, his son wouldn't have been born — he wouldn't get to live a life. And if Al hadn't done everything exactly how he'd done it, Andie wouldn't exist, either.

"It's like everything happens for a reason, you know? So I couldn't change anything, otherwise it'd all be different."

Then he'd lean back in his chair, satisfied. I resented Al's rationalizations. They made my blood boil. They were the closest he could get to apologies, and they didn't measure up.

I didn't want to admit that in my own life, back in Eugene and far away from Al, I had been doing the same thing, rationalizing my own mistakes.

Late one night, months after our breakup, Justin had invited me to his studio apartment. He said he missed me. We slept together. I woke up in familiar flannel sheets, the same kind he'd had when we were dating back in high school. It was like some bizarre *Groundhog Day* phenomenon, as if all those miserable days I'd suffered through had never happened. I'd been thrust back in time and given a second chance at the life I thought I wanted. Long story short, I thought that because we'd had sex, we were now back together. I was wrong. He didn't want anything serious. I pretended that I could be happy with that, but he saw through me. He called the whole thing off a few days later. We went back to being relative strangers. And I was back to where I started: missing classes, starving, picking my palms raw.

Stewing in my own heartache, I started warming up to the idea that I could be a bad person, or someone who could do bad things. Knowingly. On purpose. It seemed like everybody was doing it. Everyone was doing what they wanted to get what they wanted, and I just got caught in the crossfire. So why not join them? Why not get what I wanted for once?

I wanted to hurt Justin, so I circled his friends. I took advantage of our acquaintanceship and started showing up to their off-campus house. The group smoked weed each night in the attic and always left their front door unlocked. No one objected to my intrusion.

I became fast friends with Sarah, a regular in the attic who was also nursing a broken heart. We became inseparable. I fed her all of Justin's wrongdoings, knowing she couldn't keep a secret. I wanted her to spread them around. I wanted everyone to know who he really was.

Deep down, I liked Sarah. She was honest, funny, spontaneous. We had only known each other a few days when we ended up at a tattoo parlor at 11:00 a.m. By noon, we both had nipple piercings. In the attic that night, we shared knowing looks. One of us would laugh when the other winced in pain after accidentally bumping her chest with the bong. We had a secret. I liked it.

I knew I wanted to sleep with Sarah because it would eat Justin alive. But I also started to feel nervous when she and

I were alone together, in my car or in my room. I knew she liked me enough to hang out with me all the time. She told me I was hot when we went out to bars. But when we were alone together, I didn't believe any of it. I wondered if she thought about me. I wondered if she felt nervous, too. I hated the feeling; I wanted to stamp it out.

Late one Saturday afternoon, everyone was leaving the attic early — for a shift at work, or off to study for our looming midterm exams. Sarah and I were the only ones who weren't ready to leave. As the crowd dissipated, we stood silent for a second. The alternative hung heavy in the air around us until I finally said it: "Well, we could go to my place."

Maybe she kissed me first, maybe I kissed her. I only remember waking up before her the next morning. She stirred and smiled and checked her phone. I stole a few looks at her as I got dressed. Her mascara had rubbed off in the night. Her real eyelashes were blond. I hadn't known that about her; I'd never seen her without makeup. A pit grew in my stomach. I shouldn't have looked. It was unfair. I got to see her as she was. Everything she knew of me was armor, artifice.

She will hate you, I thought. *And it's too bad. She's a nice girl.*

The sinking feeling faded after I drove her home. I rationalized. Sure, Sarah didn't deserve whatever Machiavellian bullshit I was up to, but I didn't deserve what I got, either. She could hate me all she wanted. She'd have to take it up with the other guy. I hadn't started this; I was just passing it along.

Then I hit Justin where he lived. One day in the attic, one of the guys mentioned that Justin was going to be his new roommate. I left Sarah's side and started sitting next to that guy, Zach, instead. He invited me to his house parties; I let him explain how Reddit worked to me; I was the last to leave one night when he made the move I knew was coming. When he asked if it would hurt Justin if he knew about us, I pretended not to know. We hooked up for months. I always left my shoes and purse at the front door for Justin to see. I didn't feel nervous anymore. For the first time, I felt powerful, and I kept my conscience on a short leash.

Andie stayed at my grandparents' house while Al dropped me off on the North Side. I was starting to feel suffocated in the car with him. I wondered if there was any way for me to rent a car — I was too young. Still, I didn't know how many of these rides I had left in me. Al had gotten himself back on the topic of Keith, then Mia, then the past.

"Yeah, your Ma was different back then. You might not believe it, but she was. You know, when she was sixteen, she ran away to Oklahoma. Just took off with some guy. She was — what do you call it? *Rebellious*. But nah. Nah, she don't like to talk about the past."

I'd never heard anything about Oklahoma. I didn't buy it. I wanted to take an aspirin and go to bed.

"I ain't sayin' I was Prince Charming or nothin'. I know I fucked up. But when your Ma got with me, she got away from all that crap. She started to have goals."

I nodded along and let him talk, wondering all the while how my mother could have ever ended up with a man like that, a man like Al.

———

10

The Fear

Chicago, 1970s

The news said there was a clown out killing people. Mia heard about him in snippets on TV, on the radio, at school. It was snowing outside when she started hearing about that man, Gacy.

Mia will never be sure of the chronology of her memories, but she can approximate dates. It must've been January 1979; she was seven. Years later, she'll learn that the man wasn't just a birthday clown. But she didn't know any more then, no more than what she heard.

Was that the same winter — ? It was snowing when her teacher handed out candy canes. It was the last day before Christmas break, and the class spent the afternoon singing carols. After school, she walked home, let herself into the empty house, and sat with her head under the pine tree. She looked up at the lights twisting through the boughs.

Was that the same winter — ? Mia was sweeping snow off the porch when she heard a faint voice. *Help. Help.* She looked over into their neighbor's yard and saw the woman who lived next door, a single mother of a young son, standing in the snow. But something was wrong. She stood at a strange angle and seemed unsteady on her feet. Then Mia saw: The woman's nightgown was melting into her skin, smoke rising from the building behind her. She ran inside to get her mother. Ellen and the other neighbors gathered wet sheets to wrap around the woman.

Somehow, she survived. So did her son. Mia heard that the boy's mom drank heavily and had a lot of boyfriends who came and went. She was passed out that night when the boy took his chance. After starting the fire, he ran upstairs to warn the elderly couple who lived above them, saving them. The boy was sent away after that. Mia never saw him again. She wondered where he went.

Whichever winter it was, the news of a man — who was a clown, who was a killer — did not rattle Mia. The little girl was not surprised; her world was not shattered because her world had never been safe. News like that wasn't a revelation. It was confirmation. She knew there were bad people, and seeing killers and kidnappers on her parents' television set merely confirmed that fact. If it showed her anything, it was only that there were different kinds of badness in men, more than the kinds she already knew.

Years later, Mia will try to think back to her grammar school days. The memories will be discernible less by date and more by weather, the first snow in winter, the new leaves in spring. The day-to-day never changed much: Her parents, Cal and Ellen, were always working at the factory. Ellen worked the day shift while Cal worked nights. Most of the time, the two daughters fended for themselves. Jackie was six years older than Mia, and looked out for her as best as she could.

Cal and Ellen always told the girls to get inside before the streetlights came on. If they didn't, the devil would steal their soul. That's what parents in the neighborhood told their kids. Mia never forgot the threat of that monster, how the fright buried itself in her chest.

Her everyday life had enough to fear, never mind devils

and killer clowns on TV. Mia worried constantly about being kidnapped. One afternoon Jackie had come home shaking. A car had followed her as she walked past McKinley Park. The driver tried to get her into the back seat. Jackie was twelve years old; Mia was six.

After that, Jackie took her sister outside of their house. They stood on the sidewalk, facing down the block. Someone drove down the street. Jackie pointed to the car's headlights.

"You see that car? If you ever see one following you and the guy driving tries to ask you something, or tells you to get in, what do you do?"

"Run away."

"Yeah, but which way?" Mia didn't answer. "Remember? You run toward the headlights. You run the way they're coming from. 'Cause if you turn around and run the same way they're driving, they can pull up behind you and snatch you." Another car passed the two girls. Mia watched the driver, a shadow behind the wheel. "But if you run the other way, they gotta stop and turn around, so you can get away." The passing car turned the corner. She watched it disappear.

"Hey." Jackie's thin eyes were fixed on her. "You got it?"

"Yeah."

"So which way do you go?" Mia pointed down the block, at a pair of invisible headlights. The street was empty, but she imagined a van driving toward her. She imagined running.

Suddenly, Mia remembered: A year or so before that afternoon, a man in a car had stopped to ask her a question. But the car wasn't on the street, it was driving down the back alley. And she wasn't on the sidewalk, she was in the backyard. Mia was even smaller then. Her head barely cleared the top of the back gate that she passed through to meet the man at the passenger-side window. He had called out to her. "'Scuse me. Can you help me? I need directions."

As Mia approached, the man looked at her. "You know

where to buy pantyhose around here?" He was holding a map on his lap with one hand. She stood on her toes so she could see. The man held his penis in his other hand. He was sweating. Something was wrong. Before she could move, she heard the back door swing open and shut. Someone grabbed Mia by the arm, dragging her away from the man and his map, up the stairs and into the house. The door slammed shut. She looked up and saw her sister turn the dead bolt and peer through the blinds. She heard the gravel crunch beneath the wheels as the car slowly drove away.

Mia wrinkled her nose. "What was he *doing*?"

Her sister spun around. Jackie was scary when she got mad. She didn't yell; she didn't need to. "You *never* go up to a car like that."

"But he asked for directions. He wanted to buy —"

"No. Never."

Staring down the block at the invisible headlights, Mia thought about standing in the back alley with that man and his map. She was glad she had a sister to teach her things, keep her safe.

For a while, Ellen was in and out of the hospital. She was sick, but Mia didn't know what the sickness was. She and her sister would stay over at a neighbor's house when Cal worked. The woman had two sons around Jackie's age. Mia didn't sleep well there. One day she came home from school and found her cat dead. The older boy said the cat hung itself on the hair dryer cord. But she knew he killed it.

When the warmer weather came, kids at school talked about shootings around the neighborhood. Every summer Mia heard some story of a grandma who was just watching TV in her living room when a stray bullet flew through her window and killed her. Mia, filled with dread, thought of her parents. When they weren't working, they liked to sit and watch TV in their living room. What if they got shot?

Through the spring and summer of 1979, the headlines were much of the same:

1 DIES, 3 HURT IN GANG SHOOTINGS.

TEENS CHARGED WITH MURDER IN GANG-RELATED SHOOTING.

YOUTH FATALLY SHOT IN GANG FEUD.

The words jumped out at Mia from the newspapers that lay open on the kitchen table. She tried not to think about them; she thought about them constantly.

Mia didn't sleep much, even in her own bed. When she did, she sleepwalked. She could never remember what she had done; her family told her the next morning. One night, Cal woke up with a start when he heard stomping down the hall. When he reached Mia's doorway, he saw the open window. She was straddling the ledge, one leg dangling in the night air, when he grabbed her. There was no roof underneath to catch her, just a long drop. The next day, Mia watched her dad pull out his toolbox and nail all the upstairs windows shut. She shuddered, imagining what would have happened if her dad didn't wake up.

Sleep is a place you go alone. Mia learned this at a young age. She never wanted to be alone. Some nights she crawled into Jackie's bed. She made her sister turn over and face her. "You have to keep looking at me. Don't close your eyes. Least till I'm asleep." Mia didn't know what she was afraid of. It was a deep dread, a sense of doom. Her sister groaned and yawned, but she kept her promise. She kept her eyes open.

And was that the same year — ? A popular boy had started poking fun at one of Mia's classmates, a girl who was mousy and quiet and wore thick eyeglasses. Mia knew that boy — he was a jerk to her, too.

During gym class one day, Mia's eyes narrowed. The boy was ambling over to his target. She beat him to her.

"Hey. I'm your friend," she told the girl. "I'm gonna come over after school. Okay?"

"Okay."

Mia knew her family was poor, poorer than everyone else she knew in the neighborhood, but this girl had it even worse than they did. Her apartment sat above a bar, and cockroaches crawled around the floor. They sat on the couch and watched television for an hour or so. They didn't speak. But the next day in gym class, she smiled at Mia. Eventually the boy decided to target Mia again. He didn't know she'd been waiting for him. The next time he tried to come after her, Mia slapped him so hard his baseball cap spun around his head.

11

Going Away

Chicago, 1980s

Mia still couldn't sleep. She stayed up late reading *It* and *Cujo* to pass the time. Jackie laughed when she saw the library books on the table.

"What are *you* doing reading Stephen King? You hate scary shit like that."

Mia shrugged. She didn't know why she chose them, or why she enjoyed them. She wasn't afraid they'd give her nightmares; she had them most nights already.

Everyone knew Mia was easily spooked and hated all the horror movies they'd cajole her into seeing. The boys would poke fun at Mia's sweetness, teasing that betrayed their fondness for her. The tougher girls would roll their eyes and snap their gum. Later, they all ate burgers in the parking lot. One of Jackie's friends just stared at Mia, her expression equal parts curiosity, suspicion, and mild disgust.

"Wow. You're so, like, *nice*. I can, like, see little cartoon birds flying around your head. Like Snow White."

When Mia returned the books to the library, she wandered over to the geography section, scanning the US states until she found Maine. Stephen King's books were always set in Maine. She took one of the books to a table and flipped through it. She liked to imagine living in one of those Victorian-style houses. She would have a bedroom in the house's turret and look out the window onto a quiet tree-lined street.

Maybe she did know why she chose those books, and she just didn't want to think about it. Fear was her constant companion. She couldn't get rid of it. But when she was reading, she was the one in control. She could choose to be scared, and she could choose how far her imagination would take her. This kind of fear went only as far as she let it.

She couldn't control the other fear. On her first day at the local gang-ridden high school, Mia had watched a man walk up to someone sitting in a car. The man yanked open the door, stabbed the driver in the legs, and walked away. The driver screamed and bled. She saw it when she closed her eyes.

Mia was miserable at her new school. She became the target of mean girls in her class. When Rick got wind of the bullying, he told her not to worry. "I know some girls who go there. They'll be friends with you." That was worse. Those girls wore black and white: the Popes' colors. Mia didn't want anything to do with them, either. She started skipping school altogether.

At night, Mia heard Jackie and Rick in the bedroom next to hers. Cracking wood, shattering glass, a cacophony of destruction. Then the words. He would kill Mia. He would kill their parents. He would put a bullet in Jackie's fucking head. They weren't empty threats. Mia watched Rick break the windows of her parents' house with rocks and bullets. She watched her sister's wounds wax and wane. Bruises flowered and faded, bones cracked and reset.

She was sixteen years old and dating Rick's younger brother, Matt, when he called her one afternoon.

"We're getting out of here."

They were going away, he said, and she had to steal her parents' car and pick him up. If she didn't, he'd come over there and knock out all the windows. Mia left a note for her parents and grabbed the keys. When she pulled up, Matt took the driver's seat. He was bleeding; his nose was broken. She didn't ask what happened, only where they were going.

"Oklahoma."

She knew he had family there. She didn't ask anything else. Matt drove through the night, until they reached a dingy apartment. That was where they stayed. Days gathered into weeks. There were always people around, mostly her age; one of them had a little dog. Drugs, too, were always around. Even when she didn't see them, she knew who was on them. Mia wasn't allowed to leave the house, except to walk the dog.

On one day's walk, she saw some cops towing her car. Her parents must've reported it stolen. They were probably looking for her. She stopped and watched. The cops didn't give her a second glance. To them, she was just a girl walking her dog.

From a pay phone, she called her cousin. "Tell everyone I'm fine," she said. She didn't want them to worry.

Months passed. They needed cash, so Matt let her get a job at a doughnut shop. She went to work. She walked the dog. Eventually, her family found her. She never knew how. Later on, when she tried to remember, the memories stalled and skipped. It was like watching an old film.

Mia was in Oklahoma. Then Mia was in the sky. She had the window seat, next to her mother and sister. It was her first time on a plane. Snow fell as they descended into Chicago.

Chicago, 1990

Mia was nineteen when she took the train to the courthouse downtown. The notice of her court date had arrived in the mail: resisting arrest, disorderly conduct. The police records bore her name, height, and weight, along with an account of her demeanor during her arrest. The officers quoted her purported cries: *Motherfucker, who do you think you are?*

When it was her turn to address the judge, Mia told him the truth. "This wasn't me. I didn't do this, I was never arrested. It was my sister." Really, it was Rick. He controlled Jackie. She carried guns for him on the street. If she got arrested, she used Mia's name. There was no use in going to the police for help. After all, Rick's dad was a cop.

After the judge puzzled his way through Mia's story, she headed back down the aisle through the gallery. She felt lousy. She felt like a snitch. As she left, one of the bailiffs — a woman — looked at her and nodded. "Good for you," she said, and looked like she meant it.

Mia couldn't remember when or where she met Al. But whenever and wherever it was, it wasn't love at first sight. It was never love, not really. Mia didn't see a partner in him. His best qualities were the ones he lacked, things he wouldn't or couldn't do: Al was a man who would not hit her, or threaten to kill her, or shoot out her parents' windows in the middle of the night. Ultimately, he was someone who could protect her and her sister. She knew that no one else — not her family, not the police — could do it.

But Al wasn't the protector she hoped for. Mia saw her sister, bruised and broken, after Rick found her and her friend Joey together in an alley. Her sister told her it was because of Al that Rick had snapped her arm bone and held a gun to Joey's head. Al was the one who'd tipped him off. Mia was paralyzed.

Later, when Al picked her up from the hospital, she said nothing. He'd deny it all anyway, and she didn't want to cause any more trouble for Jackie. She sat silent and looked out the window. She felt like an insect in a jar; she could only watch the world go by. But she would never forget that Al could not be trusted.

When Mia let her mind wander, it strayed to the same places. *How do people start over?* she wondered. *I guess they move away.* She thought about Maine. Before long, the cloud burst. She was forced back into her body, back to where she was. And she made do.

Later that year, Jackie left Rick for good. One morning he put a gun to her head and told her, again and again, that he was going to kill her. Jackie persuaded him to let her go to work. He dropped her off at the diner and watched her walk through the front door. Eventually he drove away. She waited. Then she bolted.

Jackie and Mia hid away for weeks. They rented a small apartment in the wealthy neighborhood of Oak Park, and Mia got a job at a little grocery store owned by a Greek family. Her coworkers were a few middle-aged members of the family and some college-aged kids who lived in the neighborhood. There was a blind woman who came to the store each week, whom Mia led down the aisles by the arm.

She became friends with one of the shop's young delivery drivers. His family owned one of the grand, sprawling houses in the neighborhood, near Ernest Hemingway's childhood home and the Frank Lloyd Wright house. He was around her age, and he wasn't in college, either — though his lack of matriculation was just a protest of his parents' expectations. He wrote poetry and read it to her. He invited her over to his family's house and cooked for her. When she was home sick, he brought her ice cream from the store.

None of the people in Mia's new life knew she was different from them. She didn't lie to anyone; she just never said much. They didn't know she lived in Oak Park only because her sister was hiding from a gang leader who wanted to kill her. They didn't know Mia's parents worked in factories, or that she dropped out of high school and was studying for her GED. They knew she was sweet, dressed nicely, and spoke well. She was a regular at the local library and read *A Moveable Feast* in the park. She looked like any other North Side college kid.

But they knew that Mia's boyfriend was different. They saw Al drop her off in his truck. He and the Greek guys had an unspoken standoff every time she ran across the street into the store. They were all thinking the same thing. *What is Mia doing with* that *guy? She's such a nice girl. Why doesn't she just date the delivery boy?*

But they didn't ask too many questions. They knew it wasn't their place.

12

———

The Family Snitch

I checked into the Hyatt in the Loop, using my grant money for a week's stay. It was a relief to be alone. I fell into a dead sleep. When I woke up, it was dark. I stood at the windows that stretched from floor to ceiling. I watched the traffic, the changing colors of the stoplights so far below.

I no longer needed Al for rides. I was a short walk from just about anywhere I needed to be over the coming days: the Daley Center, attorneys' offices, et cetera. That, too, was a relief. I didn't want to be in a car with Al for a good long time.

I was done with his never-ending stories and with my own passivity. For days, I'd been sitting around and nodding. I disgusted myself. I needed to sit Al down and interview him properly. He knew this was coming, he knew about my thesis, we'd talked about all of it months before over the phone. He was always game for anything; at least that's what he said. Still, I was nervous. I asked Al to come downtown for an interview the next day. We could hang in my hotel room, get some lunch nearby. I asked him to find someone to watch Andie, so we could be alone and talk openly. In the spirit of full disclosure, I was detailed.

"I'll be taking notes and recording with a tape recorder, like all the other interviews I've been doing. Then you can tell me about the case and we can just talk."

He agreed. *"Whatever you want."*

Al called me back that afternoon. *"I'm around the block."* I could hear the sounds of traffic through the phone. *"Parking's a bitch down here. Tryna find a spot. Come down and meet me. Hurry down."*

I slipped on my shoes and grabbed my hotel key, leaving my coat and purse behind. *Would it kill him to say please?* Out on the street, I shivered in my sweater, craning my neck, searching the passing cars, cursing Al.

I heard a whistle. "Yo, Frank! *Frankie!*" The familiar truck pulled over, blocking traffic. Al rolled down the window. "Get in!"

He did a loop around the block while I tried to revive any feeling in my hands. I was too distracted to notice until it was too late: Al wasn't looking for parking. He was hungry. He took us to a Portillo's relatively nearby — though far enough away, I noted, that I'd still need a ride back. He acted like nothing out of the ordinary was happening, like this is what we'd planned all along. It happened so fast I didn't have time to feel tricked.

I chewed on the inside of my cheek. The blood rushed in my ears. I knew he wasn't coming back to the hotel with me. *Son of a bitch.* I searched for a pen in the cup holders and side compartments; maybe I could take notes on a napkin. But I came up empty. Instead of getting my interview, I watched him eat a chopped salad. I let mine sit untouched in front of me. I felt sick.

Al was talking about Andie. It made him nervous, the fact that he was so old when she was born. He worried about what would happen to her when he was gone. He leaned forward in his chair and asked me for a promise, searching for the right words.

"When I go — *whenever* I go — look out for her, you know. Make sure she stays on the — the right path. Can you do that?" I watched his focus shift; his gaze dialed in on me. I was startled. For what might've been the first time, he was truly looking into my eyes.

"Of course." I regretted it as soon as I said it.

As we drove back to my hotel, I thought about Al's arrest from 2015, that stupid trip to the chop shop. I worried that he would land himself in prison again. A few years ago, I wouldn't have cared — it was his life to ruin, not mine. But now he had a child. Soon Andie would be the age I was when Al went away, and I worried that the cycle would repeat itself. She didn't deserve to get caught up in it.

He dropped me off at the curb, and I rushed into the lobby. I let the door of my hotel room slam behind me. There, on the table — my pen and pad, my tape recorder, all right where I left them. Now that I was alone, the anger crept up my neck. I sickened myself; I had been too trusting; I'd made it so easy for him.

Fuck it. Fine. I can play this game. I was my father's daughter, after all.

I put Al out of my mind. I set off the next morning with a new resolve: If he wasn't going to budge, then I'd better get my answers elsewhere.

The federal prosecutor, Assistant US Attorney Morris "Sonny" Pasqual, cut to the chase when I finally got him on the phone. He couldn't talk to me. Since Hicks was still a fugitive, his case was still technically open — and that went for all his codefendants, too, even the ones who had finished serving their time. That was also why, I had gathered, I wasn't able to get access to certain records, specific transcripts and exhibits I wanted to see.

But, Sonny told me, if Hicks ever reappeared and the United States was able to try him in court, that'd be a different story. *Fat chance*, I thought. Of course, I didn't blame Sonny. He'd been nice enough to call me back. That was more than some of the defense attorneys did. The ones who did return my calls, I made arrangements to meet for interviews.

First up, representing Larry Knitter, was Joe Lopez. He was known by his nickname: "The Shark." His office was decorated with all manner of shark memorabilia. Figurines and posters surrounded him as he sat across from me at his desk. It made quite a first impression.

Joe "The Shark" Lopez was a real ham, a total character. You could tell he loved his niche celebrity status. He'd represented a local mob boss, portrayed a lawyer on the TV show *Chicago PD*, and he was once charged with misdemeanor assault for hitting his own client in the mouth in a courtroom lockup.

"Did you see that?" he asked me. "On the internet?"

I had. I'd found the grainy security-cam video the night before and watched it again on my walk over.

"Well, *that* almost caught me a suspension. I just got out of it last week." (Back at my hotel that night, I fact-checked him, and he was telling the truth. Ultimately, the judge found there was enough reasonable doubt as to whether he had whacked the guy through the thick bars of that holding cell because he was in fear for his own safety.)

I couldn't fact-check some of his other claims: "You know, it's funny. One of the smartest girls in high school wrote in my yearbook, *Looking forward to seeing you on TV one day being a famous lawyer.* And it turned out to be true! She wrote that back in 1973!" He smiled. "She called it."

The local papers described him as a "well-known mob attorney," who wore "flamboyant pink socks." They typed him as "gregarious," "talkative." He was, indeed, talkative. I sat in his office for the better part of an hour as he bounced from topic to topic: his TV cameos, his reputation around town, the infamous legacy of the Chicago police. *That*, I was interested in: what larger forces had enabled Hicks and his crew to do wrong, along with all the other groups of crooked cops that came before and after them.

"The corruption — it's never gonna stop." He shrugged and grinned. "It can't. It's Chi-town. This city is built on corruption."

His high-profile mobster clients had monikers of their own, embedded into their name on first reference: Anthony "Tough Tony" Calabrese, Mario "The Arm" Rainone —

Speak of the devil. The phone rang. Lopez answered: "What's up, Mario? Good. I'm right in the middle of a conference, but I wanna take your call. We have that letter ready to go." They went back and forth for a few. I smiled politely. Lopez seemed delighted by the timing, the chance to give me a peek behind the curtain. He explained his work for "The Arm."

"We had a gun case — the government asked for twenty-five; I got him fifteen years in *minimum*. It was a great victory, 'cause they had Mario on tape, telling this guy, *If you don't pay this bill, I'm gonna come over, I'm gonna cut your kids' heads off, and I'm gonna plant them in the front yard so you can watch them grow.*" Lopez leaned back in his chair, satisfied. "Yeah, he's brutal — they also suspect him of this famous murder from the '70s, of this Standard Oil executive that the mob was extorting." He sighed. "Yeah . . . Brutal."

Apparently, Lopez used to be tight with some Outfit guys back in the day. But he learned his lesson. That's what he said. "I had two grand jury subpoenas. I've almost been indicted a couple of times. I don't need any hassles."

What were we talking about again? Oh, right: corruption. I got him back on track. I let him paint the picture for me.

"What a lot of people don't realize, there's an underworld in Chicago, beyond the mob. There's drugs on the street. There's people out there pimping, taking sports books, robbing railroad stations and cartage shipments that they're selling to one another." I thought of my dad telling me about stuff he'd buy that *fell off a truck.*

"It's always going to be like that. It started like that, and I can't imagine it ever not being anything like that." I nodded. I remembered that Chicago was built on a swamp.

I steered us back to one of his other, non-Outfit clients: Larry Knitter, that old friend of my dad who got him involved in Hicks's crew in the first place. I asked Lopez to walk me through the case, to tell me about the crew and all those dealers whose houses and cars they robbed with abandon.

"For *those* guys, it was cost of doing business," Lopez said with a shrug. "That's how it was looked at. *Oh, the cops ripped you off? Then you got lucky! You didn't get arrested!*"

After the crew got busted, Knitter had ended up taking a plea deal. I read his apologetic statements from his 2005 sentencing in newspaper archives; he told the court he'd been a "follower." He was facing fifteen to seventeen years, but thanks to his cooperation with the feds, he ended up with nine and change.

That cooperation with the investigation included testifying at the trial of Larry Hargrove, the former police sergeant who'd moved to Vegas. If Eddie Hicks ever showed up, Knitter would be on the hook to testify against him, too. And there was no chance of Hicks getting a deal.

"If they catch him, they're gonna prosecute him. Look at Whitey Bulger. It don't matter. *Feds don't forgive.* That's my quote of the day. Write that down." I didn't write it down.

"I tell people all the time, if you can put *Martha Stewart* — America's best cookie maker — in prison? You can put anybody in prison. You know, she had guts. She went to trial; she lost; she did her time. I tell my clients, *She got more guts than you guys do!*"

Once I was out of questions, he asked me about my project, my past, my other parent. I explained Al's peripheral presence in my life and the move Mia made out to Oregon — a place she'd never been to, a place where she had no family.

"So she just picked the farthest place you could go without getting in the water." He nailed it. Then he turned his focus to my dad.

"A lot of good people do stupid things. Most of our clients are really good people. I mean, we have some who aren't, but most of 'em? Like Larry Knitter? Like your dad? All *good people* — you know, beyond this stuff that they do when they leave the house."

He can't really believe this, can he? I wasn't sure. I assumed this speech was for my benefit as the daughter of a man who'd "done stupid things." He didn't know that I didn't give a fuck whether or not Al was fundamentally good — or that if I'd been forced to answer definitively, I was leaning toward *not.*

"There's other people that are just pieces of shit in general, right? I don't have too many of those as clients, I don't like those kind of people. I don't do purse snatchers or, you know, street crimes." Lopez flashed another smile. I wondered if sharks ever smiled. "I do other kinds of stuff."

Bob Clarke's office was quiet. It was austere. There was no kitsch; there were no figurines. He gestured for me to make myself comfortable before he took a seat in his leather chair and crossed his arms. But I was not comfortable, because Bob Clarke did not want to talk to me.

He made it obvious. He didn't seem like the kind of guy who wanted to waste his time shooting the shit with some kid. I'd expected some of that. What I didn't expect was the skepticism, and how quiet it was.

I asked if I could turn on my tape recorder.

No, he said. He wanted to hear my questions first. His client Larry Hargrove never met my dad before the night of that raid. Hargrove was now serving his sentence out in San Pedro. So what, exactly, did *we* have to talk about?

I read each question to him from my notebook — they were only shorthand notes, jumping-off points that sounded stupid and unpolished out loud.

"Not gonna answer that," he repeated after each one. I drew a faint line through each question he shot down — I considered it a subtle, conciliatory gesture. He didn't seem to notice; his arms remained crossed.

I reached the end of my list, every item scratched out. I checked the clock and tried to think of how to turn things around in the remaining half hour of our meeting. Before I could get my thoughts together, Bob started asking me questions of his own. He wanted to know where I was studying, what kind of journalism I was pursuing, what experience I had in reporting — and how old was I, anyway? Twenty-one?

"Twenty-two." I felt myself shrink in my chair.

He wanted to know why I was working on this project about my father at all. As I attempted to answer one question, he'd interrupt with another.

"So, what are you trying to do?" Bob asked eventually. "What, you wanna be the family snitch?"

This wasn't a question but a statement. Gone was my veil of professionalism. My face grew hot. I don't remember what I said, only that I stuttered, that I felt small. I remember trying to catch my breath, like I had the wind knocked out of me.

Bob shifted in his chair. Our conversation was over. He shook my hand, said I seemed like a good kid, and handed me his card. He wished me luck at my internship next summer at *The Wall Street Journal*. "Keep in touch," he said.

Out on the street, I tossed the card in the first trash can I saw. The winter chill eased my stinging cheeks, but I got no comfort from it. I told myself that guy was a real dick.

I was terrified he was right.

I knew some members of the Family were unhappy with my search. I knew that, in their old neighborhood on the Southwest Side, there wasn't much worse you could be than a snitch. If you saw someone do something wrong, you kept it to yourself — or you joined them.

The Family thought I should leave my dad alone and let the past lie. *He did his time. Why can't she let it go?* Why couldn't I let it go? That was the real question Bob was asking. Even in the safety of my hotel room, I couldn't come up with a convincing answer. Fragments floated around my head: *My father had lied to me . . . Everyone wants to know who their parents really are . . . I deserved to know the full truth . . .*

A voice that sounded like Bob began to mock me. As it picked up steam, it became distorted. It started to sound like me. *What is it,* the voice demanded, *that makes you so deserving? What, just because some state school deemed your little project worthy of a grant or two? Because you're too nosy to be satisfied by all the court records and newspaper articles you already have? Because you can't survive a single day without wearing someone down? Do you think you're fucking special? Are you so childish, so incapable of hearing the word* no? *Why don't you do everyone around you a favor and grow the fuck up.*

Maybe that asshole was right. Maybe I was the family snitch. I shoved the thought down. It stayed there for a while, out of sight, but it floated to the surface again eventually. Each time, I pushed harder, till I was *certain* that I had drowned it for good. It bobbed back up all the same.

My last interview was my hardest-won. For weeks, I'd prodded Al to give me the number of his old defense attorney. Tom was happy to hear from me and excited to meet me. There was only one condition: Al had to send Tom a brief statement waiving attorney-client privilege. My dad made me draft it for him. I sent it to his email. (I never considered before that my dad truly existed in the current era and would know how to work an email account.) Al passed it along, I got the all-clear, and I met Tom at his office in the Daley Center. He wasn't a trial attorney anymore but rather an administrative law judge. What that meant, I had no clue. I got the sense it was a cushy gig, though, a nice place for an older guy like Tom to land.

Tom was kind. He thanked me when I asked his permission to tape-record our conversation. He appreciated the courtesy.

We started off with that 1992 raid on the Family's house, how Al'd gotten ratted out by some friend of his and the DEA ended up catching him selling steroids and weed, how he'd fucked up the terms of his probation and served those two months at the MCC before I was born.

Tom started to stumble when I moved on to Hicks. He answered my first question with a question: *What do* you *know about the case?* I hoped he wasn't testing me. I'd gotten enough of that shit from Bob Clarke. But he wasn't — he listened as I outlined the whole thing. Then he answered my questions, like why the crew would bring on my dad, a nobody.

"The biggest fear they would have would be that somebody, an undercover cop, would infiltrate what they were doing," he said. "And they knew that your dad was anything *but* that."

"And what do you think my dad was thinking, in deciding whether to get involved with Knitter and Hicks and everybody?"

"I think he was questioning how they were able to drive such nice cars and buy such nice clothes. And I think one of them — probably this guy Knitter — told him, and asked: *Would you ever want to be part of it? You don't have to do a thing. You just have to ride in the car and go up with us, and then we'll split the profit.*"

"Do you have any idea whether my dad struggled with money? Or why he might want or need —" A memory flashed, for a moment. UNPAID RENT. FINAL WARNING. EVICTION.

"Your dad did not have a lot of money, and I think he did struggle trying to make ends meet." Tom paused. He spoke thoughtfully, often interrupting himself as he found what he wanted to say and how he wanted to say it. "People that make that decision to cross that line, their thinking often gets flawed because of — because of the way in which they talk themself into — the way they tell themselves that what they're doing is *not that bad*. And they make moral judgments that are predicated on bad decisions."

He went on.

"But all in all, I would hope you'd come away with — with — with the idea that your dad, although he had made bad decisions, was genuinely a good and decent man. And that you should come away with an attitude that — that your dad would not share this information of his bad decisions with you because every father wants their children to think that they are a good person. And your dad is a good person who — who made some bad decisions."

I didn't want to talk about that. I asked more questions.

"Was my dad willing to plead guilty right away? Did he want to go to trial?"

"Well, I was a trial attorney, much like Joe Lopez is a trial attorney, and I will always try a case before pleading their client guilty. But in your dad's case, the evidence was overwhelming. They had a video of your dad up in the apartment, dressed like a tactical policeman. It would have been insanity to bring that before a jury.

"It wasn't that your dad didn't do what he was accused of doing. He did, and he admitted that to me. That was never a question. It was always about trying to convince the US attorney that he was *not that bad* of a person, that he didn't use a firearm — although they had him carry a firearm — and just the mere fact that he had one on him added an additional five years on his sentence."

There it was. Al had the gun.

As we were wrapping up, Tom pointed my attention to a photo of his children that sat behind me. One of his daughters, he said, had disowned him.

"I'm sorry to hear that." I continued to take in the smiling family portrait. I wasn't sure what else to say. I was afraid to look at him. I was afraid he was crying. "I hope she comes around."

"I hope that she comes around as well, and I — I continue to send her text messages and wish her happy holidays, and tell her I love her." He cleared his throat. "That's why I wanted to talk to you."

I turned back to face Tom, who was weighing his words.

"In thinking about what you've had to live with and experience, I wanted to be straightforward with you. I wanted to let you know, truly, what my feelings were about your dad's behavior. And whether or not you should run from him and not have anything to do with him, or whether you should try and make your relationship work."

He also made me an offer: If I ever wanted to meet again and bring Al along, he would be more than happy to do that. I thanked him. I felt a nagging at my shoulder. The mention of the gun wasn't enough. I needed to double-check. To make sure.

So I brought it up again. Tom said it again. Yes, Al had that gun. I wrote it down in my notes.

I didn't ask Tom about the red light that Al swore that he saw glowing from the camera hidden in the TV set — the one that led to his discovery of the sting. Maybe Tom could have proved Al's story as true or false. But I kept that claim to myself, because I didn't want to embarrass Al. Or, rather, I didn't want to let him embarrass himself. Because in that room with Tom and me — two strangers meeting to discuss concrete facts — it would be impossible for anyone to deny that Al's red light was a childish fabrication. Nothing more than that. I didn't want to do that to my dad, even if he brought it on himself.

I closed my notebook. Riding the high of proving a lie to be a lie, I let myself speak a little more freely.

"The gun part is interesting. It's the one thing that my dad always said — that he *never* had the gun on the night of the raid — but obviously I took that with a grain of salt."

Tom nodded. "Yeah, they gave him a gun belt to wear, so he'd look like a policeman." He paused in thought. "And I don't know why there were certain parts of this case that your dad — in his email to me, he said there were some things he didn't want me to talk about with you. But you were already aware of the facts so I didn't feel like I was —"

I no longer found it sympathetic or endearing, the way Tom meandered through his sentences. I needed him to speak up and speak clearly, because I wasn't certain of what I had just heard.

"Sorry, do you mind if I ask what it was that my dad didn't want you to talk to me about? From his attorney-client privilege email?"

"I think he did not want me to talk about — about his last case. But you already knew all about it —"

"Oh, the chop-shop arrest, from 2015."

Tom shook his head. "No, no, not the chop shop. The Eddie Hicks case. He didn't want me to speak with you about it. But I could hardly — I'm not going to be *untruthful*. You knew about the case, and you knew about the complaint, and his having a gun —"

He smiled in realization. He caught up to the understanding I was already sitting in, drowning in.

"Oh, that's funny. Maybe that's why he didn't — Maybe it was about the gun —"

"Ha. Yeah," I said. "Maybe." Tom didn't seem to notice any change in me. I thought it would be obvious, the ringing in my ears.

I turned off my tape recorder and thanked Tom for his time. I gathered my coat and purse. What Tom was saying that he'd received from Al was not the message I'd drafted. That wasn't what he promised, what we had agreed to.

As he walked me back out to the lobby, Tom commended my reporting work.

"You've really done your homework about the case. And that's why, when you brought up the Hicks case, I asked you what you knew first." I tried to smile. I wanted to get out of there. I let him finish. "But then you — you just laid out the whole thing. So that's why I felt comfortable telling you — well, telling you what you already knew."

I walked as fast as I could out of the lobby, joined the crowds. I stopped being polite. I jostled to get out of the way — why was *everyone* in my *fucking* way? I let my shoulder collide into an oncoming businessman — I let the force knock me back. I pushed forward. I didn't have to look behind me. I could feel the man turn around, his eyes searching, trying to see who that asshole had been.

Back in my hotel room, I was alone. Just what I'd wanted. Isn't that what I'd thought to myself, just that morning? How could this luxury feel so sinister now? I was alone. I had no one to call. Even if I did, I didn't know what I'd say.

So I did what I knew best. I let the chatter in my mind run free, until the overlapping words and meaning became indecipherable. Soon it was just noise, a buzz in the background as I undressed in the sleek, ultramodern bathroom, all glass and quartz and stainless steel. Yes, that was what I needed: an icy, sterile place.

I sat in front of the wall-to-ceiling mirror, under bright and punishing light, and set up shop. I didn't travel without tools: tweezers, scissors, clippers, cuticle pushers. And I didn't work haphazardly. Whatever emotions were encoded in that incessant buzzing, they couldn't reach me. Nothing could unsteady my hand. I was, as always, measured and deliberate.

I worked my way across the terrain of my body, taking the same old routes that I'd established years ago. I emptied myself in this way. I examined every single pore and follicle, prodding and picking and pulling apart. Face, chest, arms, legs, belly. I left no small stretch of skin forgotten.

I wasn't thinking of my skin as a part of my own appearance, or as an organ, or as a part of my biological whole. I wasn't thinking at all. I had no concept of pain or past or future. My mind was reduced to something like an insect's ganglia. I was all present, all instinct, all stimuli and response. The world existed in millimeters.

Sensation returned first. My body was starting to give out; my legs were numb, my hands cold and sore. I got to my feet with considerable effort. The time glowed on my phone. I tried to do the math. How long had it been, five hours? Six? I saw myself in the mirror; with bloodshot eyes I took myself in. All shades of pink and red: raised marks and angry welts, weeping some clear liquid, blood that had dried and blood that still ran.

Mutilated, that was the word that first came to mind. I surveyed the word dispassionately. That about summed it up. I gathered my tools. I washed my hands with hot water, working them over to bring back feeling. I used my ring finger to put on eye cream before I retreated to bed. In the morning, the pure white duvet was dotted and streaked, and I was scabbed and sore. The heaviness returned.

I was back in the car with Al. The heaviness remained, dulling any possible fear or guilt or dread I might've felt when I brought up Tom.

"It was a good interview, he's a nice guy. Something weird happened, though."

Al's eyes remained on the road.

"Yeah?"

"Yeah. I mean, we talked about everything I wanted to talk about — 1992, 2003, all that — but at the end he mentioned that email you sent him. The attorney-client privilege thing."

Al looked over his shoulder to check his blind spot, swung the wheel around, chewed his gum. Nothing.

"Basically, he said that *you* said he could talk to me about the steroids case, but *not* about the Hicks case. Which is weird, because that wasn't what we talked about. And that wasn't what it said in the waiver email I wrote for you."

Al raised his eyebrows, but his eyes didn't change. They remained on the road.

"That's weird. I didn't say that." I wanted to look away. I didn't want to watch him lie. But I made myself watch him.

"Yeah, I told him he could talk to you about anything you want. Like you said, in the email, and all that. Huh. You sure that's what he said? Don't know why he would say that. Weird."

I stayed silent. I couldn't breathe any kind of life into his stupid fiction. So that was it. I bit down on the inside of my cheek while Al filled the silence, rambling from one topic to the next. I saw myself sitting there. I saw Al sitting there. I saw the shapes we made, and all the lies that hung in the air. I could hold only one or two simple sentences in my mind.

One: *This is all so dumb.*

(Too dumb, even, for me to square it with my other parallel thought.)

Two: *My father has betrayed me.*

Once that second thought took shape, it invaded every contemporary memory I had of Al, from the time I first touched down at O'Hare. I had been so skeptical, bordering on paranoid. The time he told me about that stupid fucking red light, the one that never existed, he'd sat us down in a busy Dunkin' as he drank some sugar-laden coffee shit that I'd bought for him. Our table was directly beneath the tinny, distorted overhead speaker. And he spoke in such a low voice. That was the one time he let me record him. I could barely hear him as I sat across from him. The audio on the tape was impossible to understand.

*Had that been his plan? Premeditated, while we stood in the line
to order and I dug around for my credit card?*
    Could Al be so calculated? So desperate for the upper hand?
    Could my father hate me that much?
    Because that was how it felt to me: It felt like contempt.

My last day in the city was dry, gray, and cold. There were flur-
ries of snow here and there, but I found no joy in them. I'd
planned to take the Blue Line out to the airport, but Al offered
me a ride. He had something he wanted to show me.
    He pulled up outside the hotel. This time, he actually stopped
the car. As he threw my suitcase in the back of the truck, I
jumped up into the passenger seat and nearly screamed. There
was a man in the back, seated behind me.
    "That's my buddy, Donnie."
    Donnie gave me a nod. "Hey, how's it goin'?"
    I nodded back. "Hey." I contorted my arm to shake his
extended hand. I stared at Al. I waited. No explanation. No
apology. Nothing. He just scanned through some radio stations,
started telling me how Donnie was a good friend of his. He'd
done some time of his own. He and Donnie reminisced. I swallowed my own revulsion.
    We drove. I didn't ask where we were going, or why the
fuck this guy was in the car, or what the fuck was wrong
with Al, what kind of childhood head injury had he sustained
that made him *like this*. Maybe he'd make me miss my flight.
Maybe he'd forgotten about my flight entirely. I didn't care
anymore. I had nothing left. I knew the heaviness was returning to stuff my skull with cotton and make my eyes unfocused. I felt it around the periphery. I didn't have much time
before it swallowed me whole. If I was going to do anything,
I had to do it now.
    I did something that I am not proud of, something that
I've never regretted. I reached into my purse. I turned on my

recorder. I sat back and let my head fall against the window. And I didn't say a damn thing.

Eventually the car stopped. We were in some neighborhood, a stone's throw from the apartment where Al, Mia, and I once lived. Donnie got out of his seat behind me — I nodded good-bye — but he didn't go up the steps into the house. He walked around to the driver's-side window. Al rolled it down.

"Hey," Al barked. "Take one of these." He handed him a green box sitting on the center console. Had it been there the whole time? Donnie laughed.

"Girl Scout cookies." My dad grinned. Donnie gave him a few folded bills, then disappeared into the house.

I shook off the fog. I was alert again. I tried to inject a smile, a lightness into my voice.

"What was that?"

"Girl Scout cookies. Got four extra boxes in the car. I've been eating 'em like crazy. The other day I ate a whole box."

"Uh-huh. What's the money for?"

"The hundred bucks he owed me for the last five years." Al's eyes were back on the road. My eyes were back on him.

Liar.

He pulled the truck into an open spot outside a line of auto garages. I followed him inside. The smell of the tools and the oil reminded me of my grandfather Cal. It was a small comfort. There was a car, a few motorcycles. It was his buddy's garage, Al said; he let my dad use some of the space to build and fix bikes. He showed them off to me.

"Tryna get a spot of my own soon. You know, sell bikes, sell parts, a lot of my buddies are asking for 'em."

He dug into a box, pulled out a black satin jacket.

"Here."

I shook it out, smelling the years on it, and held it out before me, coming face-to-face with the familiar logo: AL'S GYM.

"Marco and I still got a bunch of stuff from back in the day, from the Gym. T-shirts, hats, jackets. Been getting friends to send me pictures of theirs, you know — a lotta people still got stuff like that. I get asked all the time when I'm gonna start selling them again."

Back in the car, Al was holding a stack of envelopes. I didn't know where they came from; must've been that box in the garage. He handed them to me, but his eyes were elsewhere. They studied the horizon. I recognized the handwriting on the front immediately. My heart dropped into my stomach.

"Letters from your Ma. Wrote me all the time back in '94, when I was locked up. Right before you were born. When you read 'em, you'll see — she really was different, your Ma."

In 1994, Mia was twenty-three years old, only a few months older than I was now. I thumbed through the bundle. I'd never thought Al would keep anything so sentimental.

I don't remember much about the ride to the airport. I'd given Al a fake departure time just in case, hours before my flight. He was never on time, not once in my life. I couldn't afford to chance it and end up missing my plane.

He told me stories I'd already heard, about Mia, about Jackie. He told me how Rick fuckin' Stratton was the root of all their misery. How Al had saved them, more or less, from his path of destruction.

"I should've just shot him," he said, shaking his head. "I could've done it. We were like best friends. No one would know."

I thought you didn't fuck with guns. That's what you told me, isn't it? So which is it? Which one's the lie? I said nothing.

"Yeah, I should've just shot him. Would've saved a lotta people. A *lotta* people. He was the fuckin' devil, man."

As we pulled around to the departures lane, I looked at the time. How had Al, of all people, managed to get to the airport early? I killed the rest of the afternoon in the terminal, turning those letters over and over in my lap.

These letters weren't meant for me. Mia didn't know they existed. If she did, she would have made certain they were all burned. She'd want them burned now. It wasn't right to open them without her knowing.

Once I was back in Oregon, I told her. I asked her to give me her blessing to read them, to give up the privacy she clung to so fiercely.

I got what I wanted. I knew I would. Mia would never refuse, not me.

13

Her Life Began

Chicago, 1994

Mia wrote to Al just about every day. She didn't have much else to do. She and her sister had left Oak Park behind. Now, Mia lived with her parents in a southern suburb far enough from the old neighborhood to feel somewhat safe. She didn't live with Al because he was in prison. He'd broken his probation — he got caught selling steroids out of the Gym. He went in on August 18. He'd be out before Halloween.

Jackie had a two-year-old daughter now and a new boyfriend — one who didn't beat her senseless. Soon Mia would be a mother, too. She counted down the days until her January due date. Right around her twenty-third birthday, she learned the baby was a girl.

Mia kept a spiral notebook in her bag so she could write letters to Al while she worked the front desk of a tanning salon. Her clean, curly script filled pages, front and back.

Mia could cry when she thought about how Al must feel, or what she would feel in his position. Trapped, guilty, ashamed. She imagined, and she felt powerless; she could do nothing about it but send him letters and magazines and money orders.

She didn't think too often about how *she* felt. If someone had pressed her to name it, she might've said she felt blue. She was lonely. But peeling back the layers was dangerous: If she went too far down, she saw what she kept hidden.

She wasn't *in love* with Al. She was *with* Al. She wanted love, and to be loved, but all she could do was give falsely and pretend to see it reflected back to her. Still, what she wrote to Al was, in some way, true. She missed not being alone. And she wanted Al to feel loved, and thought about, and cared about. She thought anyone would want that.

Besides, the letters were for Al's benefit, not hers. Only the tasks were for her: driving around to pick up Al's magazines, packing them up with care, standing in line at the post office. They made her feel useful and kept her body busy.

She wrote to him about the future, as far ahead as she could see: They would look for an apartment, somewhere in the suburbs. Mia and Jackie would decorate the baby's room together.

Mia always signed her letters in the same way:

— Me & the baby

By the end of September, Mia was almost six months along and barely starting to show when she tripped on a crack in the sidewalk. Jackie insisted they go to the hospital to make sure the baby was okay. It'd be a breeze, and they'd get lunch after. But the doctor at Northwestern Memorial told Mia that she couldn't leave. She was having contractions; she just couldn't feel them.

Mia stayed in the hospital on bedrest as her doctors staved off labor. The nurses gently prodded her for information about herself. Was she married? Who was the father? *Where* was the father? Why didn't he visit? Mia told them her boyfriend was out of town, traveling for work. In reality, he was a ten-minute drive away at the Metropolitan Correctional Center. She wasn't saving face; she lied for their benefit. Everyone was so kind to her. She wanted to spare their feelings, and she didn't want their pity.

Al was released on October 15, 1994, only a few days before Mia gave birth at twenty-eight weeks. The baby was three months premature; her lungs were underdeveloped; she weighed two pounds and barely spanned the length of the doctor's hand. Mia named her Francesca, Frankie for short.

For three months, Mia spent each day in the neonatal intensive care unit, the NICU, pronounced *nick-you*. She always brought a Snickers bar and glass of milk from the cafeteria to the isolated room where she pumped breast milk for Frankie's feeding tube. She bought the plain antibacterial soap and unscented lotion that the doctor recommended for any contact with the baby's fragile skin. She got to know the other parents whose children were in the NICU, whose cars she passed in the parking garage. Each level played a different oldies singer, a kind of mnemonic device for not losing your car. Every morning and every night Mia heard the same Frank Sinatra songs — "My Way," "The Way You Look Tonight," "Fly Me to the Moon" — to remind her where she was.

Al seldom visited. For his first weeks out of prison, he had to report to the Salvation Army per his work release and return to the halfway house before curfew. But his habits didn't change when he returned to his apartment and the Gym. *More travel for work*, she told the nurses. But the Family made their appearances. Sonia and her daughters came to pray for the baby. Mia saw their lips moving but couldn't make out the words. She only heard the low hum of their voices, mumblings of fear and invocation.

Al got upset when Mia stayed late in the NICU. She had taken to sleeping at his apartment during the few hours she was forced to leave the hospital. It was a shorter drive there than back to her parents' place, and the sooner she got a few hours' rest and a change of clothes, the sooner she'd be back with her daughter. But soon a pattern emerged. Once the evening shift started and the sun went down, it was only a matter of time before Al rang up the hospital looking for her, looking for an answer.

Mia had to hide her rage when she took the receiver from one of the nurses. "It's for you. Your *boyfriend?*" The girl's cheeky smile broke Mia's heart a little. She watched her rejoin the others. She heard their hushed chatter. *Ooooh, her boyfriend? That's so cute, my boyfriend never calls. What'd he sound like? Is he still on that work trip? When do we get to meet him? Has he gotten to see the baby yet?*

Mia turned her back to the nurses, pretending to observe the bulletin board. She knew they wouldn't need to hear her voice, only to see her face, to detect the coldness that washed over her. She wanted to hide them from it. Al's voice crackled in her ear.

"You were supposed to be here an hour ago. When you leavin'?"

Mia spared him no more words than necessary: "My child is here." But Al was like a wall. The implicit never made it through to him:

My child is here; what could ever make me leave?

My child is here; she is not yours; you have given up all claim to her.

My child is here; I am hers; you have no claim to me.

Before he could take a breath to speak, to waste more of her time, Mia shut him down.

"I'll get there when I get there."

She never went to his apartment that night. More and more often, she didn't bother showing up at all.

Mia was different now. She knew Al felt it. For years they orbited each other in separate but overlapping lives. She put up with the stories of other girls that floated back to her, because he kept her safe. But Mia didn't need his protection now. She had been given a small and precious thing that needed her. That was her world now. She was the protector.

After three months in the NICU, Mia brought Frankie home to her parents' house. The baby weighed four pounds — double her birth weight — and steroids had helped her lungs grow. But her nervous system was still developing, so sometimes she'd forget to breathe. The nurses called it a pause. They taught Mia infant CPR and sent her home with a heart monitor.

Mia didn't sleep; she listened. If a pause was short, Frankie would start breathing again on her own. If it was longer, her skin turned gray and the alarm rang out. Mia would hold her daughter upright and count to thirty. If the alarm didn't stop ringing after thirty seconds, Mia was to start CPR. It always stopped before then.

Her mother was terrified to touch the baby. "I can't, I'm gonna hurt her!" she cried, waving her hands in front of her whenever she was offered a chance to hold her. But Mia never flinched. She was twenty-three, but she had a new calm about her that made her look older. She was in control.

Chicago, 1995

TWO 13-YEAR-OLD GIRLS SHOT TO DEATH IN VAN ON SOUTHWEST SIDE.

Their names were Helena Martin and Carrie Hovel, according to the *Tribune*. The girls were in eighth grade. They were both shot as they sat in a van across from their school in Clearing, a neighborhood that the newspaper and everyone else called a cop neighborhood.

The shooter was a boy, not a man. Eric Anderson was fifteen years old, slight and pale, still a long way from growing any facial hair. He was a Pope and a cop's son. There was a turf war going on, and sitting in that van with Helena and Carrie had been two young men — rival Ridgeway Lords members. One of them was Helena's eighteen-year-old boyfriend; her mother had never approved.

Eric missed his targets; both boys left the van unharmed; both girls were shot in the head. A handful of teens, including Eric, had been arrested in relation to the shooting.

As the neighborhood's parents gathered and grieved, as the school brought counselors to comfort Helena and Carrie's classmates, the police and the news media were trying to get the story straight. The *Tribune* said one of those kids they arrested was going down for ordering the shooting. Word on the street told Al otherwise. From what he heard, Rick put out the hit that killed the innocent girls. He and Al were still friends, despite all Mia and Jackie's suffering. Al had plenty of excuses — it wasn't like Rick was the only gangbanger who came to the Gym. Besides, what choice did he have? He'd rather have Rick as a friend than as an enemy.

Those two girls were the same age that Mia was when Rick had entered her life as her older sister's boyfriend. If she'd been in the wrong place at the wrong time, she could've been the one with a bullet in her head. But Mia didn't have to think about it, because she didn't know about the shootings. She wasn't reading the news. Frankie was one year old, and in that year Mia had perfected the art of compartmentalization, tuning out the wider world with ease. In her and Frankie's little private world, nothing could get in.

But she knew it wasn't enough. Jackie escaped Rick and they made it out of the neighborhood, but it was all still too close for comfort. She knew that she and her daughter would have to leave the city one day. It was for their own good.

Mia never saw the new apartment until a deal had been made. Al found the three-bedroom — cozy, second-story, not far from Cal and Ellen — on the South Side, where the city began to sprawl into suburbs. On the first floor of the brick two-flat lived the homeowner, their new landlord, along with his wife and son. Al paid the first few months' rent up front, in cash, and the next week he picked up Mia and brought her to their new home.

As she took in the place, the owner leaned against the wall in the front room, eating mini candy bars from his coat pocket. He appeared older than he really was. Cancer, he said. Mia inspected each room, keeping up small talk so as to not make the man uncomfortable. She scanned every window-pane, every outlet. She spent a long time examining the floors. Al hovered around the periphery, in his leather jacket, chewing gum.

Mia called him over, into the bedroom across from the master, the one that would be Frankie's room. "He has to replace the carpet."

"What's wrong with it?"

"*Look* at it. It's too old, it's not sanitary, it has to be clean — she could get sick." He said nothing. "I won't bring her here."

Al shrugged — he always called her a hypochondriac — and wandered back out to the landlord. She couldn't hear Al's low voice, but she made out the man's reply. "Sure, I'll take it out. That's no problem." Then, louder, so she could hear: "That's no problem, honey — I'll get new carpet in each room for you, how's that sound?" When she returned to the front room, Al was holding his wad of cash, tying it back up with its rubber band.

The landlord asked her about the hospital where her baby had been born: Northwestern. These days, he was always going back and forth, too — doctor to home and back again. He walked them out, said he'd pray for the baby. He took out another chocolate and peeled off the wrapper.

The next time Mia came to the apartment, Al and his brother had moved in all the furniture. Boxes sat in the kitchen. There was new carpet in each room, and the man was dead.

Chicago, 1996

Mia recognized the woman standing in the doorway of the apartment. She'd heard the knocking; she thought Al ordered a pizza. Then she heard the yelling.

The woman was a regular at the Gym. She was huge — pregnant. Her eyes bulged as she looked from Al to Mia. The woman had a suspicion, so she followed Al home. And she had been right. "He — he was supposed to tell you," she said. It was all she could say.

Mia told her to leave. Behind the closed door, she made herself clear to Al. This was her daughter's home. She didn't care what he did, but it was never to cross that threshold.

It wasn't long before she enrolled in classes at the community college. She learned American Sign Language, and a professor recommended her for a job in the suburbs. An elementary school needed an interpreter. The support made her nervous; she knew she wasn't qualified. But with her professor's help, she got an offer and took it. At home, she started teaching her daughter simple sign language: "More." "Please." "Thank you."

One day, Mia created a special sign for Frankie's name. The sign for the letter "F" merged with the sign for "girl." She showed her, slowly. "Open your hand and bring your first finger and thumb together — like the sign for OK, see? — then bring your hand up to your face and trace the tips of your fingers, where your finger and thumb touch, along your jaw."

Mia took Frankie's small hand in hers, shaping her fingers into the different shapes. First the "F," and then she lifted her hand to her cheek and brought it down softly.

The days were numbered. She knew it. Al knew it. Mia would leave him, she would take their daughter, and he would do nothing to stand in her way.

Chicago, 1998

Mia started writing letters to Frankie, almost like a diary. She loved the idea of keeping them for years, until they could read them together. *See?* she'd say to her daughter, once she was older. *This is what we did together. We had so much fun. Do you remember?* Between the lines was a deeper sentiment — a persistent, living truth: *My life began with you.*

Usually she wrote on loose-leaf paper, college-ruled. One day after work, she stopped at a Borders bookstore to pick up a proper journal. She chose a blue hardcover book with a sweet illustration on the cover: a stuffed bear looking up at the night sky, at the crescent moon. Frankie would love it. She had a stuffed bear at home; she had named him Stanley.

She started the book in August, writing the first letter after a trip to Wisconsin:

> You & your dad loved the beach. It was really windy & the waves were big, but you loved it. On our way home we stopped at an orchard to pick berries & apples. There was a big brown dog sleeping on the floor of the store & you named him Duke. Your hand & face were purple from all the berries you ate.
>
> That was our first vacation.

It was a rare occurrence, for Al to be around for something like that. Al was gone most of the time. She didn't know where he stayed, the nights he didn't come home. But she didn't care; she didn't want him; they didn't need him. They had each other:

> Dear Frankie,
> Today you & I are both sick. We have a cold. I don't think either one of us feel like doing much of anything. Even though you're sick, you're still funny & delightful. You made sure I took my medicine & gave me a box of tissues.

Soon, they were feeling better, just in time to enjoy the last stretch of summer. It was a beautiful day:

> You made a book at preschool all about yourself. There's a picture of you on the front & it tells a story about you. The things you like & the things you don't. You also made pictures of your family & your house. I love it. I showed it to everyone.
>
> We played big bad wolf outside. I hid behind a pile of wood & jumped out when you were looking for me. You laughed & yelled so loud. We made a big bed on the floor & watched a movie. You're holding your bear, Stanley. You're asleep now.
>
> I love you with all my heart. You picked a pink flower for me today — I'll keep it forever.
>
> I love you,
> Mommy.

14

The Leaving

Chicago, 1999

Mia left Al on Christmas Day. She took her five-year-old daughter with her. She wasn't planning doing it then and there, but he forced her hand. When you're given an opening, you take it.

Frankie had one last unwrapped present on her lap when her parents started fighting. She only caught snippets of what they were saying; most of it made no sense until Al accused Mia of being *unfaithful*. Frankie knew what *unfaithful* meant. She watched her parents' feet, pacing round and round on the carpet. When they left the room, she followed. Down the hall, into the kitchen. She felt invisible, like a shadow behind them, like they couldn't see her if they tried.

Frankie only knew she could still be seen when her mother picked her up. She only realized that she had been crying when Mia reached out and wiped the tears from Frankie's cheek. Al took advantage of Mia's distraction; in charging steps, he raced toward their bedroom. He wanted to look through Mia's purse. Frankie saw the purse in her mind's eye. What could be in there besides cough drops and cherry Chapstick?

Her mother followed, still holding her daughter on her hip. Frankie watched Al's back grow nearer. She watched Mia's free hand reach out for him. As her forearm crossed the threshold, he slammed the door shut.

The door wouldn't close, so Al pushed harder, again and again. Mia cried out.

"My arm! My arm!"

This is my first memory. I visit it from time to time. I always have.

My first visit wasn't long after the leaving. The film was still wet then; I still recognized myself as the child in my mother's arms. The child is a stranger to me now.

I was still that child when I first walked all the way back to the start of my memory, back when it wasn't so far a walk. I walked back and back until there was nothing left, until I reached the end that was the start, and then I went a little further.

I stood in all of the dark that came before, the curtain before it rises, and then I stepped into the light. It was like the beginning of my illustrated Bible: There was nothing, and then God created light. There was nothing, and then there was the leaving.

The memory I visit now is identical to the one I visited then. Time isn't responsible for its imperfections; the blind spots, the moments of clarity, the scratches and starts, they all remain as they were. They were there when the film was wet, and they are here now, and I see:

The door wouldn't close, *I see the door* so Al pushed harder, again and again. *I see his hand on the door.* Mia cried out.

"My arm, my arm!"

I hear my mother's cries, but I don't hear the child. I feel pulses of pain on my own arm as if I were my mother, and I feel my mother's arm around me, and I hear:

"My arm, my arm!"

Then, I see nothing. I feel nothing, for a moment. The mind holds space for missing minutes, frames that were never exposed. Then, light.

Frankie blinked. She was back in the living room. She didn't know how she got there, or who had placed a new Barbie keyboard across her lap. But her throat ached, and her eyes were wet. *I see the room. I feel the ache. My eyes are wet.* Al must be leaving, she thought. He had put on his leather jacket.

"Daddy's going to work," Mia said. She sat farther down on the couch; Frankie couldn't see her. "Say good-bye."

Her father leaned down, but she didn't lift her face. Her tears wouldn't fall. They piled up on her lashes and made the room cloudy.

"Bye, baby. Love you." Al's voice sounded wet, like he was sick. He kissed her cheek; his stubble scratched her ear. *I feel the kiss on her cheek, not mine. I am not the child. I am a ghost. She sits on my lap, and I keep an arm around her. I know what she feels. She can't feel me. I'm with her, and she is alone.*

Frankie listened, *I listen*, for the roar of his Harley. It echoed down the empty street, and then he was gone.

This is where the memory ends. I leave the child where she was, before the dark returns — more lost time between flashes of what was. Sometimes I wonder who I would be if I had a different first memory, but I never wonder for long.

I still have more to tell you. I have to finish the story. I have to tell you the things I never knew. Things I can't remember. Things I hunted down. Now, who was it again? Who was it who told me Ellen was in the middle of cooking Christmas dinner when the phone rang . . .

Ellen was in the middle of cooking Christmas dinner when the phone rang. She was quiet as she listened to her daughter, stretching the phone's cord to give her enough slack to reach the oven. She turned it off. She called for her husband to go warm up the truck.

Cal and Ellen pulled up to the apartment in the old red

pickup. Upstairs, Mia was upending dresser drawers into Hefty bags. They took turns staying with Frankie in the living room while the others hauled bags down the stairs. The Christmas presents were the last to be engulfed in plastic and tossed in the bed of the truck. There wasn't enough time for anything else. Al would be home soon, and Mia didn't want him to know they were leaving until they were already gone.

So Cal and Ellen buckled their granddaughter into the center seat inside the truck and started for home. Mia stayed upstairs, doing a last pass over the apartment. Yes, she and Frankie had what they needed. Everything else would have to wait.

I listen for the roar of his Harley; it echoes down the empty street; my father is gone. Into the velvet black. A flash, a lens flare, then I'm sitting in the seat between Ellen and Cal in their pickup. I'm so little that when I want to see out the front windshield past the dashboard, I have to crane my neck. All I remember is seeing the sky open up over the road. We're driving to their house. I remember it was cold. I was in my coat.

I've always known that this was my next memory, the one that cued up immediately after the leaving. But I was never sure of the chronology, when I went back that far. I could never know just how much time had passed for every frame of darkness between the leaving and the sky — a day? A week? In my gut, I always thought it was on that same Christmas Day. Not too long ago, Mia told me she thought so, too. That the moment took place on that twenty-minute drive from the apartment to my grandparents' house, that same Christmas Day.

The knowledge doesn't change the remembering. Inside the memory — looking up at the sky, so wide above me, the truck's rumble below — I exist outside of time. The world begins and ends on that road. I was always in that middle seat. There is no place that I am coming from, and there is nowhere I am going. We never arrive; we never left.

Months later, Jackie was visiting Mia in her new house in the suburbs when they heard noise coming from the front lawn. Frankie was having a sleepover in the basement; they knew it wasn't the kids. As she came out onto the front porch, Mia saw Al's truck. Her anger rose and stopped up her throat. Dresser drawers, books, toys were strewn across the front lawn. Al stood on the sidewalk, heaving a pile of clothes onto the grass. He looked up at her, relaxed and casual, like he'd been hired to do a job.

Mia darted down the stairs, trying to keep her voice from carrying to the neighbors' windows. "Hey. *Hey!* What are you doing?"

Al didn't look at her. He just went on with his work, from the truck to the lawn to the truck. Jackie appeared in the doorway, free to say what her sister couldn't: "Al, are you fucking serious?"

He shrugged as he dropped a box onto the grass, its contents spilling over.

"What? All this shit's at my house. You don't live there no more, so here you fuckin' go."

Mia thought of Frankie, in the basement with her friends. She needed to act fast. "You need to leave. Right now." Her voice was strangled. She started loading debris into her arms. "She can't come out and see this."

Jackie followed her lead, carrying armful after armful around the side of the house to the garage. Mia watched Al lean against his truck and take in the chaos.

"I told you to leave. Go. Now." He just stared at her. "I'll call the cops."

By the time the squad car pulled up, it was dark. Al was gone. The officer left Mia standing on the porch, his business card between her fingers. A neighbor had helped them clean up Al's mess, hiding it all in the garage. Frankie and her friends were none the wiser.

A few lightning bugs danced around. Mia was already thinking, planning. She'd wash all the clothes that night while Frankie was asleep, dust off some of the toys and pack them nicely into an old plastic bin. *What a nice surprise*, she would say when she brought it inside. *Your dad dropped off some things for your new room. Wasn't that nice?*

A smile flickered at her lips as she practiced the words in her head. *Wasn't that nice?*

15

INTERLUDE II

On Discovery

Our actors leave the stage, replaced by dancers who serve as their doubles. We recognize each character by their hair and costume, only these doubles have better posture and wear dance shoes. The light shifts, the orchestra turns the page.

The name *dream ballet* is a bit of a misnomer on both counts. For one, the sequence may use a variety of dance styles; it is not a literal ballet. And it doesn't necessarily take place within a literal dream, either.

In these interludes, the storytellers are not bound to the laws of reality, so to speak. Just as we may be compelled to reach for myth and parable — the timeless, the extreme — we may also need to cast off language entirely and forgo words spoken or sung. Some stories can be told only through movement, gesture, and observation, in a space that exists outside of time.

The source of our choreography is the extensive vault of home videos recorded by my grandfather, Mia's father, Cal. He was the family documentarian. After Jackie gave birth to his first grandchild, he took up filming with his Panasonic camcorder. He shot everything: the mundane and the special occasions, hours of the grandkids playing in the yard, birthday party after birthday party. What's more, he captured it all faithfully, with a steady hand and a patient eye. Even if three-year-old Frankie was burying Mia's pocketbook in a garden bed, or Jackie's old cat was trying to eat Christmas ribbon, Cal never intervened. He called out for his wife or one of his daughters, but he stayed behind the camera and never stopped recording. I liked to imagine that this was a conscious choice, a devotion to truth, a refusal to destroy the veracity of the scene. He could only bear witness.

A couple of years back, he gave me his beloved camcorder, our old VCR, and boxes of tapes to digitize. I became the archivist. I watched every hour. I only had real memories of a sliver of the events Cal captured. Most of it was new to me, or at least gave me a new perspective. In the original aspect ratio of my memory, I might be singing the ABCs or showing off my new hula hoop. My eyes are on the camera, and the camera's eye is on me. On the screen, the shot widens, and we can see the whole scene, the entire truth. Over on the couch, there might be my mother and her sister, watching me with delight; in a chair in the corner, we might find Al, sitting silently, staring into space with a vacant, closed-off expression. I'd never even known he was there. And there are the gestural motifs, the patterned steps. The way my cousin and I open up to the camera; the way Mia, Jackie, and Ellen glide across the screen in practiced paths, ducking the camera, keeping their back to its eye whenever possible.

For this particular sequence, we draw on one tape in particular — a tape I never knew existed, showing events I'd never dreamed had been recorded. Like all the other videos, the time and date stamp hung in the lower left corner:

> PM 6:48
>
> DEC. 24 1999

It was Christmas Eve, 1999. The night before the leaving; the night before my first memory.

The actors clear the stage. Their doubles take their place. The light shifts, the orchestra turns the page.

The colorful bulbs on the Christmas tree appear to be twinkling, but it's only a trick of the light, an illusion made by the darting shadows cast onto the branches by the surrounding flurry of movement. Mia and Jackie flit around the tree, bringing presents to each of their young daughters and handing parcels off to each other, taking a seat on the floor every so often to watch the children tear away the paper and exclaim. Ellen makes slower, more deliberate rounds, leaning against the doorway or against the sofa, watching with a content smile. A television set, sitting off to stage right, plays *A Christmas Story*. Even as a stationary set piece, the screen exudes its own liveliness. And then there is my father, the outlier, blending into the couch, watching the TV.

The dancer gets Al's physicality just right. He sits still, but he is not rigid. He's relaxed but not entirely at ease. He isn't brooding in his isolation; he doesn't seem to see anything between him and the screen. He doesn't even seem to exist in his body at all. You get the sense that he was just *like this*, all the time, around the edge of everything, in the periphery.

The little girl, the one who looks like him and looks like me — she jumps and claps with her cousin by the tree; she falls into her mother's embrace, delighted by her new Make Me Better Baby doll. But soon enough Al's silhouette catches her eye. She picks a present from under the tree with his name on it. She breaks away from the group, joining him at his side. She's bouncing on her toes, watching his face as he rips the paper. His eyes drift from the box back to the TV.

The girl's departure from the group causes a slight ripple effect in the rhythm of the others, knocks them off kilter. Mia sits by the tree, shuffling boxes, but her focus is on the man. Jackie pulls her own daughter onto her lap as Ellen brings over a gift bag. If you focused on the steps of the others, you might miss her quick, fluid glances: over her shoulder to Al, back to Mia, then back to her daughter.

The dance makes clear what I never saw before. The gestures speak more than words could. Even as a child, I was always placing myself in front of Al, swaying as I followed his eyeline, trying to intercept his gaze that was always fixed behind me, focused on whatever sports broadcast or TV movie was playing in the background. I might fall back into the larger group, or take my place by Mia's side. But it was only a matter of time before my eyes would fall upon my father again, and I would try again.

And those knowing looks by the others, watching whether Al would at least make a half-assed effort to play his part — I never noticed them in my memory. I never picked up on them in other home videos, either.

On the stage, the music slows. Ellen exits stage left, to the "kitchen"; Jackie's daughter flops onto the sofa with her new CDs. Jackie clears the center stage, moving back into the doorway, facing the tree but watching her sister.

We see the shapes Mia and Frankie make as Frankie shows off her new book. They sit with their backs to us, daughter leaning into mother. Mia lifts her head into profile, in Al's direction. For the first time, he moves. He kneels down on the other side of his daughter, looking over her shoulder, completing the tableau. That is one of the only images I have in my mind of the three of us together, inhabiting the same space and time.

As the lights begin to dim — the cue for our dancers to move, for the crew to strike the set pieces and prepare for the next scene — my gaze remains fixed on the back of Frankie's head. *That little girl was in the dark*, I think to myself. She was the only one on that stage who didn't know the reality of her family, her parents, where she came from. Even Jackie's daughter was filled in, once she was old enough. Frankie would have to wait.

The Greeks called it *anagnorisis*. Aristotle wrote all about it in the *Poetics*, this essential part of a tragic plot, what we translate as "recognition" or "discovery": the pivotal and startling discovery that takes our hero from a state of ignorance to one of knowledge, which typically also results in a reversal in fortune for said hero. (See also: Oedipus.)

Around the same time that I was learning of this *anagnorisis*, I was reading a book I'd gotten at work, from the "free" shelf near the newsroom's book review team: *Sophocles and the Language of Tragedy*. In my mind, I linked my discovery of *discovery* with my reading of Simon Goldhill's passage on dramatic irony:

> The audience is placed in a position of superiority to the characters on stage and responds to the action through this knowledge: irony lets an audience see itself as *le sujet qui sait*, "the subject who knows."

I thought about this balance of inferiority and superiority — who is kept in the dark and who is not — as I thought about the nature of the tragic turn of recognition.

I was the last one to know the truth of where I came from, the terrible truth about my mother's suffering and sacrifice.

And, in no way giving my plight the same weight as Mia's, I felt tricked when I thought about how I was the last to know. I felt foolish; it tasted bitter. (For what it's worth, I also felt like a pathetic sack of shit when I admitted all of this to myself. *Poor you. You, You, You.*)

It reminded me of that uneasy feeling in my belly, the one I got whenever I spent too much time over at the Family's house when I was a kid. I am an actor in a play I've never read, the only one who hasn't learned the steps, hasn't been told their lines. (To this day, I have this exact recurring nightmare — set in an actual theater, with actual actors. No Family in sight.)

I knew that I wasn't kept in the dark out of malice or cowardice, but that didn't change the fact that I had been stuck there all the same. Now, like it or not, I could never put that knowledge back in its box, anymore than I could change the past itself.

16

———

The L-Word

The summer after I graduated college, after I left Eugene and never went back, I moved to New York City for an internship at *The Wall Street Journal*. I lived out of two suitcases that carried everything I owned, renting a room in a women's dorm, like the one from *The Bell Jar*. I brought my worn copy with me and reread it on the rooftop overlooking Midtown.

When people asked how I landed that big break, being from some state school out West, I always told them I got lucky. I knew I was being modest. It wasn't just luck. By my senior year, I was working full-time as a staff reporter at Eugene's family-owned daily paper, *The Register-Guard*. I earned a salary; I was even eligible for benefits. I did it all while taking a full load of courses, writing my thesis, winning scholarships, and finding time for all of my self-destructive extracurriculars.

I had worked hard, but I'd also caught a break. A pretty big one, I thought. Out of the dozen or so intern spots at the *Journal*, the new Pensiero internship gave extra weight to state-school applicants, and especially, it seemed, to University of Oregon students. (The internship's namesake, former deputy managing editor Jim Pensiero, was a proud Duck.) Even when I laid out all of the facts that might make me a worthy candidate, I firmly believed that the only reason I'd made it to the final round, let alone got the job, was because I just happened to be a reasonably big fish in the right small pond.

One afternoon that summer, I sat in a conference room in an outlet store suit, surrounded by other recent grads with more prestigious pedigrees, trying to look like I belonged. We listened to some of the *Journal's* top decision makers discuss the paper's ethics and standards. Someone asked them about the debate among media critics over what to call it when President Trump said something that wasn't true. A lie, or a falsehood — or perhaps a *deliberate* falsehood?

I hung on every word of the panelist's answer: To say someone lied meant you knew their statement was intended to deceive. The prevailing view, as I understood it, was to proceed with caution and to rarely use the L-word.

My mind whirred for the rest of the session, returning over and over to the same question: Did Al *lie*? I knew what Al told me was false, but was it a lie? I knew the memories he shared with me were self-serving and fanciful, but did he know that?

I went back, again, into the depths of the literature. Without the extensive resources of the Knight Library and my unlimited JSTOR access, the work looked different. I downloaded PDFs of photocopied articles, marked up by their rightful owner, and kept printouts in a stack by my twin bed. Next to them were my binders of thesis research: Al's court records, old news articles about Hicks, the letters Al wrote to me while he was in prison, the letters Mia wrote to him.

First, I needed a rigid definition. The scholars gave me variations on an overarching theme: that lying was an act of *deception*, a deliberate behavior aiming to give another person false information and induce *false beliefs* in them — and the beliefs are false so long as the liar thinks they're untrue.

The thing is, we all do it. We all lie, every day, and the act of lying is essential to our daily lives. Think about social interactions, small talk, ease of conversation. To tell the naked truth about everything all the time, to give an honest answer to any question, would not be conducive to a normal or well-adjusted life. It's part of our human social contract. *Some* lying is allowed, or even required, to do right by ourselves and others.

But if we were to play one of those tedious games of word association — *I'll give you a word, you say the first thing that pops into your head* — given the word *liar*, we wouldn't shout out, "A good friend!" or "Ideal spouse!" or "Someone I'd want to go into business with!"

The ways we all think about those who deceive us are well-worn paths leading back to myth, to archetypes like the serpent in Eden. In religious doctrine and other ancient texts, you will find precisely what humankind has made of liars, and you will recognize it.

I found it interesting that some of these scholarly conceptions of lying made another distinction: That it is a deliberate *attempt* — successful or not, it doesn't matter. Nor does it matter whether the false belief is factually incorrect. What matters is the intention — that I wanted to trick you, I wanted you to believe a falsehood, and I did what I could to lead you into that trap.

In the study of deception, scholars pose the same questions I confronted in my weeks of worry over the L-word: When does *lying* turn you into a *liar*? When should we label someone as such? How do we keep the score, how do we determine the toll that this action will take upon them and whether it is warranted? Whether it is accurate?

We've all lied at some point, usually taking our first stab at verbal deception around the age of three — an important step in our cognitive development — but it strikes me as wrong to call us all liars. It deflates the word, takes away its weight and meaning. I found the other ways scholars took to determine its appropriate deployment more compelling. We can take into account the relative frequency of a person's lying, when they choose to lie, and the consequences of those lies.

The way I see it, the small to moderate amount of socially adaptive lying that we all expect from one another is handily outweighed by all the truth we tell in every other context, at least most of the time. The scales start to tip if someone tells me too many white lies, or tells them too often; or if their lie is larger, more consequential, with a less altruistic underlying motivation.

In all these definitions and discussions, I held on to one key determinative factor — something that made a lie a lie: To lie, you must intend to deceive.

I knew Al lied to me when I was a child. I knew he lied to others in his past; you don't end up having a child with a woman that's not your live-in partner without lying to at least a couple of people. But I never knew if Al's latest untruths were intentionally deceptive, or at least I felt I hadn't definitively proved them to be so. I didn't know if that was something I could ever prove. But if they were, then Al did not simply earn the label of *liar*. If they were, he was a *pathological* liar.

The literature makes clear just how serious the consequences are for someone labeled a pathological liar. After all, pathological lying isn't recognized as a diagnostic entity. Other diagnoses may come into play, ones that do appear in the *DSM-V*; deceit is among the symptoms of psychopathy and antisocial personality disorder, for instance. It comes with each respective territory — the lack of empathy, the malice. But scholars set pathological lying apart from each of those disorders. Not that some of these liars aren't malicious, and not that their actions aren't destructive, but they are not always, as one article put it, "sinister."

I felt personally vindicated when I read the authors of that same article address the previous work of another scholar, who had argued that pathological liars were generally harmless. These authors "kindly" disagreed with his assessment. These authors found that "pathological lying carries a heavy toll, damaging relationships, causing dysfunction in many domains of life, and ultimately leaving a wake of distress."

Thank you, Curtis and Hart, I said in my head, to the article glowing on my screen.

It didn't help my unease to learn that, in addition to confabulation and all of those other ways our own memory can steer us wrong, lying can screw with the way memories are recorded. It can sow doubt.

To tell a lie requires brain power, cognitive resources diverted from other concurrent processes, like filing away the experience as memory. Researchers found in an experiment that those who were directed to lie during an interview showed trouble with memory. They forgot the lies they told in the interview. They got their wires crossed, thinking they'd lied about something that they'd been honest about. Compared with the group of people who were directed to be honest, the lying group retained fewer memories and had more *non-believed memories* — things they remembered but weren't sure actually happened The conclusion? Lying can disrupt memory; more lies mean more opportunities for memory to go wrong.

My conclusion? Al has a history of lying a lot. Maybe it diminished his abilities to properly remember. Especially when I thought about the *way* Al lied. He didn't use the relatively low-bandwidth techniques like false denial or feigning amnesia, simply saying things didn't happen or that he didn't remember any of it. He engaged in *fabrication*, creating entirely new versions of events out of whole cloth.

All this fabrication would demand that much more work from his mind. He had to make up that whole new story. Then, for the attempt at lying to be successful, he had to remember all the details and particulars of that whole new story *and* retain the whole original truth. That would leave his memory considerably under-resourced and, understandably, prone to error.

Maybe this became a cycle, a self-perpetuating pattern. Maybe his untruths were a product of broken memory, not of deception. Maybe he didn't meet all those key criteria of lying: *He* didn't intend to plant in me a false belief, because he didn't know or believe it was false.

This wouldn't change the fact that he told me a lot of bullshit. This wouldn't erase the feeling I had that he *did* know it was bullshit. This would muddy the waters just enough for him to win a mistrial. It would give me the wiggle room I needed to escape my own dreaded conviction: that my father, whether he knew it or not, held enough contempt for me that he would deceive me.

As I pulled apart each layer of the case that sat in front of me, I only had more questions. If Al was aware of the distorted reality he built around himself, would he ever leave it willingly? If he asked himself whether he lied — to me or to himself — what would his answer be?

Deeper still: Was I wrong about Al? Could I be wrong?

I'll give you an example: When I was twelve, Al told me a story about the day I was born. He was in the elevator, going up to the NICU to see me and my mom.

"A guy gets on, and I look up — it's *Gary Fencik*. You know Gary Fencik? Plays for the Bears, huge at the time. And I always thought he was a big guy, people said he's six-one, six-two. But I'm in the elevator, thinking, *There's no way this guy's six-one. I'm taller than he is.* Anyway, his girlfriend was having a kid on the same day as your Ma. And that same day he went and played for the Bears. Ain't that crazy?"

I wondered if any of it was true. I let Al's track record with the truth make the judgment for me. No deliberation, no fact-checking. The story was bullshit.

Then, years later, in talking about all of the stupid stories my dad tried to sell me as fact, I recalled the story to Mia.

"Oh, I remember that," she said. "What was his name? The football player?"

My heart sank. "Gary Fencik?"

"Yeah. I think I met him, too, or maybe it was his wife. I barely remember."

"But — are you saying you remember the story he made up, or that it actually happened?"

"That it actually happened."

"Fuck." I rubbed my eyes. Mia watched me with worry. The question returned, pecking at my brain. *Am I wrong about Al? Am I wrong? Am I wrong? Am I wrong?*

There is a type of memory, *autobiographical memory* — it's what it sounds like. It's the group of memories of our own lives, recollections that underpin our identity and self-conception. We know memory on the whole is generally trustworthy, and we know that it is fallible and vulnerable to distortions. In selecting and saving autobiographical memories, our minds are naturally prone to protecting our self-esteem, making it easier for us to see ourselves as the good guys, as characters we want to root for. Scholars point to this propensity as a potential explanation for *fading affect bias*, in which memories associated with unpleasant emotions tend to fade more over time than those associated with pleasant ones.

The literature is full of examples: studies in which people recalled their high school memories as better than they really were; in which people's memories became more positive as they aged; in which people saw the choices they made in the past as the better option than the ones forgone, simply because they were the ones they chose. To continue to live, we must see our life as worth living. And so our brains give us a helping hand in this aspect of our survival.

Interestingly, this effect isn't seen so much in those who are *dysphoric* — the academic catchall term for the pathologically depressed and anxious and the like. They don't experience this effect that is thought to be part of a "healthy coping process."

I wondered if I fell into this dysphoric category; I probably do. I wondered if my need to know interfered with these neurological coping mechanisms; the literature suggests it does.

I wondered if a life unexamined would be easier to live; I knew I'd never find out.

These memories that gloss themselves over and reshape themselves, that tint themselves in rose — what was I to call them? Were *they* falsehoods? *Intentional* falsehoods? Untruths? Lies? Would those memories take on a new identity if we became aware of their distortions and still continued to believe them? Then did they become lies, with a capital *L*? Then did we become liars?

I asked myself, was this another excuse for Al's distorted reality? Maybe I could avoid the L-word entirely, chalk up his fantastical and ever-changing stories to mnemonic self-preservation and healthy coping mechanisms. Or did he *lie*? To me? To himself?

And if I was going to ask it of Al, I had to ask it of myself: *Did I lie?*

17

Lies I Tell Myself

I don't smoke.

I said this to myself in the morning hours, during the winter after my twenty-seventh birthday, as I sat on my balcony, smoking a cigarette with my coffee. I started most of my mornings that way, after my husband and I left our Brooklyn rental behind to buy a Harlem co-op. It was peaceful, looking out onto the courtyard. Sometimes I'd have a second cigarette out on the street, as the light faded in the evening; on rare occasions I'd have a third. I never enjoyed that one as much; it usually made me nauseous.

I never smoked before we moved. I'd only just started. And there were days and weeks where I didn't smoke at all, so I told myself: *I don't smoke.*

That doesn't mean I believed it. I interrogated myself as I brushed ash from my jacket. What precisely did I mean when I assured myself, *I don't smoke*? I supposed I meant that I was not a *smoker*; I was addicted to neither habit nor substance, neither the cigarettes nor the nicotine; I didn't miss them when I wasn't smoking. This was just a phase I was going through for reasons I couldn't put my finger on. But I couldn't leave it alone. I pestered myself, mocking myself: What, then, would make me a *smoker*? How many cigarettes would I have to smoke, how many packs would I have to buy?

What milestone would mark the transition? What goalpost would I shove back?

I had no answer for myself, and I sure didn't appreciate the questions.

I don't smoke.

This is a lie I still tell myself, in the winter after my thirtieth birthday. The denial is less emphatic; it's a bit more tongue-in-cheek. But deep down, I still believe it.

I don't smoke because I've spent my life dogmatically opposed to smoking. I always hated the raisin smell of the filters, the bitter smell of the smoke. The smell that hung around the Family, wafting from my grandmother's Pall Malls. Yet I smoke nearly every morning and enjoy it.

I don't smoke because I know I will not smoke forever.

I don't smoke because I started in my late twenties. *Smokers*, real ones — they get their start in high school or earlier. I know people who took it up when they were children. They've never known life without it.

I don't smoke because it's a shorter sentence, an easier explanation. A more truthful, nuanced answer would be too wordy. *Oh, I only smoke sometimes: like when I'm feeling hopeless or tired or hungry, or if I've had a few drinks, or if I'm outside, or if I feel like it, or —*

None of this makes it less of a lie.

I don't smoke because I don't know who I would be if I did smoke. The Francesca my friends know, the Frankie my family knows — no, no, she would never smoke. Not our Frankie. She's too smart, too *good*, to take on a habit that she knows is bad for her. She knows better.

I don't smoke because I feel shame when I think of all the late nights Mia spent in the NICU, all the work that went into growing my small lungs after I was born. They were a gift, and who was I to take them for granted, abuse them for no good reason?

———

There are other lies I have told myself, to keep the shame at bay. Some are not so succinct; some are harder to wrap my arms around. *I am a good person. I am a kind person. I am not selfish. I am not vengeful. I don't hurt people. I don't enjoy hurting people.* They ring true, most of the time. But at the times I repeat them to myself the most, they usually feel like a lie. At those times, I am usually feeling shame.

Here is an example. During that first summer I lived in New York, I met a guy named Adam through my phone. I was lonely and I didn't know anybody outside of work. He proposed a date at the Museum of Modern Art. I'd never gone to a museum with a stranger before. I was relieved that he looked like his photos, and I tried not to talk too much. Adam was kind and funny, but reserved. He cracked jokes in a low voice that made me lean in toward him, and he smiled without his teeth. I couldn't tell if he was shy or trying to keep a mask in place. By the time we reached Monet's water lilies, I got a real smile out of him. I relaxed.

At the end of the night, I invited myself up to his apartment. He kissed me, and I settled into his bed. I unzipped my dress and let the straps fall to my hips. Eventually he pulled back.

"I really like you," he said.

"I like you, too."

"So maybe we could wait."

"Oh. Sorry." I sat up. "Do you not want to?"

Adam's eyes widened; I hadn't hidden the hurt well enough. "No! No, I do. I just —" He smiled and shrugged. "I want to see you again. So maybe we could wait." My heart swelled. I'd never known that was an option before — not with guys my age.

We spent nearly every night together after that. We went to museums and bookstores and bars near his East Village apartment. I liked that he read books I wanted to read, that he knew the city better than I did, that he wanted to talk to me about art and politics and religion. We commiserated about the prejudices of our older, devout relatives — mine Roman Catholic and Southern Baptist, his Orthodox Jewish. He was warm and understanding and, best of all, he liked me as much as I liked him. I wasn't alone anymore.

After a few weeks, Adam frustrated me. He made it a point to denounce his privilege as a rich white guy, but he only hung around other rich white guys. When I pointed it out, he'd look downcast and guilty. "I know," he'd shrug. After a month or so, he told his parents he had a new girlfriend. My Italian name tipped them off to my shiksa status, so he lied that I was half Jewish, on my mom's side. He asked me to keep up the lie when we met up with his more traditional friends.

"By the way, if anyone asks, you're Jewish. But only if anybody asks." He assured me nobody would. I agreed and kept my hurt feelings to myself.

I moved on from Adam at the end of that summer, but I took my time letting him know that. I waited until after he borrowed his dad's car to help me move into a subleased room in a Brooklyn apartment. A few days later, I broke up with him in a text. *I'm not doing anything wrong*, I told myself. *Adam treated me as something to hide. This is justified.*

This was a lie. I just wanted to hook up with one of my new roommates with a clear conscience. By the time the guy's sublet ended a few weeks later, I'd moved on to the next in a succession of guys and girls, none of whom ever said they liked me or wanted to wait. I was back to old habits. As always, they bit me in the ass.

Within a couple of months, I was alone again. I asked Adam to meet me at a bar. We apologized to each other and picked up where we left off, spending nearly every day and night of the next six months together. We became increasingly codependent, insisting we were only friends. I told him we wouldn't sleep together, and he agreed; we broke the pact after a few weeks. We still fought about the same things, and I ducked out of view when he FaceTimed his parents before Shabbos. We went to parties together and left with other people, returning to each other in the morning. I thought it was better than being alone. I thought it was what I deserved.

Something shifted between us after New Year's. Adam took us out to dinner and a movie on Valentine's Day. We didn't call it a date, but old couples smiled at us as we walked back to his apartment. I stopped going out with other guys. I started telling Adam that I loved him, and he said he did, too. I told myself I wanted to convert to Judaism. I told myself the lies didn't hurt me anymore. I told myself things would all work out, even though I knew better.

One afternoon, Adam called me. He said he couldn't see me anymore. I remember him saying that we had *to call this what it is.*" His words stood out to me then because they knocked the wind out of me. They were the exact words my stepfather said to me, over the phone, the last time we spoke. I question the veracity of the detail. I don't trust it because I know it's possible that my mind transposed the memory, placing dialogue from one painful event into another. But that is how I remember it, so that is how it was.

Our minds are made for finding patterns and gleaning meaning from them. Here, a pattern emerges from the facts.

One:

My father left me when I was a child; he did not take care of me.

Two:

My surrogate father cut me off once he was relieved of his legal obligation to care for me.

The rule of threes does not apply; one recurrence is enough for the mind to declare its conclusion: *Fathers love and care for their children unconditionally. Yours do not. The proverbial lightning struck you twice — so what does that say about you?*

I'm not stupid. I caught its meaning: I am the common denominator. I am the problem, the root of the malfunction. I am unlovable. It is the simplest explanation, and so it must be true. And if I am the problem, how should I feel? Ashamed, of course.

The mind points to the supporting evidence: My first boyfriend did the dishes and left without warning. Adam said he loved me, then he said we should call this what it was. The mind ignores nuance, waves away any interruption — *But there was warning before Justin left, wasn't there? And wasn't I the one to leave Adam first?* The satisfaction of making meaning outweighs whether any of it holds water. The mind's work is done. But the shame sticks around. It begets bargaining — *If the shame is here for good, then what's the difference if I do something bad? What's another drop in the bucket? What's another drop in the sea?* And then come the lies.

I started to see, for the first time, the lies I told myself. They'd been blending into the wallpaper for so long; they had become part of the set dressing around me, and they no longer registered to me as anything but furniture. But I couldn't pretend I didn't see them anymore. I knew I could no longer ignore them. I saw how Al's life was built on the lies he told himself, and I knew I wanted a different kind of life. Even if it was harder. Even if it made me miserable. *Let's not shit ourselves here* — that became a familiar refrain. I needed to see things as they really were, and see myself as I really was.

So long as I'm coming clean, why don't we walk back to that scene — my last day in Chicago. It needs a closer look.

Let's see. There's Al, watching me thumb through that stack of letters Mia wrote to him when she was twenty-three — the letters Mia didn't know existed, that she would've burned if she did.

And there I am, right there, counting the envelopes with

greedy eyes, measuring the weight of my plunder. We remember what happened next, don't we?

It wasn't right to open them without her knowing. Once I was back in Oregon, I told her. I asked her to give me her blessing to read them, to give up the privacy she clung to so fiercely.

Those words are true, but what I told you was a lie. Now, don't feel bad, don't feel dumb — how could you have known? You couldn't have. I'll fill you in:

It wasn't right to open them without her knowing.

Sitting in the terminal, waiting for my flight, I knew it wasn't right. But I was tempted. There would be no witness. There would be no evidence. The envelopes were already open. No one would know if I read one — just one. No one would know if I lost control and read the whole stack.

I went back and forth, back and forth. The whole time, I truly believed that I had the power to choose right or choose wrong, that at any moment I might put them away and breathe in deep relief that I could be good. And the whole time, I knew what I was going to do.

I read one letter, just one, from the envelope at the top of the stack. She was writing to Al while she was at work. She was pregnant with me. She was imagining what our life would be like, together. Then I bundled them back up and tucked them into my backpack. Just one; a slip, not a slide.

But I didn't stop because I was overcome with my sin, or because I came to my senses. I stopped only because I had suddenly started to cry.

Reading her letter, I felt the great expanse of time between my young mother and my young self collapse, folding in on itself like an accordion. It felt like a vision, or a miracle; something that, if I put words to it back in the Middle Ages, would clinch me a sainthood; something that, if I put words to it nowadays, might land me in an institution.

I didn't see a ghost. The reception desk at the tanning salon where she worked didn't come crashing into Terminal 2. But I had the undeniable sense that, for as long as I was reading, only a thin membrane separated me from the scene of her writing. Ten real minutes of her life laid over ten real minutes of mine. I reach for figurative language to close the gap between what it was and what I can tell you. It was a double exposure . . . no, a filter over a lens . . . no, it was mono sound split into stereo . . . no, a one-way mirror . . . no . . . no . . .

Anyway, whatever it was, it made me cry. I couldn't risk tears falling onto the letters, or a Good Samaritan asking if I was all right, so I stopped reading. I got on my plane; I got off my plane; I went home.

Once I was back in Oregon, I told her what Al had given me.

I didn't tell her anything else.

I asked her to give me her blessing to read them, to give up the privacy she clung to so fiercely.

And we remember how it ended, don't we?

I got what I wanted. I knew I would. Mia would never refuse, not me.

18

David Rose

Detroit, 2017

One September morning, a man walked down his street with a granny cart in tow. He didn't know he was being watched.

A squad car pulled up beside him. The man didn't move his head to look. He kept his pace. He was crossing the intersection when the officer and his partner approached him. The officer asked for his name.

"David Rose."

"Date of birth?"

"March 11, 1956." The man was more than happy to show the cop his driver's license, bearing that name and that date and his face. The officer just looked at him.

"You know, David Rose is deceased. Died in 2010."

The man smiled, unfazed. "Not this David Rose."

If you blinked, you would have missed it. Later that day, during the eleven o'clock news on channel four, after the lottery results and an ad for a personal injury lawyer, the man's face appeared on-screen: the old FBI mugshot from his WANTED poster. Underneath, the chyron read: FUGITIVE COP CAUGHT IN DETROIT.

A male anchor's voice narrated. "After a fourteen-year search, a fugitive officer from Chicago is back in federal custody. Sixty-eight-year-old Eddie C. Hicks was charged with federal drug conspiracy charges when he skipped town in 2003. Well, he was arrested this morning here in Detroit by the FBI Detroit violent crime task force."

Seventeen seconds of airtime, then the face disappeared and the chyron was replaced: BREAK-IN AT POPULAR LOUNGE BAR.

Hicks hadn't spent all of those fourteen or so years hiding out in Brazil, like the authorities suspected. He'd spent a good amount in Detroit, a stone's throw from home, and he'd kept busy. Back in 2011, *Chicago Tribune* reporters had been investigating Chicago-area fugitives like Hicks and how they managed to enrich their families while continuing to evade capture. The reporters weren't the ones to track Hicks down in Detroit, but what they exposed stood to embarrass law enforcement and seemingly poked holes in the notion that Hicks had disappeared to some faraway country, never returning home in the time he was on the lam.

After all, back in 2003, Hicks had a wife he was leaving behind. He and fellow former CPD officer Carol Pierce tied the knot six days before he vanished. On the day after that missed court appearance — Hicks's first full day on the lam — he signed papers to have his police pension checks mailed to his and Carol's home on the South Side. His disappearance didn't stop the checks from coming, more than three thousand dollars each month, and Carol kept cashing them. When the feds finally noticed about a year later and got a subpoena for copies of several recent checks, they saw Hicks's signature clear as day.

Even so, they let Carol keep making the deposits — possibly, the *Tribune* noted, because they were hoping the trail of money might lead them to Hicks.

The pension board, for their part, seemed to be powerless: Hicks had never been convicted and sentenced. In 2005, Hicks signed paperwork instructing the fund to wire his monthly benefit payments directly into his Chicago Patrolmen's Federal Credit Union account. No more bothersome checks.

Hicks also had a son, Anthony, who was an active-duty cop himself. In 2005, Eddie Hicks's signature appeared on land records giving his son a gated three-story brick apartment building on South Phillips Avenue. That property had been the collateral Hicks posted to secure his $150,000 bond. Despite Hicks not holding up his end of that bargain, nobody seized the building. And, the *Tribune* found, Anthony used the building to secure a $217,500 mortgage — which he did not repay.

It seemed like Hicks was untouchable — even as a fugitive, he was able to do what he wanted, in this case enriching his family from afar. But sometimes, all it takes is some journalistic intervention to get things moving. The *Tribune* was working on the investigation, reaching out to the pension board about Carol receiving Hicks's benefits. At first, they implied their hands were tied. After that initial response, they decided otherwise and suspended Hicks's pension.

When the *Tribune* reporters sat down with Anthony Hicks for an interview, they brought along a copy of the 2005 deed that bore both his and his father's signatures. Two notaries had verified the elder Hicks's signature and attested that they saw Hicks sign the papers. What did Anthony have to say about that?

Anthony claimed he was "baffled," said he didn't sign it with his father, that he hadn't seen his father since before he disappeared. He declined to answer any questions about that unpaid mortgage.

Carol and Anthony weren't on trial here, so to speak. If either wife or son had seen more of Hicks than they claimed, or if they knew more about how he was spending his time in hiding than they disclosed, of course they'd keep it to themselves. Why would they blow up his spot? They were family. You don't snitch on your family.

———

About a month after he was picked up in Detroit, Hicks was sent back to Chicago. That October, he sat shackled in a court-room as the federal prosecutor, Sonny Pasqual, asked that Hicks be kept in custody: "Needless to say, he is a serious risk of flight." Hicks's attorney didn't object.

19

Paths of Least Resistance

Al texted me the news before I had a chance to confirm it myself. Eddie Hicks was arrested in Detroit. He was alive, he was found, and he would be brought to justice.

I was at my desk in the WSJ newsroom, having earned an extension on my internship that kept me on through September. I was the last one left of the summer interns. I hoped that their willingness to keep me here longer was a sign that they might want to hire me one day.

I excused myself from my desk when I saw his message. I called him and got a few minutes of scattered takes from Al. There'd be a trial for sure; the guy looked old as fuck now; he was probably going to die in prison, even if he only had to serve time for running away.

Talking to Al didn't make me feel better. Since defending my thesis back in the spring, I'd spent months living in a new place, doing new things, and not thinking too much about my dad. It had been nice. I knew I would dive back into the case, renew my search, return to Chicago. The idea of getting answers, of some closure, excited me, but the idea of seeing Al again made me tired. Like my head was filled with lead or some other heavy molten metal. I didn't know which feeling I should suppress and which one I should follow.

I was also nervous. I'd covered arraignments and some other more minor sentencings back in Oregon, but this was bigger. The stakes were higher. I didn't know what I'd find once the evidence and the exhibits were all brought into the light. I felt panic in my throat. I didn't know what to do, or who to tell.

I still had Brent's number from school. I texted him. He made time for a call. I took it in a corridor of the newsroom that I'd seen other reporters duck into for important, hushed conversations. I don't remember exactly what we talked about. I remember my hands were shaking. I remember trying to steady my voice. I tried to be honest about my struggles to get my foot in the door as I applied and interviewed for entry-level jobs as a reporter. I was afraid I wouldn't make it. But I had nowhere else to go. And I was afraid of what would come my way whenever Hicks was put on trial.

I'm hesitant to say that I *remember* Brent's words, knowing how our minds compress our memories to capture the gist. I debate myself in my head: *Maybe it's better to say that I* think *I remember what he said, I think. Or does that give the impression that I doubt what I remember?* There has never been any doubt in my mind; I knew the words well; I repeated them to myself over the months that followed, to bring myself comfort. *So then what's the problem? Am I afraid to say them with certainty, because they were so important to me?*

Stop. That's enough. Just get on with it. Please.

"Well," Brent said over the phone, "*in order to make it there, you need talent — which you have. And you need to be brave — which you are.*"

In that moment, I tried to believe those words were true. I returned to my desk and got back to work.

The start of 2018 marked the end of many things: my complicated relationship with Adam, my post-internship unemployment, and my revolving door of roommates and sublets. I found a one-bedroom rent-stabilized apartment in Ridgewood, Queens. I took out a cash advance on my credit card to cover the broker's fee.

That year, I learned to make the most of the little I had. I found most of my furniture for free or cheap on Craigslist. I used dollar-store pushpins to hang the only decor I had: photos of my family, cut-out poems, and a print of Frida Kahlo. The building had a no-pet policy, but some months in I began to hear barking from the stairwell. Encouraged by my rule-breaking neighbors and my off-site landlord, I went out and found my best friend, a black-and-white kitten with wide, expressive eyes. I named him Jiji, and he and I settled into the first home that was ever just mine.

That was also the year I met Ryan.

When people ask how we met, I have to tell the full story. If I only tell them the gist, I get raised eyebrows and have to explain: "Wait — let me finish —"

I met Ryan on Craigslist. (Let me finish!) The existential pressure of my first year out of college and the monotony of my ten-hour workdays had gotten the best of me. I couldn't afford a therapist and I didn't want to increase my antidepressant dosage, so I decided a hobby would fix everything. I started painting, using canvases and brushes I collected for cheap from Craigslist. When I saw a listing for oil paints, I haggled with the anonymous seller and set a date for pickup.

Ryan was the seller, and we met at a café in Queens. When I arrived, he was reading the latest *New Yorker*. This impressed me. I hadn't made it through a single issue in the growing pile on my dresser. I hadn't read anything in weeks: Reading made me think of writing, and I couldn't do that, either. All I could do was look at my phone.

Ryan was also handsome. I instantly regretted driving such

a hard bargain over the paint. When I handed him the cash, I insisted on giving him an extra twenty dollars, bumping the price back up to what he'd asked. I wanted him to like me. We chatted for a while as he finished his coffee. He was an artist, he grew up in New Jersey, he was in his late twenties. He spoke softly; I leaned in to listen. I was reluctant to leave.

But after an hour, he had to go. I reached down to grab the toolbox filled with my new paints and yanked the handle up. The box didn't budge. Oil paint is dense as fuck, apparently. There was no way I could get the box home myself. Ryan offered to carry it for me and walked me home. He said we should meet up again sometime.

I fell in love quickly. I was impressed by Ryan's mind, which was always whirring, and by the effect he had on others. Whether he was talking to me or a waitress, an old friend or a work colleague, Ryan was genuine and charismatic, without any pretension or performance. He seemed to move through the world with ease. A singular thread ran through each facet of his personality: He seemed to really know who he was. I felt like I had been chopped up into a hundred different people, each playing a different part and doing a shitty job at it.

We went to museums and galleries; we stayed up late in my apartment reading poetry; we talked. The subject of Al was broached quickly when he saw the stack of binders and documents in my bedroom. I told him how afraid I felt as a kid, and how lonely.

Ryan said he felt the same way. He told me a story, a memory, from when he was eleven. Every morning, after his parents and brother had left for work and school, Ryan made his daily rounds. He walked through the house and said good-bye to each empty room, wiping away tears before getting on the bus. He was so lonely all the time, he said, even when he was a kid, and he never understood why. When Ryan told me that story, I understood him. Together, I thought, we would never feel that loneliness again.

A few months in, I met a new side of Ryan, one quick to anger. Not the stereotypical masculine anger, red-faced and bellowing. It was quiet and quick, like a snake's strike.

When I met this new Ryan, I was sitting on the kitchen floor of his new apartment. He had recently broken up with a long-term girlfriend and had been living out of a duffel bag in temporary quarters. We were cleaning the place when I got a text from an old hookup. I laughed out loud. I didn't mean to. It just struck me as so funny to see the guy's name pop up on my screen all those months later. I had forgotten he existed, and the text itself was so forcedly casual, some laid-back joke meant to reel me into meeting up with him for an afternoon. I was laughing at the boy, and at myself. *I can't believe that actually used to work on me.*

Ryan smiled. "What is it?" He thought someone sent me a meme. I told him through giggles, showing him the message. The more I spoke, the stonier his expression became. The more his brows knit together, the more I stumbled and stuttered.

He cut me off. "I don't think that's funny. You think that's funny?" he said. His mouth was a hard line. "I think it's pretty fucked up, actually, you telling me about someone who used to fuck you. I don't really want to think about that. How's that supposed to make me feel?"

The room shrank around me. The air grew heavy. He was a stranger now. I watched his back as he grabbed the mop. I got to my feet. Pins and needles ran through my toes. "I'm sorry," I said to his back. I held my breath as I walked out of the room. I didn't want him to hear me cry.

I reached the doorframe when his hands spun me around. He hugged me. "Hey. I'm sorry. Everything's okay." His voice was gentle now, familiar, and desperate. Ryan pulled back to search my face. "Forget everything I said. Everything's fine." I nodded and tried to smile.

These bouts of anger and depression appeared more frequently. Eventually they stopped ending with his stricken apologies; all I got was more stony silence. I walked on eggshells. Ryan picked fights that lasted hours over things I thought were inconsequential. When I told him about my past relationships and issues with men, he became jealous. I saw my own fault in it: I overshared, expecting Ryan to react with the same blasé attitude that all the guys my age approached sex with. How many of them had told me about other girls they were seeing before I had time to get dressed after? I didn't stop to think that Ryan might feel differently, that he might feel how I felt before I had toughened my own skin. But his jealousy didn't fade with time or understanding. It became an ad-hominem attack he wielded in every argument. Eventually I only saw the man I loved in flashes, long enough to get my hopes up before this other man replaced him. Sometimes I worried he'd never come back.

I wasn't blameless. Early in our relationship, Ryan came clean: There was some overlap between his drawn-out breakup and our tentative first weeks of dating. This lit a small fire in the back of my mind that fed on my insecurities. Another lie, shortly after, about getting coffee with his ex-girlfriend fanned the flames. I couldn't stand being lied to, I told him. He promised: "Never again."

That Christmas, we were decorating a tree at his place. Ryan was looking for his old ornaments and lights. He'd gotten rid of all the old stuff from his past relationship — *I don't want to remember any of it*, he'd said, *what do I need all that for?* — but we found a grocery bag of old holiday cards and cheap ornaments with their names on them. He said he'd toss them later. A few days later, I was in the apartment by myself. A nagging thought led me down to his basement storage. I found the grocery bag he said he threw away.

I lost my fucking shit. I ripped up the cards and smashed the plastic and glass, leaving the debris on his living room floor to find when he got home. My heart pounded in my ears as I walked to my apartment; I didn't recognize myself under the rage. To me, the discovery was a betrayal and a warning: If he lied to me once, he could lie to me again. To Ryan, it was no deception; it was just a bag of trash he hadn't taken out yet.

It took hours for the fury to fade and my eyes to clear. It was like I woke up from a dream. I saw the glitter under my fingernails, the thin red cuts on my palms, the dried blood. I saw what I had done. Shame crept up my legs and climbed the notches of my spine. I felt its grip on the nape of my neck. Before I could draw breath, its heavy hood came down.

Ryan forgave me, again and again, as I forgave him. We resolved to take care of ourselves and each other. On my end, that meant curbing my compulsion to know everything. In past conversations about our exes, I had interrogated him for hours. Not so much out of jealousy as from an unending curiosity. I wanted to know everything about them, what brought them together, what caused them to part. I wanted to know every life he lived before I met him.

But I couldn't wear him down, like I wore down everyone else in my life. Once he told me, gently, "I don't remember every conversation I ever had with them. I can't tell you everything." After that, I tried to bite my tongue. I wondered if I could ever let anything go.

On his end, Ryan finally went back to a psychiatrist. As a teenager Ryan had taken Lexapro and Prozac, but he spent his twenties self-medicating and white-knuckling. In some ways, it had worked: He was successful at work and in his studio, and his friends never would have guessed he was in so much pain. But we agreed that his old strategy wasn't working anymore. For all their side effects, the new pills did their job: We fought less; his moods were less erratic; he seemed lighter.

I left my apartment behind when the lease was up and moved in with Ryan. I didn't feel too bad trashing most of my furniture — it had come from the sidewalk in the first place, after all. Our cats became brothers. Our lives intertwined.

We still had low points. His new medications were constantly being adjusted, and every few weeks there would be a period of tapering and withdrawal. During those days or weeks, the old barrier was built back up between us. No matter how I tried, I couldn't get him to talk to me. I let myself keep one foot out the door: I looked at subletting rooms in the neighborhood to get out of our shared apartment.

That was when I thought of Al.

"I'm getting real sick of all the shit," he said to me once. He was venting about his girlfriend, Andie's mom. He didn't like her much; they fought all the time. I assumed he cheated on her, based on his overall history with women and a few targeted Facebook posts she once made about Untrustworthy Men. I took his complaints with a grain of salt. I nodded along all the same.

"Probably gonna end up moving out. I don't have much of my stuff at her place anyway. I keep most of it at your grandparents'." He shrugged. "Always been like that, you know? I always wanna have a place that's mine, just in case."

"Me, too. I always feel better if I can keep one foot out the door."

"A foot out the door — exactly." His eyes met mine with a recognition that made my stomach sink. "Exactly."

All my life when I thought of Al, I thought, *I want to be nothing like you.* But there it was: like father, like daughter, even if only in that one way. One was enough to fill me with dread. I worried that if I went looking, there'd be more.

One afternoon I called Mia. I asked her whether she thought Adam would have been a better match for me.

No, she said, she didn't think so. She reminded me about the lie, about my ambivalence toward him. I was half listening. I asked her whether she'd be mad at me if I ended up back with him. I hadn't spoken to Adam in more than a year, but I kept him in the back of my mind as a hypothetical safety net, ignoring the fact that he had his own life that I was no longer a part of.

"Of course not. I would never be mad at you."

"Okay, not *mad*. But would you be disappointed?"

"No." I heard her take a breath. *"But I want you to know that it doesn't have to be Ryan or Adam. Those aren't your only options. There are so many people out there. You don't have to settle for anyone who doesn't make you happy. I don't want you to do that."*

"I know."

I walked home as the light turned blue. I imagined what the future might look like: Ryan and I, separated, in new apartments. And I pictured him as a child, alone and dressed for school, saying good-bye to each room in his empty home. Then I ran the tape back and played it again, breaking my own heart all over again. The pain was too great. I couldn't bear it. I loved him. I could never leave.

That night I found Ryan at his drafting table. I took stock of the tight line of his mouth and his furrowed brow. The wall was up. I wrapped my arms around him; I pretended not to feel his shoulders stiffen. I held on.

Ryan was diagnosed with borderline personality disorder. I knew he'd gone to a psychiatrist for medication, but he hadn't told me that he started therapy, too. He only told me about that development after his therapist referred him to a specialist. (She had a hunch that he might be bipolar, or something along those lines, but couldn't diagnose him.) It wasn't long until we got the final, formal verdict: BPD. The disorder characterized, per the *DSM-V*, by instability: unstable emotions, unstable relationships, unstable sense of self or identity. One of the first descriptions I heard of the illness came from psychotherapist and BPD expert Marsha Linehan: People with borderline personality disorder, she had said, "are like people with third-degree burns over 90 percent of their bodies. Lacking emotional skin, they feel agony at the slightest touch or movement." I had seen that agony firsthand. Before the diagnosis, I had cursed its unknown source, lamenting my inability to save the person I loved from such pain. I wished I could take it from him, bear it for him. I feared he would suffer forever. After the diagnosis, my heart soared.

That specialist referred Ryan to a local hospital, one that had a renowned intensive BPD treatment program. For a year, Ryan devoted himself to group and solo therapy two days a week. We bought all the books that his team recommended. I read about "emotional dysregulation" and "rejection sensitivity." I understood him in a new way. The well of patience I thought had run dry renewed itself. Over that year, I watched Ryan do what Al never did: try to be better. He did the work to manage, understand, and overcome his pain.

There were still hard days. The loneliness still found me sometimes. I was tired. I was the only one who knew about Ryan's diagnosis, all that he went through, what we both had to endure. Sometimes, when I felt weak and selfish, I wished he would tell his parents, or one of our friends, anyone who could bear some of the weight for me. We could take shifts. I could take a break.

One morning, I found a note on my desk in Ryan's careful, clean hand:

I'm sorry.

I know I've been irritable.

I'll be better today.

I still worried about Ryan and me; whether he'd leave me for someone else, or whether I wouldn't be strong enough to get through the hard times. But as much as I had doubt, I had a faith I couldn't shake that a change would come — so long as I fought hard enough to earn it.

I felt that faith in my love for Ryan. Somehow, I still had it for Al, too. I couldn't pretend I didn't see the difference, though, between the kind of man my father was and the kind of man my partner was. Ryan heard me, saw me, and tried to change; Al did not.

In the meantime, my father and I would keep up our play-acting — a sorry attempt at familial normalcy. Every so often a birthday text, a few Instagram likes would drop in like pebbles into a pond. The surface would ripple, as if there was life down below. But the small, shimmering waves would lose their strength, the water would settle and grow still. The surface would return to its natural state: smooth, reflective, as if impenetrable, as if nothing lived below but silvered glass.

It was easier to keep up the charade. But how long could I keep it up? How long would I tolerate Al as he was? How long until tolerance turned into acceptance?

20

_____

The Shame

The wheels of justice turn slowly. Hicks was arrested in 2017, but he wouldn't stand trial until 2019. That was just fine by me. In fact, I hoped they'd slow down a little more. I wanted more time. I was afraid to finish what I'd started.

In the meantime, I had plenty going on to distract myself from the countdown. After months of unemployment, I had landed a full-time job as a reporter, back at the *Journal*, covering markets in real time for WSJ and the Dow Jones Newswires. It wasn't a sexy beat by any stretch, but I didn't mind. Not long after I was hired, I got a little surprise: Our commodities reporter was leaving, so guess who got to learn all about wheat and corn? In addition to finding my way around the stock market, I tracked the rise and fall of the futures prices of cattle, soybeans, and hogs. In addition to my growing Rolodex of stock analysts, I started making calls to livestock traders. Pretty much all of them were in the Midwest, and many were based in my old hometown, the home of the Chicago Mercantile Exchange.

It felt strange to dial in the familiar area codes, to hear the traders greet my call in familiar accents. I fought off strange impulses. I wanted to ask my sources, *Does the name Eddie Hicks ring a bell to you? Eddie Hicks, corrupt cop? No? What about Al's Gym? You ever heard of an Al's Gym?* Eventually, the urges went away.

I tried to stir up some excitement within myself about the markets, but I couldn't help but become bored. I told myself it was just part of the process: My life was stabilizing; I was taking root in a new place. *It's a privilege to be bored*, I told myself.

How could I be bored, anyway? I'd made it! Back to the *Journal*, back to the place I thought I'd only dream of. *I finally got what I always wanted — now enjoy it!* I told myself. I guess I was too loud; my fear heard me. It saw an opening and pounced, poisoning the thought. *I finally got what I always wanted — now I have something to lose.* I felt the ground move. *What if I lose it? What if —* And then I was falling; I landed in the familiar trap of magical thinking. *Now you've done it. You've spoken it into existence. You've told your own future. That is, unless you do all that weird stuff you hate doing, like tapping your toes in the exact right way or clearing your throat a hundred times. But that's just a Band-Aid, a temporary fix. You really want to save yourself? Well then you better find a good mask and keep it on tight.*

I hadn't wanted to admit it, but I had begun to feel a certain dread. I was neither dumb nor blind. I saw that the elite national journalism scene that revolved around Manhattan was a small world, and most of the people in it had very different lives compared with mine. Many of my colleagues went to the same Ivy League schools, or the same Columbia master's program, or even as far back as the same private New York high schools. They seemed to assume the same of others, including me. It was my job to maintain the illusion.

The months passed by. I couldn't talk myself out of being bored by soybeans and tariffs and supply-and-demand forecasts — no more than I could talk myself out of my weekly imposter-syndrome panic attacks. I became exhausted and depressed in short order. I gained weight as I cranked up my meds. I couldn't stop yawning. All I wanted was a good night's sleep, but my worries kept me up. I drank a lot of coffee instead.

I was drinking my coffee in the newsroom when I noticed a sign above the kitchenette sink. It had never caught my eye before.

ONLY THE AMBITIOUS READ THE WALL STREET JOURNAL.

I stared at the shapes the words made. I didn't know who the message was for. *The sales team sat somewhere around here, didn't they? Maybe it's for them, like a motivational poster, to reinforce their belief in the brand.*

I made my eyes focus. I read it again. ONLY THE AMBITIOUS.

I was ambitious once. I wasn't so sure I was anymore. I was too tired. I didn't want to volunteer for more work, to get my byline out there, to angle for a promotion. I wanted to go to bed. I wanted to think less.

Maybe I hadn't even come by that virtue honestly, if I had ever truly possessed it: *ambition.* Yes, I had worked hard. I worked hard because I had to. I was ambitious because I couldn't afford not to be. I had to eat.

If I was no longer ambitious, then it was only a matter of time until someone in the building got wise to my unearned presence, my wasted salary. They'd notice my mask and confiscate it. Then they would do the right thing. I wouldn't even hold it against them. I'd get fired. I'd lose my employee subscription to the *Journal*; I'd be too broke and unambitious to pay for my own. And then, at some point, I'd die.

Ah, well. I drank my coffee.

I got dinner with Brent the next time he visited New York. I knew I wouldn't be able to shake off the listlessness that had settled upon me, but I tried my best to hide it. He congratulated me on my early-career triumphs and told me about another *Journal* reporter he had worked with, back when that reporter was still a journalism student in Oregon. Another hometown hero.

"When I met you, it was just like when I met him — I *knew* it. I knew you both would just —" He whistled as he pushed his hand off the table, taking the form of a jet ascending. "You'd just *take off*." There was that familiar sickly feeling — gratitude, enveloped by shame.

That night, I sat on my living room floor, digging through my old college papers. There it was: a recommendation letter Brent had written for me:

> I had heard of Francesca Fontana before I met her . . .
>
> Francesca possesses a gift for storytelling, investigation and empathy . . . yet she takes none of these natural qualities for granted. She has emerged from a difficult upbringing with a focus and determination to earn her way into journalism . . .
>
> I've known few young journalists who match Francesca's promise.

Back then, I'd held the words close. I thought I didn't deserve them; I hoped that one day I would. *I knew . . . You'd just take off.* I held these words close, too. And, just like I had back in Eugene, I tried to trick myself into thinking they could be true.

I got a new therapist, whom I hoped could help me cool it with the work-related rumination and dread. I was coming around to accepting that my OCD was, in fact, OCD. She encouraged me to talk to Ryan about it. I was optimistic; I thought it might bring us closer in the wake of his own treatment.

He didn't say much when I told him. He raised his eyebrows at me. I rambled to fill the silence.

"I mean, *I* think I have it. And not just me — so does my therapist. And so did the other ones I saw, back in Oregon."

"I really don't think you have OCD," Ryan said. He thought I was exaggerating; he thought it was irresponsible for my therapist to talk diagnoses. He spoke dismissively, with an edge, as if I had done something offensive and wrong — like I'd parked in an accessible spot without a placard.

I looked for a solution. I spent four hundred dollars on a diagnostic visit with a psychiatrist specializing in anxiety disorders. After my appointment, I asked the office to send me documentation, any kind of proof — a letter? A certificate? The administrator emailed me back a copy of my invoice, virtually unchanged. I looked closer. In one of the columns, they had added a diagnostic code. *Close enough*, I thought.

I printed the invoice. I showed Ryan. He shrugged. I shredded the invoice. I felt ashamed.

Shame and guilt are two different things, I've learned. It took me a while to grasp their difference. In my mind, shame was the root of guilt; shame was what made you feel guilty about something you did or someone you were. The experts tell me otherwise.

Both are self-conscious emotions — feelings that guide our behavior by nudging us toward actions that our societies value and away from those that alienate us from one another. But guilt stems from our disapproval of a specific behavior or act; shame comes from our disapproval of our whole self. You feel guilty that you did something bad, not necessarily that you *are* bad. But shame scrutinizes *you*, the self.

What does it feel like, the so-called shame experience?

Nothing good! I thought to myself, reading through scholars' answers to the question. When we experience shame, we feel exposed; we feel we are shrinking; we feel powerless; we feel worthless. When we feel ashamed, we want to hide.

Earlier, I told you that I was neither dumb nor blind. Maybe it's more of a case-by-case basis — otherwise, *how* did it take me all those years to see it? That, for most of young adult life, I had been feeling near-constant shame? I thought this state was normal; I thought it was a consequence of being me, of being the person I was, of doing the things I chose to do.

Shame has been called the least desirable emotional experience. It is more painful and more damaging than guilt, so it makes sense that we try to skirt it as best we can. We avoid doing things that bring us shame, or we run from the shame we bring our way. This is a typical human response to typical human shame.

But what about the atypical? What about the extreme?

Central to my experience of OCD was the idea that I was inherently and irredeemably bad; I was doomed. I brought ill fate to others, and it was my responsibility to protect others from the harm I would bring down upon those around me. Unsurprisingly, studies have observed "greater levels of shame in those with OCD in comparison with healthy controls."

The condition has other hallmarks; some call it the *disease of doubt*. The doubt and the fear work hand in hand. They sent me running back into my apartment each morning, only minutes after I'd left. I needed to make sure that I hadn't inadvertently opened all of the windows and lifted their screens, inviting our cats to escape and fall to their deaths. You know, the kind of stuff you do when you're in a hurry to get to the office; the stuff that totally slips your mind.

The doubt also drives excessive pattern-seeking. It takes our natural human impulse to make meaning and learn from life and puts it into overdrive.

I can see now that my obsessions have been most dangerous and detrimental when they were the most "rational." The one that has always loomed largest? My need to know. *I must find everything, fact-check everyone, trust nothing.* It may be maladaptive and unhealthy in many contexts, but in the field of journalism it's a feature, not a flaw.

This need can also be justified when considered within my own specific set of circumstances: I have a father who lies, a mother who buries her secrets. Maybe if I didn't have anything to dig into, I would have seen the behaviors sooner for what they really were. Maybe I would have spared myself some pain.

You know what? Maybe I *am* dumb and blind after all. I sure was back then. I didn't see the damage. I only saw the rewards promised by the hunt. Once again, like the lightning that struck me twice, I learned the wrong lesson.

I don't know how many years had passed — demarcations of time have been losing their edges, congealing together — when I returned to that strange sign by the kitchenette. I was sitting at the same table, drinking my coffee, when I saw it. My stomach dropped.

THE TRULY AMBITIOUS READ THE WALL STREET JOURNAL.

That wasn't right. I knew what it said. I had been certain. That weird slogan had been the source of that day's shame-spiral, however long ago it was. ONLY THE AMBITIOUS, it had said. ONLY THE AMBITIOUS.

How? How could I have gotten it so *wrong*? I thought back to my perfect model of memory: *My mind is an office . . . I am a clerk . . .* How childish it seemed now — my little fantasy, my playing pretend — in the face of my great failure, and all of the doubt it ushered in.

My mind is an office; I am a clerk; I am kicking in the door.

I storm down the aisles of desks and typewriters to my file-cabinet memory. I fumble with those *tiny, motherfucking, keys,* before throwing open each drawer. I tear file after file from its assigned home, in pursuit of the record that betrayed me.

Where is it?

I have no concept of order and protocol. Folders fly open behind me, their precious contents spilling across the floor. I trample records that land underfoot. My fellow make-believe clerks gasp. A woman shrieks — the *horror!* — the *desecration!* Someone, somewhere, pulls an alarm. I hear nothing but the roar of a freight train. I am nothing but a vessel of ruin.

My rage propels me into a state of annihilation. I wrestle the drawers from their tracks and let them crash to the ground. I upend my empty cabinet. I pick up my Smith-Corona and then I smash it down. Its metal arms snap; the keys bounce and scatter. I lay waste to everything in my path.

Sensation returns as the roar fades. My breath is ragged. My body is sore. I've destroyed all that I can. I am alone.

The office has been long evacuated. The alarm continues to blare, warning no one. I stagger over to my chair. The heaviness returns. I dig through the desk for my pack of smokes and lighter. I ignore the blood and ink on my hands. I ignore the sign hanging over the card catalog:

NO SMOKING, NO MATCHES, NO OPEN LIGHTS.

I take it all in. There will be nothing to salvage, and that's probably for the best. I'd started to have a sneaking suspicion that it wasn't memory, but *my* memory that could not be trusted, that bore such flaws in its design, that had been programmed to deceive me.

THE TRULY AMBITIOUS READ THE WALL STREET JOURNAL.

I sat there for a long while, reading the words that I'd gotten so wrong.

Ah, well. I drank my coffee. My body was too tired. I'd let myself spiral later, about whether I'd ever trust my own mind again.

21

INTERLUDE III

On Tragedy

No one could tell me that Rick Stratton was dead. No one I trusted, at least.

I called the county coroner in Oklahoma. I called the Chicago offices that deal with the bureaucracy of death. Some court records listed his first name as Richard, but other sources online suggested it was his middle name. I had no hard proof that Rick was, beyond a shadow of a doubt, dead.

But I was obsessed. I couldn't stop searching.

I scoured the internet from my phone, searching through strangers' social media. All I had were a few Facebook posts. Random guys from the neighborhood, wishing Rick to rest in peace. I clicked through photo galleries and found images of Al and his friends smiling at a "memorial" held in a pizza joint. They used the hostess stand as a makeshift pulpit.

Al's words echo back to me. I'll let them echo back to you now. He only kept Rick close all those years to protect Mia and her sister.

I should've just shot him. Would've saved a lotta people. A lotta people. He was the fuckin' devil, man.

That's what my father told me. Those photos, that memorial — they say different.

Still, all I had was Al's story: Rick Stratton was living in the Oklahoma town his family hailed from — the same town Mia was taken to by his brother all those years ago. He wasted himself down to bone. He was half the weight of his old iron-pumping frame — all the meth. Al told me he talked to Rick on the phone weeks before the news of his death drifted back to Chicago. He didn't say what they talked about. He didn't repeat his story about keeping him close as an enemy, not a friend.

According to my dad, the word on the street was that Rick died in his house, from an overdose or a heart attack or some shit like that. His dogs fed on his corpse. When the authorities found the remains, what was left of the man weighed seventy pounds.

This is a story. I can't tell you if it's true. I don't know if I believe it. But it's all I have.

Like a Greek fuckin' tragedy, ain't it? Al let out a bark of a laugh over the phone when he told me the story. *Eaten by his own dogs. Fuckin' karma.*

Greek fuckin' tragedy. Tragedy with a capital *T*.

It is not in the business of dealing just deserts and calling it a day. After Herakles kills his wife and children in a god-commanded rage, Euripides does not end the hero's life. It's not so simple. Herakles is spared one suffering and will endure another — life with the knowledge of what he has done. But he is walked offstage held by the hand of a friend who promises to care for him in his sorry state. Is he deserving of that small comfort, of that sympathy? Does it matter?

In tragedy, there is always a fulfillment of an inevitability, a necessary suffering or foretold transformation. We do not have gods or Fates pulling strings, but we do have cards dealt to us that are out of our control, that you could call predetermined — who our parents are, for one. They shape us and we have no say in being shaped by them, though we can go on to make our lot better or worse through our own actions. And we all have our fatal flaws, which certainly may be a group effort — the result of some combination of who we come from and who we choose to be.

So, in tragedy, we may not get what we think we deserve. We may not get any measure of justice. In coming out the other side of tragedy, we may not be condemned or redeemed. But we are forced to come out the other side. We are forced to confront what we cannot bear.

The chorus, the witnesses, the all-knowing audience — they are the ones with the privilege of perspective. They're *the subject who knows*. They see who we are from every angle, and so they can see what may need to happen to us in the end. Not as cosmic retribution or exoneration, but as an evening of the scales.

We can evaluate some familiar case studies through this lens of Greek fuckin' tragedy.

Rick Stratton was a man who terrorized and felt no remorse. His massive physique was his pride and his power. So we can see what may need to happen to him. Whether fiction or fact, Al was right in one respect: The story of the dogs was a fitting end.

My mother, Mia, buried her past to create a new life for herself and her children; she valued privacy above all else.

Al refused to see himself as he is, to see his past as it was.

You can see what may need to happen to them: a daughter driven to dig.

Were this a tragedy, I would be the protagonist — *proto-agonist*, the first actor, the one who got the stone rolling down the hill in the first place. The stage was set long before I came along, but I made the first push when I set out looking for answers. I couldn't let things lie as they were. If I could, if I had never chosen to search, all would still be as it was. But I reached for veracity, in my compulsive need to know. I wanted to find an honest father, an end to the lies, an absolute truth. For years,

I told myself that Bob Clarke was just a dick, a typical Chicago defense attorney, and that he was wrong about me. But I had to sit with the possibility: Maybe Bob Clarke was right. Maybe I was the family snitch. Maybe I still am.

And — I can never stop the *what ifs*, the endless branches of possibility — what if he *was* right about me? What if that fact is another terrible truth, another discovery that stands to reverse my fortune? Would I be able to live with myself? I don't know. I don't have an answer.

Here's what I *do* know, what I can only tell you here and now, in this intervening period: Even after each of our fates play themselves out, I never let any of it go. I never discard the stacks of paper, the criminal records and arrest logs that I gathered for years. I still have them. I find myself still search-ing, retracing my steps. I review all the court documents I already know by heart and chase small details that have no real importance. At work, I spend my lunch breaks on hold with my alma mater, trying to get access to my student email account so I can plumb its depths for every minor record of who I was then. Even though I know the search will yield nothing: There is nothing to find. I know the administra-tive policies. My account was erased long ago, likely within a month after I took my diploma and ran, left Eugene and never went back.

Now allow me to take my place alongside the others: Rick, Al, Mia.

I was the daughter of a man who said he'd tell me anything I wanted to know, only most of it turned out to be lies.

I was the daughter of a mother who would never lie to me, only she clung to her privacy that had helped her survive, that she thought would save me from a similar fate.

I had started something that I could not stop. Because if I was still searching, then there was no ending. If I was still searching, the future was like Schrödinger's cat: There was still the possibility of an honest father, an end to the lies, an absolute truth. If I stopped searching, I would have to open the box and see the certain end.

So you can see what may need to happen to me.

22

————

The Trial

I told myself that 2019 would be my year.

I was training for the New York Marathon. I rewarded myself for a record-breaking no-picking streak with my first-ever professional manicure. I finally got my New York driver's license. Everything was looking up.

That autumn I'd be turning twenty-five. Ryan called it my quarter-centennial. By then, Hicks's trial would be over. My search would be done. I would know as much of the truth as I could ever hope to know about Al, Hicks, and the case that had consumed so much of my life.

I had decided that I would try to write about the trial for the *Journal*. Even if all the top editors passed on the piece, even if the final draft ended up living in a folder under my desk, I was going to write the story down. Then, I hoped, I could move forward. I could think about something else.

In March, I used up the lion's share of my vacation days to fly back to Chicago and watch the proceedings. I stayed in the same old guest room in my aunt Rosie's apartment, in my uncle Marco's building. Al dropped by for dinner; we talked about the case. I felt the strangest sense of déjà vu, flashbacks to that first college research trip. I didn't want to admit it, but I had hoped that I would feel differently at twenty-four than I had at twenty-one. *Have I grown up at all? Or have I just gotten older?*

That night before the trial, I couldn't fall asleep. I shut my eyes. I remembered that first night in Chicago. Al and I had made pizzas together. I felt the same thing back then: *I don't think I know what I'm doing.*

I arrived early to the courthouse downtown, wearing one of my work blazers, armed with a reporter's notebook. In the courtroom, I watched Hicks arrive, handcuffed in an ill-fitting suit. I recognized him from the WANTED flyers. He was seventy now; he looked older than he did in the mugshot, but not by that much. I couldn't stop staring at him. I'd been looking at his face for years, never once believing that he would be found, that one day I'd get to see what happened for myself. I trembled in my seat. I wasn't afraid of Hicks or angry at him. But his presence rattled me. It was like seeing a dead man brought back to life; he had been made real. The compulsions I thought were tamed returned in full force. I tried not to pick at the scabs of old wounds I'd worked so hard to heal. I sat on my hands and bit the inside of my cheek until I tasted blood.

It wasn't long before Al's old friend Larry Knitter took the stand. I didn't know what to expect; I'd never met him before. Before the trial, I requested his criminal court records. In 2002 — a year after he was arrested in connection to the fake raids, mind you — Knitter was arguing with his wife when he told her he was going to kill her, then himself. He grabbed his Colt Mustang and a five-round magazine from the closet and took his aim. She ran in fear for her life. He ultimately pleaded guilty to aggravated assault. I thought he sounded like a real piece of shit. Al sure knew how to choose his friends.

When Knitter lumbered up to the stand, I wondered if he recognized me as Al's daughter, if I looked enough like him to be recognizable. My dad had tried to describe him to me: "He talks like he's got a mouthful of rocks."

Al was right. In a low mumble, Knitter told the court that he served more than nine years in prison for his role in the fake raids. Now he worked as a teamster. He had to explain what that meant to the jury: "I drive a truck."

On the stand, Knitter laid out the inner workings of the crew. Each raid went through a similar routine: The four men — actual cops Hicks and Hargrove, civilian employees Moran and Knitter — met up at the precinct's gym to go over each operation. Hicks and Hargrove got tips from drug dealers on who to target, where to find them, and how much money or dope the mark had stashed away in his house or car. Moran typed up a fake search warrant; Knitter, a mechanic for the Chicago Police Department's motor pool, swapped out the plates with out-of-commission ones on the CPD cars they would use.

Then they'd gear up. Knitter had two equipment bags he took on every ride. One bag held his bulletproof vest, guns, gun belt, flashlights, and license plates. In the other were tools, a sledgehammer, and a crowbar.

"Did you also wear gloves when you went out on these jobs?" the prosecutor asked.

Always, Knitter said.

The reason?

"If I punched somebody in the face or in the mouth, I didn't want their saliva or any type of things on my hands."

"And why *else*?"

Knitter thought for a moment. "Because of fingerprints, too."

Their busiest years were 1994 and 1995. In the spring of 1995, Knitter shattered his left hand in a bar fight. "Broke my fingers off," he told the jury. This was a problem, given he was a mechanic. He had a solution. During his next shift, he placed his broken hand in a car door and slammed it shut. He collected workers' comp insurance, sued the city for pain and suffering damages, and was relieved of his duties for the rest of the year.

The day after Knitter left the doctor's office, his hand in splints and bandages, the crew went out on another ride. They were "sitting on a house" in the south suburbs, occupied by a married couple and their kids. The whole thing was a bust. When Knitter muscled the homeowner into opening the industrial safe under the staircase, it was empty.

There was one silver lining. Knitter found a nine-millimeter Ruger in the bedroom and stole it. He kept it until the day he was arrested, when his equipment bags were confiscated as evidence. The prosecutor presented it to the court. I knew that gun. It was the gun Knitter gave Al before the raid, loaded, the one Al said he never carried.

By 2000, the crew was down one man. Hargrove moved to Las Vegas, retiring from the force and their side hustle. Ahead of a job in December, they needed a replacement — someone who was big and could keep his mouth shut. Knitter knew just the guy, an old friend of his.

"Whose name was?"

"Albert Fontana."

There it was. His name, entered into the trial's record for the first time. I held my breath, as if any sudden movement would break the room's focus on the man in the witness chair and all heads would snap toward me.

That time, Knitter told the court, Al declined this offer; the three men went on the ride anyway. That raid, on December 21, 2000, was the FBI's first sting, but they didn't know that yet. They went out again on another job on January 31 — another sting. Knitter asked again. This time, Al said yes.

TV monitors were wheeled to the front of the courtroom. The prosecutors pressed PLAY and there it was: grainy VHS video of the raid itself. I watched in black and white as Al entered the apartment, wearing a baseball cap and leather jacket. He approached one of the cameras hidden in a television set. I saw his face clearly. It was like he'd stepped out of my memory.

I held my breath. I waited for the moment Al told me about, where I'd see him realize that the drug house was too clean, too bare to be legitimate. I never saw it, because it never happened. After the trial, I requested a copy of the video and rewatched it for months. I wasn't looking for evidence to exonerate or damn Al. I just wanted to see the face from my memory, from before I knew so much.

The session broke for lunch. I shuffled out of the courtroom doors with all the others and kept walking. I left the courthouse and told myself I was weak for leaving. I couldn't bring myself to go back. My bare hands froze in my unlined pockets as I wandered.

What was I even doing? For the first time, I saw myself as if I were a stranger. There I was spending money and time I couldn't afford to waste, chasing down proof of what I already knew. All so I could prove a small fraction of my dad's lies to be lies, even though all the proof in the world would probably never get him to admit any of it.

I had a life all my own back in New York that stretched out ahead of me. The revelation shocked me. How had it never occurred to me before? I didn't have to be there, in Chicago. I was not bound by law or contract to return to my father, to the Family. I could go home and just stay there. No one would come after me, least of all Al. In that moment, I felt a relief that Mia must've felt when she was around my age, when she realized that she could go away and have a better life — that she *had* to go away to build that life for herself.

A few days later, Hicks was found guilty. I couldn't bring myself to go down to the courthouse that day. A thick fog had rolled in over me, and I stayed in the guest room, in a deep sleep. After it was all over, I realized that all that Al and I talked about the entire time was the trial. We texted before court; I called him during breaks; we debriefed each night during dinner with the Family. If I thought back, that's how it'd been for years. Now we had nothing to talk about.

In the car on the way back to the airport, I tried to find new topics. The past was always a safe bet. I brought up my teenage years.

"Yeah, you remember that time you bitched me out on the phone?" Al laughed. I couldn't pretend it didn't hurt. I didn't say anything. I didn't need to; like always, he just kept talking. I remembered that call; I remember how much I cried and how angry I was that he didn't give a shit about me. I guess that wasn't what stuck in his memory. I didn't want to examine the reason for the lump in my throat as he drove. Forget his daughter's feelings, reckoning with his own mistakes. All he'd heard over the phone that day was a girl bitching.

The spring came and went; the summer came and went. After weeks of sitting in front of blank pages and banging my head against a wall, I'd drafted an essay about the trial and how I learned the truth of why my father went to prison. Al gave me his blessing to write about it all: the Hicks case, our relationship, his criminal record. I pitched it to a WSJ editor, and, to my surprise, they went for it. I found out on my twenty-fifth birthday that it was officially moving forward. But before the *Journal* could publish the story, I needed to go back to Chicago. I had to make sure that Al had a chance to respond to what I'd written. And they'd hired a photographer to get portraits of us to run with the story. Both directives filled me with different senses of danger, of what could go wrong.

I flew out for a couple of days. I took Al to a sports bar on the North Side. I had no recorder, only a pen and pad and the text of my essay glowing on my phone. I went over the story from start to finish, beat by beat. I explained each statement I made of what he claimed happened the night of the raid and compared it with everything the trial showed me. I saw the gun he carried, the one he said never existed. I saw him on video in the fake drug house; there was no moment of realization, no glowing red light.

Al talked the whole time, a low, rapid monologue. When he agreed with something I said (usually something he had told me), he nodded vigorously. When I said something that contradicted him (like my mention of the gun or the light), it was like he never heard me.

"Yeah, I saw the light and I was like *no friggin' way*. And that's when I knew it was a setup, the whole thing was a setup."

At the end, I explained the essay's conclusion. Twice. The first time he was still talking over me. I had to interrupt him. What I was afraid to do as a daughter, I had to do as a journalist. I had to make him hear it.

"But — wait a second — I just need to make sure you heard this and have you respond."

I told him that, in comparing his version of the story and all the plain facts from the trial, I didn't believe him. I told my father, for the first time in my life, that I thought he was lying.

"So what do you think about that?" I asked.

He shrugged. He was looking through me. "People believe what they believe," he said. "You believe one thing, I believe something else."

I paid the tab and struggled to sleep that night. I wondered if that was it; if after everything I had worked so hard for, that was all I'd get from Al.

When I got back to New York, I sat down with my editor. "All he would say is, *People believe what they believe.*"

"Really!"

"Yup. *You believe one thing, I believe something else.*"

The editor leaned back in his chair and laughed. "Well, there's your ending!"

I laughed, too. What else could you do but laugh?

23

The Aftermath

Al called me the day the *Journal* published my essay about the trial. He was manic. I barely had time to duck into a phone booth in the newsroom before the words tumbled out.

He didn't know the story was on the front page of the paper. (It wasn't on the front page of the paper, just the front page of a section inside the paper, I thought to myself.)

He didn't know I'd mention his 2015 arrest, when he picked up stolen motorcycle parts from that chop shop. (Yes, he did. I explicitly told him I would mention the arrest.)

He hoped the Family wouldn't read the story, especially his own father. He thought he looked like an asshole. (I didn't know what to tell him there.)

I tried to comfort Al without backing down from the truth or giving credence to his veiled accusations. After airing his grievances, his pace became less harried. He took a rare pause.

"I didn't know you were listening."

In the story, I recalled the weekends I spent with him as a kid, how when his cell phone rang he'd lower his voice and wander away, how I always wondered who was on the other end.

"I didn't think — you were a kid, I didn't know you —"

He trailed off, leaving a beat of silence before he was back on track, resuming his rapid-fire monologue. Andie's mother would give him shit for the story. His parents would give him shit for the story. He felt like a real asshole.

For the first time since I was a teenager, I let my annoyance show. I laughed at him.

"Well, it all happened," I said.

"Yeah. Yeah. I know."

"And it's a big deal for me, to have this story out there."

"I know. I'm so proud of you. You're a good writer. When I read it, I felt like you sounded — you wrote like someone who was older. You know?"

I smiled. I couldn't help it. That was all I wanted to hear. I disgusted myself.

Then Al started wrapping up, in his usual way. He was sorry for putting me through all that, for not being a good dad, for going away all those years ago. My smile faded; my fatigue returned. Before I could speak, Al began to counter each sin with a retroactive justification.

"But, you know, if I hadn't messed up and gone away, then you and your Ma might not've moved to Oregon. And you might not've gone to the same school, or even be a journalist, or have gotten as far as you have."

He went back and forth, as if he were speaking to his double. *That's what it's like in his head, all the time*, I thought. *It must be exhausting.*

"And who knows, you know?" he said with an air of finality. *"Maybe if I hadn't done all that stupid shit, you'd have nothing to write about."*

Why do we apologize? Because we feel guilt or shame; because we want to repair a relationship; because we want to do right after doing wrong.

When I left Oregon, I had taken the miserable cold years and boxed them up. I thought I'd get around to examining them at some point, once I was ready. I thought I had control. I didn't. Three apologies — or attempts at apologies — made their way to me, jolting me from the present and yanking me back into a past I longed to leave behind.

Justin followed me to New York during the summer after college. He claimed he was visiting the city, where he knew no one but me, "just for fun." He pestered me daily to see if he could see me. He made me feel sorry for him, so I agreed to dinner.

Justin was chasing something: a romanticization of our past, or a stroke of his ego, or absolution of his guilt. He alternated tactics, flattering my success and postgrad momentum, then peppering in callbacks to inside jokes I'd forgotten. I didn't pretend to laugh like I used to, and I watched him deflate. I sat back in my chair, observing him closely, trying to understand him. I wanted to tell him he was selfish. He had no right to demand my presence, to follow me into my new life. Wasn't he ashamed of all the hurt between us? Wasn't he embarrassed to act like I was frozen in time until he wanted something from me?

I kept this to myself and paid the tab. "It's good to see you," he said as we parted. I didn't say, "You, too." Again, his face fell.

I was at work when my phone lit up. I had a message from a guy I hooked up with for a few months in college. I cringed at the memories that returned to me. I'd forgotten him. He wanted to offer me "a formal apology."

I skimmed it: *I was dishonest and emotionally manipulative to you during our time together . . . I was extremely naive and imma-ture . . . I'm sorry for the way I treated you . . .* I never finished reading. I never replied.

My former stepfather, Keith, sent me a letter. He was making his amends. I don't know if he asked for forgiveness. I don't know if I read until the end. Years later, I only remember one sentence: *I'm sorry if you felt abandoned by me.*

After each of these attempts at apology, the same sick feeling returned to the back of my throat. It felt like returning home after a break-in. Nothing had been moved or taken, but the violation remained. I didn't accept their apologies. I didn't ask for them. I didn't need them. What I needed was to be left the fuck alone.

I thought about the people who hurt me and the people I hurt, about whether I forgave them and whether I wanted forgiveness. I always had trouble understanding forgiveness, starting when I learned about original sin from the Family. I never had my Communion, but I tagged along to church enough to get the message: You *must* forgive others. You *must* ask the Lord for forgiveness. (And of course there's the correlative: If you ask and if you atone, he will always forgive you.)

I didn't have any issue with accepting apologies because an apology is for the person you hurt. You can accept an apology and not forgive, because forgiveness is a two-way street. I didn't think we owed anyone forgiveness. I still don't.

We are not good or bad. We do and we are done to; we are the offender and we are the aggrieved; we are the bullet and we are the wound. There's no way around it. To some, I am nothing more than the pain I caused them. I am my worst. There is no absolution. It can't be undone. We are not exonerated by apology or forgiveness.

But don't let me stop you. Seriously — forgive yourself anytime you want, as many times as you want. Go ahead, knock yourself out. It won't mean a damn thing to the people you've hurt. Only our actions can distance us from the damage we cause. We are not good or bad. We choose to do — good or bad — and then we choose again. We are what we continue to do.

When I thought about all of this, my mind wandered, as

it always did, back to Al. He apologized all the time, but the words were empty. I told him it was okay for his sake. I never really forgave him. I wondered if I wanted to. I wondered if I ever would.

For months after my WSJ story ran, Al kept calling me, every time in the middle of a breakdown. Each one escalated in severity, and soon he was sobbing into the phone and saying he should kill himself. His custom motorcycle work had become too much to handle; he was behind on rent for his garage space; he owed tens of thousands of dollars to his landlord and customers. He told me he wished he was dead. He asked me to forgive him and to take care of Andie. I spent hours on the phone with him. I told him I loved him and that everything would be okay.

During our call, we went in circles. I laid out possible solutions: He could sell whatever parts he had, work out payment plans with his landlord, move in with his parents to make his cash last longer. He never acknowledged them. It was like I never spoke. He just returned to his refrain: "*I'm screwed. There's no way out of this. I wish I were dead. I'm better off dead.*"

I wondered if he was waiting for me to offer him money. Maybe he was. Or maybe this is just what happened when Al had nowhere to hide from himself. Either way, I never offered him any money. Either way, I felt sick. *You made him like this*, the shame said to me.

One day, Al told me he bought a big bottle of pills. He wanted it all to end. Ryan watched me drop my work to talk him down, taking the call out on our stoop. I brought a notebook with me, jotting down everything he said because I wanted to remember it, and I couldn't remember anything anymore. I thought of Mia's long lapses in memory. I used to wonder how it was possible for her to not remember so much of her life. Where could it have all gone? Now that I was miserable most of the time, I understood.

Here, I call myself on my own shit. *I wanted to remember —* that wasn't the only reason I wrote it all down. I wrote it down because I knew my father. He'll swear something to be true one minute and denounce it the next. I was stashing away evidence to catch him in the next lie. Maybe someone else would look upon that scene with some amount of sympathy for me, whether it sprang from understanding or from pity. Not me. When I stepped back, all I saw was a cynical, calculating daughter proving herself unlovable as her father sobbed in her ear. She was indefensible; she should feel ashamed. With that, the shame took its cue, wrapping itself around me.

When I came back inside, Ryan told me it wasn't fair for me to be Al's only lifeline. I bristled. I said it had to be this way. I needed to keep the line open between us for my reporting. *There it is again*, the shame said. *Always fucking double-dealing.* I didn't want to admit that I was afraid the calls would stop coming if I refused him, that he wouldn't want to talk to me anymore. *And why should he want anything to do with you? You're the reason he wants to die.*

I started having variations of the same dream. I still have it from time to time. I'm searching my apartment for something I've lost when I find Al. Sometimes he's alive, sitting in the corner of the room, refusing to leave. Sometimes he's dead. I'll open a drawer in the nightstand to find his corpse folded in a grotesque, impossible way to fit inside. I try to cry out but choke. Sometimes the Family appears to tell me that I am what killed him. Sometimes I'm alone, but I still come to the same conclusion. After waking up, I'd drift through my day in a fog, sending the same words into a void, over and over. *Please don't let him be dead because of my dream. Please don't let him be dead because of me.* It wasn't praying, but it was the closest I ever got.

After almost a year of these episodes, I made a decision. My phone had lit up with two missed calls and a message from

Al: *"Call me."* Usually I'd redial without hesitation, thinking he could be in danger, thinking time was of the essence, thinking that if I hesitated, I could be too late.

This time, I put my phone down. I wrote out a script on a legal pad. Then I called him back.

When he answered the phone, Al started into his usual list: He was fucked; he wanted to die; he was a horrible father. But this time his voice wasn't ragged. It was calm, casual, like he was telling me what he had for lunch. I could hear a TV blaring in the background.

I interrupted him and read my script. I told him these calls were hard for me. I needed him to find someone to talk to about all of these issues. I couldn't handle being responsible for his life from so far away. It hurt that he only called me in crisis, that he never asked about me. I could hear him not listening. He interjected at odd intervals, with, *"No, baby, I don't want you to feel that way,"* and, *"Of course, of course."*

In the background, I heard noise like a stadium. I realized he wasn't paying attention to me. He was watching TV. Wrestling, it sounded like.

I hurried through the rest of my little speech and hung up. A shudder ran through me. I felt like I was in a horror movie. I heard shrill violins.

When I first reunited with Al, I thought I only had to dig deep enough and prove myself worthy enough to know the real him. But there was nothing under the mask. That day, I saw he wasn't hiding anything: This was truly all he was.

After that day, after I pretended that I had been heard and pretended I had to get back to work, after he told me he loved me and missed me and he'd talk to me later, Al stopped calling. A variation on the old journalistic adage came back to me.

If your father says he loves you . . .

24

If Your Father Says . . .

If your father says he loves you, check it out.

It was inevitable that I'd get here one day, right down to the heart of it all. It feels silly, melodramatic, to seriously approach the question: *Does Al love me? Did Al love me?* That's what I'd been asking all along, really, if I peeled away the layers. I wanted to know if Al would tell me the truth if I asked him, put my needs ahead of his for once, do something selfless. All of those are things that you do when you love someone. He did not do those things.

This was a serious charge — that Al may not love me. Of course, he would be innocent unless I proved otherwise, and I took my burden of proof seriously.

I had skipped closing arguments in the Hicks case back in Chicago — I slept the whole morning instead. I was too drained to bring myself to get out of bed. But later I got that day's transcripts from the court reporter. I read them thoroughly. The judge told the jury that they would hear closing arguments; then she would instruct them. But she changed her mind and swapped the order: instructions first. As judge, I'll take my lead from her and start by addressing the jury — which is also me.

As juror, your first duty is to decide the facts from the evidence that you saw and heard from Al in the entirety of your relationship. The second duty is to evaluate the facts and determine whether the prosecution has proved, beyond a reasonable doubt, that your father does not love you.

The defendant has not entered a plea in response to the indictment. He hasn't said anything at all. He doesn't even know we're here. But I'm sure if he were asked, he'd shake his head at the charge and say — *'Course I love you, baby girl. What're you talking about? 'Course I do.*

Remember, the defendant is not required to prove his innocence. The burden of proof is that of counsel — which, of course, is me.

Those are my instructions. Now let's start with defense counsel, which is also me, and which posits that the following evidence is exculpatory:

ONE

He told me he loved me. Ever since I was a child.

TWO

He remembered things about me. Like when I was a kid and he was telling his sister to pick up pizzas for a birthday party, Al would always make sure she knew that I didn't like meat toppings. Or like when I was a teenager and I told him I was into theater. He got a friend to get us tickets to the Broadway tour of *Shrek the Musical*. I would never have picked *Shrek*, but I was shocked by our seats. We were right in the front. I'd never been so close to the stage.

THREE

He was moved to displays of emotion. He cried on the porch when he was leaving me to go to prison on that night in 2003. He cried when he saw me for the first time in years — that was in 2016. When he drove me to the airport the last time I saw him, back in 2019, he texted me after he dropped me off: *"Sad."*

FOUR

While he was in prison, he wrote me letters. No one forced him to do that. He showed consideration — he used printed hand-writing during the early years, till I was older, around ten, then he switched to cursive.

FIVE

He kept old photos of me. Of us. Some of them he framed.

SIX

I could make him laugh. I got a genuine one out of him when I was around seven. I was using the word *ass* to mean "donkey." He found it hilarious.

SEVEN

He was proud of me. He complimented me on my grades, on my intelligence. Especially as I got older, he said I was "beau-tiful, like your Ma."

EIGHT

He told me we'd talk about it all one day: about what he did, and why he went away. That allows for an inference: that he cared about my experience, about making things right, about telling me the truth. There was intent to do good.

Eight? That's *it*? All right.

I — the prosecution — will begin with rebuttals to the defense's arguments regarding each piece of evidence. I'll work in reverse order:

EIGHT

He told me we'd talk about it all one day . . . His intent to do good. Well intentioned or not, what did he actually do when he got out of prison? When did he ever talk about his case or his time in prison without any trace of selfishness or deception?

SEVEN

He was proud of me. Was he? Or was he proud of himself for spawning such a smart kid, for how his children reflected upon him? When October rolled around each year, and he posted photos of me and of his other daughter on Facebook, thanking God for his two beautiful girls, was he just waiting for the dopamine hit? All the adoration, the fawning praise that filled the comments?

SIX

I could make him laugh. I got a genuine one out of him when I was around seven. That's the only real laugh recorded in memory that involved something I said. Usually, it was him laughing at something *he* said, and it always seemed joyless somehow. And the joke being my inadvertent swearing — was that me making him laugh, or him laughing *at* me?

FIVE

He kept old photos of me. And of himself. Those photos reminded him of a better time, when I was less complicated and he was greater and his fate hadn't played out yet. Are a father's keepsakes valuable forms of parental love when that father never calls?

FOUR

He wrote me letters. Yeah. He was in prison. There wasn't much else to do, was there? Not to mention the requests for favors that each letter contained: to send him photos from the Family, to remind others to call him. I was a child messenger, doing his bidding, sustaining his ties to his external life. And what happen when he got that life back? When he got out of prison? The calls dwindled, didn't they? The letters stopped. Maybe I got a birthday card or two. But now that he was back on the outside, he had better things to do.

THREE

He was moved to displays of emotion. He cried . . . Yes, he cried. He could've been crying because he was losing his freedom. He could've been crying because seeing me put into stark relief all of the years he spent away. He could've been crying for himself.

TWO

He remembered things about me. Pizza toppings . . . Musicals . . . This is getting depressing. Plus, remember who paid for those tickets? His married female "friend" from the Gym — not to be confused with his actual girlfriend at the time! — who pecked him on the lips when they thought I couldn't see them. I apologize, your Honor, I digress. Did Al ever know the name of my high school? Medications, allergies? How I got home from school each day? Where I was in the world at any given moment? How could he? He was never there. He didn't want to be.

ONE

He told me he loved me, ever since I was a child. Jesus Christ, that's proof of nothing! That's why we're all here! *If your father* says *he loves you —*

All right. This jury has heard enough. No, this Albert Fontana did not love you — me — us. Are we done now?

With our judgment? Yes, we're done. But there's more to consider before we enact a sentence — mitigating factors, like remorse or restitution, or diminished responsibility.

The thought has crossed my mind once or twice, so of course it must be thoroughly examined. *Maybe he didn't love me because he couldn't love. Maybe he's genuinely incapable of it.* If that were the case, I could absolve Al of some of his liability — if I found that he suffered from some mental disease or defect, any abnormality that would lessen his culpability in his not loving me. And I had a growing sense of what that might be.

Narcissism has gone through an interesting cycle in our age of normalized mental health care and therapy terminology making its way into our colloquial vocabulary.

Many people use the term *narcissist* when they really mean "selfish." Similar, in some ways, to casual usage of *being so OCD* — another kind of shorthand. What they really mean is that they keep a clean house, or they enjoy having order in their lives, or they're Type A. It's a system of colored sticky notes, or a bookshelf alphabetized, or a spotless kitchen. They don't mean any harm by it; they're trying to express themselves. But the fact remains that these specific terms each serve a specific purpose, they have a proper meaning, and those meanings are the ones I strive to use here.

True narcissism — clinical narcissism — isn't just being a selfish asshole. (Though, to be sure, *selfish* and *asshole* are two words you might use to describe a narcissist.) I thought Al was selfish for the lion's share of my life, even in my childhood, but I'd never gone out in search of his pathology until 2019, around the time of Hicks's trial. I'd started seeing a new therapist for guidance and support in my relationships — with Al as well as with Ryan. I told her the whole story about my father and me, all the way back to my childhood. I told her about our reunion, about all the ways he seemed different from my grown-up vantage point, all the ways I feared he remained the same.

My therapist said she wasn't in a position to diagnose him, but she did anyway. Based on what I had shared with her, she believed Al displayed some serious narcissistic tendencies. I was only a layman, but I thought I agreed with her. I also worried that she only came to that conclusion based on my own flawed, biased retellings. So, because I could never let something be simple, I could never *believe* without an exhausting hunt for unimpeachable *fact*, I did some research of my own.

I already knew the etymological roots of *narcissism* — I remember reading about Narcissus at the family computer, during my summer of Greek mythology. The psychological study of narcissism isn't quite so ancient, dating back a mere century or so. And as a diagnostic entity, it's basically an infant. After all, the Narcissistic Personality Inventory was created in 1979.

I went to the diagnostic bible, downloading a copy of the *DSM-V* that had been published in 2013. As I scrolled through, looking for narcissism, the text was so riddled with typos and errors that I thought I'd downloaded a phony copy and would soon have my laptop overrun with malware. Headers were written "*Spmatic* Symptoms" instead of "*Somatic* Symptoms." The authors had even described pedophilia — wrongly — as a "sexual orientation." Turns out they'd rushed this edition to print, or something like that, and ended up with an embarrassment on their hands. As someone prone to obsessive and compulsive fact-checking, the entire thing gave me some kind of vicarious panic attack. When I finally found the revised copy, I was able to focus. I found the entry I was looking for, and I skimmed its contents:

Narcissistic Personality Disorder

Typical features of narcissistic personality disorder are variable and vulnerable self-esteem, with attempts at regulation through attention and approval seeking . . . characteristic difficulties . . . maladaptive traits . . .

My eyes glazed over. I'm sure yours did, too. So I bookmarked the pages and moved on, turning instead to journal articles discussing narcissism more widely. I wasn't looking to pin a personality disorder on Al when I wasn't even sure if he was in the narcissistic realm.

Let's start with the narcissist himself, and his internal experience. In a nutshell, the narcissist has an inflated self-importance. Some called it entitlement, a feeling of inherently deserving more than the rest of us. (See also: self-centered, egotistic, arrogant.) The literature also emphasized another essential characteristic: a pattern of *grandiosity*, meaning an unrealistic sense of superiority.

All of these clinical criteria for narcissism, they seemed to fit Al like a glove. The impaired capacity for empathy: Al's muted, strange reactions to emotionality displayed by me or anyone else; the way he did things that hurt people without giving that hurt a second thought.

And there were the largely superficial relationships. All of his girlfriends and flings from the Gym that floated around in my childhood, his deadbeat friends from the neighborhood who flooded his Facebook comments, the mothers of his children who didn't speak to him.

The narcissist's existential pursuits, the fountains from which he gets his fill of meaning, revolve around three main areas: achievement, materialism, and reflections of glory. And they, too, were all there for me to identify: Al's Gym; the wads of cash my dad liked to flash, the bikes he rode and built; the hyper-local kingdom he built around himself; his shimmering, self-made myth.

In understanding what narcissism is, it's valuable to understand what it isn't. This self-importance that the narcissist has in spades is sometimes conflated with an excess of self-esteem. I liked that some experts pointed this out and debunked it. Like them, I thought there was a significant difference.

Unlike someone with healthy and robust self-esteem — the way we value ourselves and our worth — the narcissist feels intense need for validation and admiration from others. People with true self-esteem don't need all of that admiration to sustain them — they don't share that fragility of narcissism, the hypersensitivity to criticism and the defensiveness to any possible threat to their ego, their entire sense of self.

Narcissism is a defense against excessive shame, one scholar wrote. Counterintuitive, no? That's what I thought at first. I always saw Al's core problem as his *lack* of shame. Despite the Family's strict piety, he seemed to evade the affliction of Catholic guilt. I figured it was just my luck to inherit all the shame that slid off his back, that he repelled like oil on water.

"Who knows?" I joked to Ryan at the time. "Maybe Catholic guilt skips a generation." He didn't laugh.

But now I could see that Al's shamelessness wasn't necessarily his fatal flaw. In the mask model of narcissism, a conceptualization with its roots in psychoanalysis, the narcissism is the "mask" that protects him and hides his deep insecurity — that hides, in famed expert Otto Kernberg's own words, an "empty self."

There were other hypotheses, other models and ways of thinking. But wherever I turned, I found common foundations: pride and shame, the two self-conscious emotions. I knew about shame, all right. I didn't know so much about pride.

There are two versions of pride that the literature compared: authentic and hubristic. I knew *hubris* from the Greeks — that often fatal flaw of god-defying arrogance. While authentic pride comes from the actual achievements that build a healthy self-esteem, hubristic pride has no such basis in reality. It is aggressive, competitive, and maladaptive. But for the narcissist, hubristic pride reigns supreme because it can be manufactured. He doesn't need to achieve anything to get a steady artificial stream, one that's reliable and easier to come by than the real thing.

So the narcissist survives by snuffing out shame and flooding himself with a counterfeit pride. This winning combination allows him to do what he wants, when he wants, flouting the confines of our social contract. The literature says so: Narcissists are prone to aggression, and they have an increased likelihood of committing white-collar crimes. Like I said — it was fitting Al like a glove.

To my surprise and delight, one of the academic sources cited a personal hero of Al's, the great Arnold himself. They quoted Schwarzenegger from an interview he did with *Rolling Stone*:

> Around the time of grammar school I had this incredible desire to be recognized. [. . .] I got the feeling that I was meant to be more than just an average guy running around, that I was chosen to do something special. At that point, I didn't think about money. I thought about the fame, about just being the greatest. I was dreaming about being some dictator of a country or some savior like Jesus. Just to be recognized.

This was not self-esteem. This was neither a stable confidence nor an assured contentment in self. This was something else, something that moved, something striving. A God complex, as

Ernest Jones called it. After all, we saw where it led Arnold, down his path of developing a superhuman shape. (Not to mention a command of considerable political power as governor of the country's most populous state.) It was no wonder that Al found such an idol in Arnold, and such satisfaction in the same pursuit: defying man's corporeal limits and attaining a likeness to the gods.

But a man is not a god, and most men must wrestle with that fact throughout their struggle toward superiority. They are forced to jostle for position among the others, the background players on the stage. It's a bit of a catch-22. Without all of these extras, these bit parts that support the star's turn, the star is alone. He is nobody special without them. But with them, the star has less free rein. They're always in the way somehow; he has to negotiate his choreography around them, expend some of his energy on dealing with their presence. And to rise above them, he must put them down — enough to keep them in their rightful place, but never so far down that they decide to leave the stage.

It seems so obvious, as we step outside the narcissist's circle of self and into the larger surrounding circle of his outer life: his family, friends, coworkers, subordinates. Here is the narcissist's double bind. What sustains them has the power to destroy them. They see admiration as their natural right, the order of the world; criticism or dismissal shatters this world. The shame fills the room; the shame feeds his aggression and his rage. Scholars aptly call this process "humiliated fury" or "the shame-rage cycle." (See also: Al's spiral after my story was published. I hadn't meant to do it, but I had ignited another turn in that cycle. I hadn't kept to my role.)

That's the thing, about living in the world of the narcissist. He'll cast you in many roles, as many different You's, depending on the scene. You are a competitor for survival: Your success means his failure. You are the object of his affections, so long as you do nothing but build him up. Otherwise, You are the albatross around his neck; You are the scapegoat for his failures. You are the one he will leave holding the bag.

The narcissist doesn't live with his head in the sand, not necessarily. He probably knows he loses his shine in relationships quickly, that he has to act fast. He knows where he likes to be best: in the spotlight, in a position of power, in arenas that show off his strongest suits. In the unlikely event he ends up in a therapist's office, he will be loath to give up his superpowers. Everyone else should fix themselves; *they're* the real problem here.

That doesn't mean that the narcissist is a total antisocial nightmare to others. Sometimes Al did good things. Sometimes he helped others. When a cousin of mine needed a place to crash, Al invited him to share his apartment for a while. He spent time with his mother, his father, his sisters and brothers. Once, when he dropped me off at O'Hare, he silently palmed me forty bucks. But the literature accounted for this, too. It might've been that he cared more about being seen as generous or thoughtful, rather than acting purely out of genuine goodwill.

In *The Handbook of Trait Narcissism*, a book that became such an important resource for me that I kept my digital copy open on my laptop for weeks on end, I highlighted this passage about the narcissist's self-awareness:

> Recall that narcissists have some insight into the fact that their reputation wanes over time. Because narcissists use social contexts to maintain their self-image, they are motivated to seek out short-term relationships where they thrive in order to see themselves in a desirable light.

Jeez, I thought. *That must make it hard to have a family. To have a kid.* In Al's world, relationships among kin could never become short-term or severed, because of the importance placed on the Family by the Family. That would surely cause him shame.

So what is it, down at the core of all narcissist's interpersonal issues, that explains (as one scholar put it) his "failure to be enduringly likable"?

It could be the low empathy that he tends to exhibit. His natural state is to be unmoved by the suffering of others. But *low* empathy doesn't equal *no* empathy, the literature makes clear. His deficit is not necessarily an absence; just because narcissists tend not to engage in an empathetic process doesn't mean that it's impossible for them to do so. He *can* do it — for example, in a scenario when clinicians explicitly instruct him to. But even then, scholars think he might be feeling less compassion and concern for the other than distress for himself, that he must feel all these *feelings*.

This raises another question in my mind: *If he's not incapable of empathy, why doesn't the narcissist use it?*

The simplest answer is another question: *What would empathy do for him?*

Nothing. He's got no motivation to empathize; in fact, he's motivated to *avoid* empathizing. It makes it easiest to get what he needs from the world. If he doesn't relate to someone, their pain can't hurt him, and he can take them for all they're worth.

The narcissist is a man made of paradoxes: extremes of pride and shame, idealization and devaluation, strength and fragility. And he is a man who lives in constant threat; at any moment, he may find that his crowd of fawning devotees looks more like a lynch mob.

I am not an expert in anything, and certainly not in psychoanalysis or psychiatry. But I believe Al is a narcissist, pathologically speaking. I believe that the literature speaks for itself. And so, after months of printing hundreds of pages of research, reading dozens of articles, losing hours upon hours of sleep,

I determined that I had proved enough to myself. You heard the jury. Al did not love me, not in a genuine way, not in the way that parents should love their children. He could not love me, perhaps; his capacity for love may have been diminished in the same way his capacity for empathy might have been. Those were the mitigating factors I presented to myself. They were the closest I could get to an understanding of who my father was to me, and who I was to him.

At the very bottom of things, I guess it came down to a question of remorse. I watch a lot of courtroom footage, trial recordings — especially murder cases. Before the judge imposes her sentence, I'm always on the edge of my seat when the defendant rises to make a statement. These statements are usually addressed to the victim's family, who deliver their own testimonials on the effect of the defendant's crime, how they have suffered from their loss. I'm usually listening to see if the defendant will manage to eke out any kind of remorse.

When I thought about these kinds of emotional phenomena, I laid them out like this in my mind. In one place, there was guilt — *I feel bad for doing this.* Then, next to it, there was both regret and remorse, merged together — *I feel bad for doing this; I wish I hadn't done this.*

Over time, I started to tease the latter two apart, give them their own space. Regret became: *I feel bad for doing this; I wish I hadn't done this; I wish I had done something else; I wish I didn't have the consequences I have now.*

Remorse, too, grew: *I feel bad because I hurt someone; I wish I hadn't done this. Not because I was caught. Not because there are consequences. Because it was wrong, and I know it was wrong, and I feel the weight of what I've done. I feel for those I've hurt. I deserve the consequences.*

Al talked about his regrets all the time, but he never seemed to have any true remorse for me to use in my deliberations, in my consideration of what sentence I would give him. The closest thing I could think of was all of his suicidal ideation. But that was tricky.

Narcissism is a defense against excessive shame. But what happens when the shame sneaks past all of the narcissist's defenses? What happens to the man when he sees himself for who he is?

His world shatters.

There seems to be a myth that narcissists don't tend to commit suicide, that threats of taking their own life are usually manipulation tactics. Part of me — an ugly, secret part of me — always hoped this was the case, so that I could put aside my panic that Al would kill himself and that it would be my fault.

I found the words of Leo Sher, a medical doctor based in New York, in a 2024 letter to the editor he wrote for some Croatian psychiatric journal. Sher cited studies suggesting that narcissistic personality disorder is, in fact, associated with suicidal behavior. It seemed Sher was speaking directly to me, because he left no room for me to wiggle out of it. He got more specific, cited another study's findings that "depressed older adults with narcissistic personalities" were at increased suicide risk. Al was an older adult; I considered him to have a narcissistic personality; he was depressed. Three for three. Fuck.

Suicidal behavior in these people, Sher wrote, could be an attempt to defend themselves against narcissistic threats; revenge against narcissistic damage; a product of their desire to abolish an imperfect self. Al had suffered narcissistic injury, hadn't he? A blow to his clinically fragile self-esteem, dealt by his own daughter's contemptuous hand?

Did I have contempt for Al, as I once felt he had for me? I wasn't sure. But I underlined one study's particularly savage remark about the psychotherapist's duty to narcissistic patients: These clinicians must "resist the descent into contempt that is so common for all of us."

What the author, Glen Gabbard, was saying was that the stakes were high. Suicidal behavior, Gabbard wrote, is a clinically significant but underestimated cause of mortality when it comes to narcissistic personality disorder. In the desperation to protect his self-image, or the intense shame of being exposed, death could feel like the only way out of such devastation, to go through what he could not bear.

Sure, Al could've been trying to guilt me into giving him money, or exploiting my love for him for his own emotional gain. Or my worst fear could've been a possibility. I had to live with that uncertainty.

Even as I sit here now, at a safe distance, buffered by an accumulation of time passed, I feel the chill. In all of this remembering, I can see myself as I was then, sitting on my old stoop, after I'd talked Al off the ledge for the umpteenth time. The old shame rushes in.

Wasn't my father suffering? I ask.

Yes, it answers. *Yes, he was.*

Was it my fault that he suffered?

Yes. Yes, it was.

Shame has no facts to back up its claims, and I don't ask to see any. My vigilance is gone. I accept the blame; I welcome it. Someone has to carry it. It might as well be me.

I just wished I wasn't left to draw my own conclusions. I wished that I didn't have to compare Al to entries in the fucking *DSM* to understand him. But I had been left to my own imperfect devices. The whole thing was starting to feel like a fool's errand, like trying to finish a puzzle when you know there are pieces missing. Eventually you just scrap the whole thing, right? Isn't that the logical thing to do? What's the use in all the work if you'll never get the whole picture?

25

———

Collateral Damage

Long before I began this story, I knew the ending I wanted to write. I never let it take a complete form in my mind, and I never wrote it down; I didn't want to jinx it. There's nothing left to jinx now, so I'll let you in on my little secret.

I always imagined that one day, once I had all the facts and knew what to make of Al, I would go to him. One last chance for him to redeem himself. I would lay out everything I knew of him and then I'd wait. I'd hold the line. Then Al would finally break. There would be confessions, tears, pleas for forgiveness. Then I'd have to make up my mind: Accept my father and a life lived with him, or deny him and live my life without.

But this was a fantasy. Al had shown me, over and over, who he was. I knew what I was to him. None of it was human, none of it was love.

I was a dog, decently trained, dumb as rocks. If he was feeling low, all he had to do was whistle and I'd race to him. Even if I knew better, even if I knew that sometimes a whistle ended with a swat of the newspaper or a kick in the ribs, I came anyway. Until I didn't. Bad dogs get put down.

Then I was a trophy, a framed photo to leave on the mantel where people could see it. I was an extension of his sovereign self. Everything I achieved could be traced back to him. If I was beautiful, he was the source of my beauty. If I was smart, it was his intelligence I inherited. If I lost my shine, I could always be taken off the mantel. But my stock was still up, so there I stayed.

I couldn't delude myself anymore. There was no future here. The kind of appeal I hoped for will never come from Al. That ending would never be. Al was a dead-end road that I let myself wander down anyway, waiting all the while for the sidewalk to end. I knew I would have to leave him in the past, his chosen home, and grieve for the man I knew and the man I thought he could be.

But I couldn't bring myself to do it then and there, when I first knew it, on that day in 2020, the script in my hand. I couldn't bring myself to do it in the weeks that followed, either. I spent all of 2021 dragging my feet. We texted here and there, but I didn't know how to do it, how to cut that cord. I'd have to figure it out.

I knew that without my own intervention, I'd never see my father again in my life. He had never visited me in Oregon. He never came to New York. He would never seek me out. I'd always know where to find him. I knew that, whenever I'd had enough of him, all I had to do was not go back. That would be the end. He wouldn't fight it.

I wondered if I'd ever be able to let this all go. Maybe I didn't have to write it down. I could do what everyone else does: relegate the stories to mere memory and move forward without them.

"All I will ever want is to move on from the past," Mia said to me once. "I have the good parts that I want, and I let the rest go."

One day, maybe I'd do the same. But the past hadn't let me go.

"Why not wait till everyone's dead?"

Mia was the first one to voice the question; I knew everyone was thinking it. That is the usual way to tell these kinds of stories. Wait till all the players are buried, safe from whatever the fallout may be. Mia knew the answer, but she asked anyway, while we drank coffee together in her kitchen. "Wouldn't it be easier that way?"

Many assume that Al is dead already. Brent did, that day in his office. So have editors, friends, acquaintances. Do they make that assumption because I'm telling a story no sane person would tell with its subject still aboveground? Or is it because I speak of Al in the past tense without realizing it?

I told my mother I couldn't wait. The story was ready to be told now, so I had to tell it.

Another time she asked me about fiction. Couldn't I write it all as a novel, change all the names and leave the rest as it is? I could, but I didn't want to.

"Then it's not a true story," I stammered. "Part of what makes this story worth telling is that it all *happened* — it happened to me, and to you."

I told her I'd use pseudonyms for most of the players. Jackie, Rick, Keith, Adam, Justin — these are not their real names. She, however, would remain Mia. I apologized and rambled about my reasoning. Something about how in naming Al it was only fair to name her, too. Something about apples to apples. She took it in stride, as she took everything. It was just another sacrifice of her privacy for my own gain, my "art." Another debt thrown on the pile, another source of shame.

I feel guilty using her name. I don't feel guilty using Al's. Why? I tell myself it's because he made himself a public figure: *The Chicago Tribune* named him long before I did. Many of his mistakes sit in the records of federal and county courts. But my self-interrogation never ends, nor does my self-flagellation. I imagine the Family sitting around the kitchen table, shaking their heads. Someone says what they're all thinking: *How could she go against the Family like that?*

So why not wait until everyone is dead? I give myself reasons.

Because it is a true story.

Because people can live an awfully long time.

Because this is a story I want to tell now, not when I am older and wiser, not when the years and nostalgia may have clouded my view.

Because it is a good story. This answer I have to pull out of myself, like yanking a sore tooth. This answer is less morally defensible, less noble. But it's true. It's a damn good story, and I'm a writer. What else am I supposed to do with it? Live with it?

Because in telling the story, I can finally put it down. I can leave it on a shelf and see what it's like to live without its weight on my back.

Because . . . *Because* . . . *Because* . . . Eventually I stop coming up with reasons. I will tell the story, regardless of what comes after.

With that certainty, all that is left to consider is collateral damage.

I can only echo Joan Didion, who said before me that writers are always selling someone out. And of course, there are the words of Janet Malcolm, who goes for the jugular: "Every journalist who is not too stupid or too full of himself to notice what is going on knows that what he does is morally indefensible." In this story, I am no different, no less culpable for what I have chosen to do. The very least I can do is take stock of the casualties.

Will telling my story ruin Al's life? *Ruin* is a hefty word. I pull the question apart into more manageable pieces.

Will telling my story prevent him from making a living, or securing gainful employment? No. He told me before that he hates to work for anyone else; he wants to be his own boss. And he is. He has rebuilt his former kingdom and resurrected Al's Gym — same name, new location. (And not for nothing, but any background check would give a human resources officer a truncated version of his criminal past. Again, the records stand for themselves.)

Will telling my story ruin his reputation? In many ways, no. The Family stands by him, as they always have. His friends, with their similarly checkered pasts, stand by him. I am the bad actor, not him. I am the one who won't move on. I'm the family snitch.

But I am showing Al to a wider world, far beyond his sphere of influence, revealing him to those who would never meet him otherwise. That is my burden to bear. God knows I will bear it.

My only solace is bittersweet, remembering that Al gave me his blessing, in his own way. *Who knows? Maybe if I hadn't done all that stupid shit, you'd have nothing to write about.*

And what about my mother? As I began to write, I started sharing pieces of this story with Mia — the parts she didn't already know, the parts she hadn't lived through. During one phone call, I read some drafted pages to her. I don't remember which ones, but I remember her reaction. She gave some praise, then paused.

"But is that how you really felt? Or is this just material?"

This wasn't the first time the topic of material had come up in our conversations. *Material*, though never explicitly defined, was implied to be the distortion or exaggeration of truth to make for a better story. I don't remember when exactly it was that the concept first came up between Mia and me. It might have been 2022. I'd written an essay for the *Journal* about my grandmother Ellen's death. Mia gave her blessing, and a warning. She delivered it with love, and with severity. I remember the precision of the words she chose: *"Make sure you only write what's actually true. Do not exploit my mother's death."* We always say what we mean, she and I.

Or is this just material? I should've seen her question coming, but I didn't. It knocked me back. For the first time, I starkly saw that my mother knew less of me than I thought. In my life, I had always known that Mia, if no one else, would understand me. It was a given, a rule of the universe, like gravity. Now there was a crack in the foundation, and I felt uneasy. I felt myself floating away from solid ground.

I told her that it was how I really felt. I told her that it would never be material. I didn't tell her how much it worried me that she could think I was capable of writing something that wasn't true. I didn't tell her what appeared to me in the shadow of her question: that there was a sliver of me that she didn't yet know.

Why do we write? To understand, and to be understood.

I know that Mia will read this story one day. I know it will be hard for her. *Just another sacrifice*, the shame reminds me. But it's a small comfort to know that, whenever she does, it will close the gap between who I am now and who she knows me to be. She will understand me then, I think.

26

_____

How Does It End

It's hard to know how a story will end when you're still in it, when you and the players are still deep in the fourth act and have one more to go. It's harder still for me to admit that at each turn, at every ending that wasn't, I have been tempted to deceive you.

Not egregiously, of course. I would have never fed you an ending cut from whole cloth, like that fantasy I was afraid to write down: Al and I settling into a happy conclusion. That would have been a creation, a fiction. I would never stoop so low. I would show you only things that happened.

That doesn't mean I couldn't deceive you, depending on where I cut the film, like right after our first reunion in Chicago, with Al's promise to tell me the truth.

Or after Al gave me those letters, and I saw Mia's life as it was for the first time.

Or after the trial of Eddie Hicks, before Al's miserable spiral, before I heard him watching wrestling — the discovery of that terrible truth. That's roughly where I left it when I wrote it all down the first time, when I published my essay in the _Journal_. None of the rest had happened yet. I could've cut it there. But I didn't.

Where were we? That's right, 2021: the year of dragging my feet, at least when it came to Al. Seeing who he really was, digesting the reality that he didn't love me, fighting through that wave of grief — I kept that process to myself. In the meantime, I kept busy. I had my own life that I was building, and I was determined to stay that course. Starting with Ryan, the man I loved, the man who changed — the man I had married.

On Christmas Eve in 2019, Ryan and I had eloped at the Multnomah County Courthouse in Portland. Over the next couple of years, we took on the unpaid full-time job of trying to buy and renovate a co-op apartment in Manhattan. In 2021, we closed on our beautiful home: a snug two-bedroom overlooking a courtyard. Ryan designed colorful tile layouts for the kitchen and bathroom walls in his signature artistic style. Between his beautiful designs and the glossy new kitchen, Mia said it was like we lived in a magazine. She told me that when she visited, as we sat on the balcony.

I loved that balcony so much. I woke up with the birds that sang from the willow tree. I drank my coffee at our little blue bistro table. Jiji joined me at the window, curling up on the sill inside, as we shared the same view of the birds. During our first summer in the apartment, I took up gardening. I grew flowers, peppers, herbs. I filled the space with life.

I loved that balcony nearly as much as I loved the Study. Ryan had his art studio, a sprawling loft space in the Bronx, so we decided to use our second bedroom as a study. That was the proper word for it — it was a study, not an office or, even worse, a home office. We freely admitted to ourselves and each other that "the Study" felt foreign in our mouths at first, just as "husband" and "wife" had in our first months of marriage. They felt affected, somehow — pretentious, somehow — at least at first. But in each case, we quickly came around, and the words bent naturally to our wills.

Ryan let me have free rein to design the Study. I chose a deep forest green for the walls, walnut bookshelves and desks. I filled the shelves with a hundred or so volumes of my growing library.

I dusted my typewriters. Ryan helped me carry in our beloved gray armchair. It cradled Jiji and I, as he slept and I read. I spent all my time there — all the nights and weekends that Ryan spent working away in his studio. I created an archive for my writing and a database for my collection of books. I bought yellow circulation cards and cream-colored adhesive pockets from a library supply store. It was no matter that I didn't yet have any close friends of my own to come and borrow my books. I hoped they'd come later. When they did, I'd be ready. I filled out each title's card, slipped one into the back of each book. With a simple, custom stamp, I left my mark in ink: FROM THE LIBRARY OF FRANCESCA FONTANA.

I loved to flip to the back of a book and turn the circulation card over in my hands. I ran my fingers across the lines, where all the borrowers would one day sign their names.

The cards remained empty.

Still, I was happy. I tried to do something I hadn't done in a long time: I tried to take care of myself. One day, as I worked in the Study, I realized that I hadn't smoked for a few days. There was a pack sitting half empty in my desk drawer, but I didn't reach for it. I realized that, most of the time, smoking was a pleasure I allowed myself for the sake of being selfish. There were also times when smoking was something else. Sometimes I smoked when I didn't want to, when I felt the diminishing returns of the nicotine. But I went through the motions anyway, and there was no pleasure in it.

I saw that I had wanted to punish myself. *You want to ruin those lungs your mother gave you? Go ahead. You don't deserve them anyway.* Once, a woman on the street turned her head at the scent of my smoke. Her eyes landed on me. She wrinkled her nose. I surprised myself. I fought a smile. I tried not to laugh — didn't she know? It was cute of her to try, but her disdain was nothing compared with the vise grip of my own conscience.

I wondered what my life would be like if I stopped punishing myself. After all, people can live an awfully long time. Begrudgingly, I decided to give it a try. I bought the kale and the spinach and the oats, ignoring the voice in my head warning of contaminants and bugs and *E. coli*. I dragged myself to the gym, running a mile in seven minutes. I took myself out for walks around the Central Park Reservoir. I surprised myself. It wasn't so bad after all.

Now, *that's* an ending, isn't it? Wouldn't it be nice if I cut the film here?

I was in the Study, pacing circles on the rug, when I had my last conversation with Al. It was in the spring of 2022. I'd found out — from a cousin, not from him — that my grandmother Sonia was dying.

I had been lucky. I had made it nearly thirty years without experiencing any major loss on either side of my family. However, that meant that the icy dread that washed over me when I got the news was unfamiliar, frightful.

That same month, I learned that Mia's mother, my grandmother Ellen, was diagnosed with cancer. I had plenty of love and affection for Sonia, but I'd never gotten to be as close to her as the rest of my cousins. I paid my respects and showed her my love when I made my pilgrimage to her kitchen. But Ellen had taken care of me from the time I was small. I could still remember how soft her hair was when she let me comb it for her, her eyes closed. Her voice, too, was so soft, when I cuddled up next to her, when she sang "This Little Light of Mine" under her breath. I couldn't imagine a world without her in it.

As soon as I heard about Sonia, I called Al. He answered on the first or second ring. We talked. At some point, his voice grew thick and I thought he might be crying. I wanted to ask him why he didn't call me sooner. If she'd been as sick as this for months — like my cousin had told me — I could've made time to see her or at least talk to her on the phone. Did she know I had been kept in the dark? Or did she think I didn't care about her, since I hadn't called? But there was no time for that now. Al told me she was expected to die within days. I kept my mouth shut. I listened. I tried to offer comfort.

Eventually, the conversation became stilted. We'd said everything there was to say about hospitals and illness and love and loss. I wasn't sure what to talk about. I didn't need to worry. Al's voice regained its usual gravelly tone, and he started telling me old stories, like always, about some mischief he and his buddies got up to in the past. A friend of his who'd gotten locked up back in such-and-such a year for such-and-such a crime. Another shiver ran through me. I had no grounds on which to judge him, his mother was dying, but I found it unnerving, the way he just picked right up again with his same old shit. And above all, I realized just how boring that same old shit had become to me.

Sonia died the next day. Al texted me the news. I don't remember the last time I spoke to her. I never got to say good-bye.

That summer, Ellen rapidly declined after completing rounds of chemo and surgery. I drove out to my grandparents' house in rural Wisconsin to help care for her in her last weeks. I struggle to write about it now. I'm still in the grief, even years later.

I don't know how Al found out that Ellen was sick. I don't know whether he knew I was with her, caring for her as she did the hard work of dying. But I assumed he must've found out, because during one of my first days in Wisconsin, he called me. I let it go to voicemail. By the time he called again, not a minute later, the rage had taken hold. I silenced the call and snuck a cigarette out of my purse. Walking down one of the wide country roads, with every exhale, I released my contempt for my father — if that's what it truly was. And I remembered my love for him.

I never set out to tell this story because I hate my father. I'm telling this story because I loved him once.

Eventually I was left smoking filter, but I knew what had been done. I had reached the end.

That was our real ending, between Al and me. There was no fanfare, no last confrontation, no final plea for his honesty. It was more like an Irish good-bye. That day, I just stopped responding. I couldn't bring myself to block him right away, so for months I still got texts from him on Mia's birthday, on my birthday, on various holidays. He sent me old photos at random hours. I let them sit in my phone and gather dust. I let his call go unanswered. I let the thread between us go slack. Eventually, on some random, unremarkable day, I paused my crossword to block his number, block every road he had to get to me. It took maybe a minute, all while I stood waiting for the train. I went back to my crossword.

That is how I buried my father. I dug a double grave, for him and myself, the person who loved him.

In the months that followed, I was at an all-time low. I thought I had buried the shame, too. But it could not be so easily confined. It consumed me and telescoped time around me, blended the years: '22, '23, '24 — who cared what year it was, so much of it was all the same. My old compulsions returned in stronger, stranger forms, and I found new ones. I began to crack my neck. I'd never been able to do that before, not even as a kid. Simply trying to roll my neck from side to side had always made me squeamish. I'd hated the sensation.

Not anymore. One day I sought release and found it in some small tweak of my chin. I had to replicate it, of course. And then it grew, until I was constantly twisting and contorting and jerking back and forth in pursuit of that "just right" feeling that OCD promises but never makes good on. I tried watching myself do it in the mirror. I assumed I'd look like anyone else I saw at work or on the train, leaning their head to the side, getting some relief in their cervical spine, then moving on with their day. I did not look like that. Whatever I was doing, it wasn't casual and relaxed. It didn't look natural. It looked like I was having some kind of fit. The awkward angles and strange motions made me swear to myself that no one would ever see me do it. Later, I read about extreme risks of neck manipulation: aneurysms, strokes. I thought I was scared straight. I swore to myself, again, that I'd never let it get that far.

I shouldn't have bothered. Soon I was cracking my neck for half an hour without stopping, then an hour, then more — as long as I could before the ringing in my ears forced me to sit down and get my balance. When it got especially bad, I started losing my grip on the compulsion entirely. I'd be thinking about something horrible while standing on the train platform, then I'd be cracking my neck. I'd try to stop; it'd only get worse. I noticed people moving away to keep their distance. They must've thought I had a tic, Tourette's or something. Once, some tourists stared at me. Humiliated as I was, I couldn't stop. I just stared back. The next day, I would be unable to turn my head in either direction.

Then I started pulling out my own hair. First it was in private, only a few strands at a time. The odd coarse or curly hair. Again, it snowballed. It followed me to work. At my desk, I'd twirl a lock of hair around my fingers. When I thought no one could see me, I'd snap my arm down. If I did it right, and I always did, the whole lock came out clean as each hair was ripped from its follicle at the same time. I came to love the sound, the dozens of stinging *pops* that I was never sure if only I could hear.

I was ducking into the women's restroom and hiding clumps of hair in my pockets. I couldn't throw them into the trash, on the off chance anyone went digging through the garbage and recognized the hair length and color as mine. I felt delusional. But when I looked in the mirror, I still looked normal: I only pulled from the lower regions of my skull, leaving the top layers undisturbed. I had a thick head of hair to start with, too.

But before long, on the sides and back of my skull, patches began to thin. Then they became bare, save for a few light strands poking out here and there. I could see the tattoo on the side of my head peeking out behind my left ear. Soon I had ravaged my scalp, the entire expanse from the nape of my neck up the back and sides. I shaved it bald into an undercut, a style I hadn't worn for years, and continued to hide in plain sight.

Honestly, I just didn't care anymore. I thought that if I punished myself enough, the forces of the universe would keep Al from killing himself, so I sought out all manner of punishments. I smoked more and ate less. I welcomed bad haircuts and accidental burns on the stove and fights with Ryan that kept me sleeping on the couch, seeing any bad fortune that came my way as a good omen. The suffering was my way of balancing the scales, restoring order to the world, in the way that only I could.

Ryan was overwhelmed by my sudden decompensation, and he was confused. Since when did I have OCD, anyway? (*Did he not remember our conversation? The four hundred dollars I wasted? Did that make so little of an impression in his mind?*) So far as he could tell, I hadn't shown any symptoms for all the years we'd known each other. Only now, totally out of the blue, I was pulling out all my hair and wreaking havoc on my neck. What was going on? I didn't know what to tell him.

Soon I started feeling like my brain was busted and my soul was rotten and that I might be better off in the ground. One night, while Ryan was at the studio and I was sick with the flu, too delirious to navigate my keypad, I asked my phone some questions: "Hey, Siri. Is it suicidal ideation if you don't *want* to

die, but you think you *should* die?" "Hey, Siri. If I don't wanna
kill myself, but I don't wanna be alive right now — is that
suicidal ideation?" "Hey, Siri. If I'd kill myself on the condition
that I get brought back to life in ten years, like a long coma, is
that suicidal ideation? Is that even anything?"

Each time, she displayed the same old hotline to call. No
answers.

"Aw, c'mon. Fuck you." I tossed my phone out of bed and
heard it hit the wall.

When I realized that I might literally no longer be able to live
like this, I sought out treatment. I entered an exposure and
response prevention program at the same hospital Ryan went
to for his BPD treatment. The compulsions got worse before
they got better. My clinicians told me that would happen, and I
had relayed that to Ryan, but he was still upset. I wasn't getting
better, it seemed to him. I got the sense — rightly or wrongly —
that he thought I wasn't working hard enough. I tried harder.

After some months, I "graduated" from my solo exposure
work and entered group therapy. My clinician strongly recommended another group to me, a family support group program
for patients to complete with their parents or spouses. I told
her we were absolutely interested. But when I asked Ryan
about the group, he balked. He was too busy with extra work
and his studio. He was overwhelmed. He'd had some recent
injuries and was at long last free of follow-up visits and other
appointments. He couldn't do it. He wouldn't do it.

I asked him if he would reconsider down the line, maybe in
six months. He equivocated. He stressed that I should focus
on working on myself first. He was still finding strands and
clumps of my hair around the house, after all. I wouldn't admit
to myself that I'd been stunned by his refusal. I'd read so many
books about BPD, done so much research and supported his
treatment. I'd looked for support groups for patients and their

families, wishing for something like this group that the OCD Center offered. If the roles were reversed, I knew I'd have made the time. But I didn't let myself dwell on that. Otherwise it would've broken my heart.

On a sunny afternoon, around my twenty-ninth birthday, I left work early on a Friday. I told one of my editors that I was ill. And I was, in a way. I'd been sitting at my desk, admiring the late-afternoon light streaming in from the windows, when I felt a cold sweat wash over me. A sudden burst of pain on my left side radiating out from my shoulder and down my arm. A tightness in my chest. I couldn't believe it. I was having a heart attack. At work.

I was lightheaded and clumsy, having to use only my right arm to gather my things and sneak out to the elevator, my left arm hanging at my side. I recall only one cohesive thought: *I can't have a fucking heart attack at work. That would be so embarrassing.*

Instead, I wandered into a Walgreens and found some aspirin. The checkout line was far too long, and the pain was getting worse. I shoved some cash into the hand of a security guard and left, chewing on a grainy bitter pill. I couldn't figure out my phone's map — my eyes were growing heavy — so I called 911 to ask for walking directions to the nearest ER. Despite my weak protests, they sent an ambulance instead. *Still embarrassing*, I thought as an EMT helped me into the back. *But better than dying in the newsroom.*

After an EKG, X-rays, tests, and hours of waiting, the doctor felt comfortable sending me home. He had ruled out a heart attack and stroke. He wasn't sure what was causing my pain. Maybe neuropathy — a pinched nerve — something like that.

Mia was relieved that I'd gotten myself to an ER and that nothing dire had been the cause. After a couple of hours, Ryan showed up at the hospital. He wasn't happy. He was trying not to show his frustration, to say he was glad I was all right, to make the best of the evening as we took the train home, but it seeped out all the same. Again, I was surprised — that he was upset, that he didn't seem the least bit worried or loving. It seemed like he thought I'd made up the symptoms in my head, out of anxiety. Again, it hurt my feelings.

"You shouldn't have gone to the ER. And you *definitely* shouldn't have gotten an ambulance."

"I was just calling for directions . . . and I was in really bad shape, when I looked up my symptoms . . . they were all pointing to a heart attack —"

"Yeah, because it's the internet and that's what happens when you look that stuff up. But see? You're fine."

"I'm not fine." I moved my left arm as much as I was able, which was not much at all. "This side is still fucked up, I'm in a lot of pain — the doctor said I'm safe to go home, not that nothing's wrong. If it still hurts on Monday, he said —"

"I know, I know, I heard you. I'm just saying, it really seems like this is an OCD thing and you've *really* got to get it under control."

That night I resisted sleep as long as I could. I was afraid, and the fear made shapes and shadows on the ceiling. *The ER doctor was wrong . . . the Big One is coming for me . . . don't close your eyes . . . you won't wake up . . .*

I woke up in the morning to a short burst of relief and a long drip of shame. I felt like such an idiot. The weekend passed; the pain slowly subsided. One night, I was googling pinched nerves when I was struck by a memory. That afternoon on Friday, before the heart attack that wasn't a heart attack, I had been cracking my neck. *Why hadn't I thought of that when the doctor mentioned neuropathy?* I thumbed through possible answers:

Because I thought I was having a heart attack — I was thinking about my chest, not my neck.

Because I was in a lot of fucking pain — I didn't have the clearest head.

Because I'd ramped up my smoking lately — it sure seemed possible that all that selfishness was coming home to roost.

Eventually, the simplest answer came to me. Why hadn't I thought of that twenty-minute span I'd spent in the bathroom cracking my neck? Because my life now occurred in the breaks in my compulsive fits, not the other way around.

I avoided the topic with Ryan. In secret, in a small part of my brain that I tried not to dwell in, I knew he was wrong. I knew what I had felt. It wasn't just an OCD panic attack.

But he was still right about the OCD, I thought. *Just not in the way he thought. It was from cracking my fucking neck.* That meant I was still wrong, which meant that it was my own fault if my feelings were still hurt. *Tough shit. Move on.*

_____

27

Nostalgia

Nostalgia creeps in quietly. Its paws are padded; it makes no sound. One day you're walking through the park. Some sense — the scent of rain, or the chill in your boots — transports you to the past for half a moment. A small voice in your head purrs. *Maybe it all wasn't so bad.*

A few years ago, before we got married, Ryan and I were walking down Ludlow Street in Manhattan when he pointed out his old dorm building from art school. That was where it found me. I imagined visiting Eugene with Ryan.

There's the university library — did you ever know it's actually "the truth will make you free," not "will set you free"? I know, right? I thought so, too. And there are all the campus bars. And if you go down that street and take a left, you end up at my old apartment — fuck, what was that place called? Eugene Manor. Man, how could I forget?

I knew the facts of the memories — that I had been sick and sad during those years, that the autumns were hopeless — but all the old vitriol had evaporated from the sights and sounds that rushed back to me. Before I could catch and interrogate the thought, it came and went: *Maybe it all wasn't so bad.*

I had made an enemy of nostalgia. I was dedicated and vigilant. It found me anyway.

_____

If the purpose of memory is to learn, what is the purpose of nostalgia? To cope.

Nostalgia — from Greek, *nostos* and *algos*, the pain of returning home. The wish to go back and find things as you left them, when you know that you can't go back. You may realize they were never that way at all, that you long for a home that never existed. It's a peculiar state — doctors used to think it was a disease — and still scholars debate whether nostalgia is healthy or maladaptive, whether it encourages social bonds and acts as an emotional balm in hard times or signals a poor adaptation to life's changes or trauma.

I know people are more likely to see the past as happier than it was as we age. But I want to remember things as they truly were, so I fight the siren song of nostalgia.

Of course, there are times I feel nostalgic for genuinely good times. I feel a warm ache when I hear the albums Mia played in the evenings of our first Oregon summer; when I remember my brother as a baby, his eyes growing heavy before he nodded off on my shoulder; when I find old photo-booth filmstrips of Ryan and me. These moments are not as complicated as others, like when I remember falling asleep with Al on his worn recliner in his office, long before he went away. Less warmth, more ache, because I know what comes after.

But there are times I wish I'd stop resisting. Then nostalgia would work its magic. I might become a person who owns sweatshirts from their alma mater, who cheers for the football team and shares throwback photos, who maintains decades-old friendships for the sake of the tradition. But I can't. I keep my watch.

My parents are polar opposites when it comes to nostalgia. Al ignores all but the good times that he remembers or invents, the highlights, the hits. That's where he lives; his longing for the old days seems so great that there's no barrier between his present and his past.

Mia feels none of the nostalgia she hears about from her sister. They had the same childhood, the same struggles, and yet Jackie can reminisce on Facebook. She can stay in touch with Joey and all their old friends from the old neighborhood. Mia knows no one from her past, and she likes it that way. She has a few nice moments that she keeps close to her, but the rest looms too large. What she can't will herself to forget, she boards up and leaves behind.

Looking at my parents, I saw two paths: You ignore the past, or you want it back. Is there no other option?

I think there is. I opened myself up to the past, let it consume me, and found a way forward as I build a new life for myself. My mind finds new places to wander, and I let it roam. I am not so haunted by my father, not anymore.

Lately, when I do think of Al and our double grave, there is no great sadness. I mostly feel relief. Panic comes only when I imagine myself, decades from now, falling victim again to sentiment. Trusting my imperfect memory to show me Al as he was. Letting the thought cross my mind: *Maybe it all wasn't so bad.* Going back to my father and believing time and age might change him. Going back to see if it might turn out this time.

But I won't, I tell myself. *I won't go back. I won't let myself forget.*

Nostalgia does good for our relationships with ourselves and others, for our *self-positivity* and *social connectedness*. The narcissist is likely to care far more about the former than the latter. In fact, studies show that nostalgia doesn't serve its social-connectedness function for grandiose narcissists. So when I wonder how Al remembers, and what he gets from his memories, and why he chooses to live in the past, I can understand. And when I wonder how he remembers me, and what those memories mean for him, and what self-positivity he can drain out of them, I can understand.

I'm a little surprised that I don't feel any nostalgia I need to resist when it comes to Al. I feel something for Frankie, my little self. But for my father? The memories don't carry any kind of spell for me, even as time widens the space between him and me.

When nostalgia finally finds me vulnerable, as I am now — when it strikes me between the ribs, as it has now — I'm in a place I never thought I'd be. After all, I never imagined I would choose to leave Ryan.

I left in the summer, a few months before my thirtieth birthday.

I wasn't planning on it. The whole thing took us both by surprise. I came home one night and couldn't stop sobbing. I thought I needed a break, that I might need to be somewhere else for a while. I had the feeling that I might not be able to hold on anymore. I took it all back when I saw Ryan's face. I told him to please forget what I said. I didn't know what I was talking about. But the next night, I crossed the threshold of our apartment and burst into tears. I had to go.

The leaving itself was sudden, but looking at it from a distance I could see that there was a kind of accumulation taking place.

Yes, I had been lonely. I had been depressed. I had been suffering from my compulsions. But I was working on it, and everything was looking up. I had gotten everything I ever wanted: a clean, warm, happy home that I owned; a job that made that home possible; a partner I loved, with whom I got to share that home. I was putting myself out there, making new friends. I was trying.

But loneliness has a way of coming out sideways. And I spent a lot of time alone. Ryan had his studio practice, and every week or so he'd end up pulling an all-nighter or two, letting himself get swept into the flow of his work. Sometimes I got a little blue after a couple of nights by myself. But I was all right. I had a rich inner life, I thought. Still, from where I stand now, I can see that I was doing weird shit. If I knew I was spending a weeknight alone, I'd sit at my desk in the newsroom until the cleaners had come and gone, wandering around the building like a ghost. Or I'd hunt down a happy hour, clinging to shreds of affection from the new friends I made. I made them playlists and bound them handmade books. I was always there for the last round, no matter how early a meeting I had the next day, trying to cajole everyone into *just one more* without seeming too pathetic. Then I'd make my way home, drowning out the silence with the same three documentaries on repeat. I'd trade my suit jacket and trousers for my "inside clothes" — usually covered in old paint or ink, always subway-germ-free. I'd feed the boys, make myself air-popped popcorn for dinner, and fall asleep in my jeans.

I didn't think anyone could see through my act. But one of my friends, a fellow reporter, saw something and said something. We were wrapping up a deep talk over coffee about families, generational cycles, and where our lives had led us. I alluded to all my past struggles: with love and relationships, with grief and shame, with loneliness. I spoke of all of them in the past tense, breezily, as if I wasn't lying awake at night reading the terms of my life insurance policy — arranged to be split three ways, among Ryan, my brother, and Mia — and doing the mental math of whether I was worth more dead or alive. I'd forgotten about one of the hazards of befriending another journalist: setting off the finely tuned bullshit detector.

"I think you're lying to yourself. I think you're really lonely."

It wasn't an indictment or an insult, nothing like that. It was just an observation, something seen and shared. For me, it held up a mirror and let me get a good look.

Something inside me cracked open that day. I was afraid. I walked all the way home from my office in Midtown to our uptown apartment. And when I made it into our home, my body knew I was leaving before I did. All the sobbing I did that I couldn't understand.

If I am honest with myself, I was lying to myself. I tried to sublimate my needs. I tried very hard for a very long time. And I was not strong enough to continue. I loved my husband. I wanted to take care of him. I wanted to grow old with him. I still have all the love, and I still mourn that path that I wasn't strong enough to take, the life that I've taken away from us both. But I knew if I had carried on, the love would have rotted from the inside out as my loneliness and exhaustion turned into resentment and bitterness and contempt. I couldn't bear to witness such a cruel disintegration, let alone be complicit in it. I believe I will never forgive myself for what I've done to us, for what I've chosen to do.

I tried to describe — poorly — what had compelled me to leave during a session with Ryan and our therapist. The only analogy I could think of was a game of Double Dutch — a game I've never played. I had been on the edge of something for a long time, something I didn't understand. I could only feel surges of urgency from time to time, like counting the slaps of the ropes on the pavement, trying to make sense of the rhythm as you look for an opening to jump in. But the ropes twirled too quickly, and an opening never presented itself, so I stayed in the dark, aware only of that rhythm I didn't understand. Then there was a beat — an opening — and instinct took over. My body knew before I did. I took the opening. I jumped. I got a hotel room that weekend, and I never went home again.

For weeks I lived in hotels and short-term rentals, seeing Ryan each week during our regular couples therapy session — which had become "uncoupling" therapy. We wrestled through the question of why, figured out how to move forward through the separation, made space for all our grief.

Early on, I had to contend with the possibility that my blowing up our life together was self-destructive. Ryan suggested it might've been, or at least that it was rash. But I didn't think it was a giant act of self-harm or some premature midlife crisis. All the same, I questioned myself the entire summer. For all the relief I felt at being lonely by choice instead of by circumstance, I was homesick. I imagined taking the train back uptown and using my keys to let myself in and curling up on the couch as if I'd never left. It was torturous, the lure of comfort and an end to the suffering I was doing alone in southern Brooklyn, in a neighborhood I didn't know.

I thought of Ryan back at home, alone. However difficult it was for me to be away, I knew the pain of living among the remains must've been worse. I imagined him tending my garden without me. After my leaving, he mentioned that he was keeping up with it. I had always hoped it would be something we'd do together, maybe on lazy Sunday mornings. But it never came together like I'd imagined, and I gardened alone.

And I thought of the Study, my chair and my desk. My library, my circulation cards, all gathering dust. I thought of our cats, whom we'd have to separate. I thought of every single thing I loved about Ryan, every time he made me laugh, the sound of his keys in the door when he came home.

It's only a train ride away. The siren song. *You're so close. Why torture yourself? Why not go home?*

I knew I couldn't go back. If I did, I would only do something worse in the long run.

And here, the doubt comes in. Could I trust my memories? The ones that underpin my understanding of why I had to leave, could they be distorted by my ever-fallible mind?

And here, the nostalgia. It's always the same playbook: It dims the lights and fires up the projector. There it is: the supercut, the highlight reel, moments representative of everything you love about this person, every hope and dream you ever shared with them, all on an endless loop.

See? This is what you had, what you threw away. This is how it all really was. You can't trust all those other memories, all that fake shit you've been playing back in your head.

Its tone alternates; it keeps you off kilter; its voice beckons, then it mocks.

See? You think these are rose-tinted, but you're wrong. That's just what reality looked like. All those other memories, those are the filtered ones. Just look what you've done to them! All drab and washed out, you stripped them of all their color — you and your bad attitude.

I couldn't help but notice that I was the one doing the leaving. That had never been my modus operandi, historically speaking. The men in my life, more often than not, are the ones who end up out the door first. I think back to that breakup with Justin — *we were really just kids then, was I ever so young?* — and that night he came home, did the dishes, and left. This time, I was the one who came home and shook the foundation. And I think of that Christmas Day, the leaving, my first memory. How Al might've felt, coming home and finding the apartment empty.

These parallels do little for me, but ruminating about them is something to do. They come and go regardless, whether I ask them to or not. I might as well watch them as they float through, like looking for shapes in the passing clouds.

I still feel what I felt in the summer, in the immediate aftermath of my leaving.

I believe I will never forgive myself for what I've done to us, for what I've chosen to do.

That belief is now joined by a new fear.

I will never forgive myself. I'm afraid that I might.

28

On Cycles

Myths are all about cycles, parallels, iterations of the universal. I don't go looking for them, like I go out searching for everything else. And yet I find them everywhere.

Some of them aren't too hard to spot, like in Al's cycle of fatherhood. I'll take one liberty; I'll ask you to set aside the fact that he has *three* children — me, his son born a couple of years after me, and Andie. But right now, we're dealing with daughters.

One. Al's daughter was born in October 1994.
Two. She's given a boyish nickname: Frankie.
Three. Al went to prison when she was nine years old.

We know the rest from there. Now, the reiterations:

One. Al's daughter was born in October 2013.
It's statistically insane, in my view, that he managed to have a daughter on the exact same day *again*. But the next recurrence wasn't chance or fate.

Two. She's given a boyish nickname: Andie.
This was a choice. This is where the tension built for me. As she and I both grew older, in our separate worlds that over-

lapped for only a couple of cumulative weeks, I thought often about her ninth birthday. Reminded me of *Sleeping Beauty* and how those fairies must have ruminated with each passing year over the prophecy, asking whether the princess would prick her finger on that spinning wheel before she turned — what was it, sixteen? My birthday would come and go. I would tell people how old I was that day, and in my head I'd do the arithmetic. *Three more years. Two more years. One more* — I hoped Al wouldn't continue the cycle, make an innocent kid suffer simply because he, who was her father, couldn't manage to live an honest life. I'd done my time already, and I would never wish it on her.

Three. Andie's ninth birthday came and went. Al remained free.

Here the pattern is broken. I feel slightly ashamed to say that Al surprised me. I'll admit that I felt bitterness toward him — for doing something right by his daughter, the one who isn't me.

I never set out to tell this story because I hate my father. I'm telling this story because I loved him once. Here, I'll add a postscript. I don't think I ever hated Al. I think I had other complex emotions. I think I held a lot of grief. But if I ever hated him, it's for this: When Andie was young and I was back in Chicago, he was careless. He built me up in stories he told her before I even landed at O'Hare. She called me her "big sissy." He had her draw me pictures. She looked at me with curiosity and affection. I returned it as honestly as I could. But I knew my visits with her would only last as long as my tolerance for Al. By cutting Al off for good, I'd cut her off, too. I imagined telling him off to his face: *How dare you make her love me, only to force my hand in leaving you. How dare you do that to her. How dare you make me hurt her. How dare you make me like you.*

It's only fair to reckon with my side of that street, too, and answer for the sins that are mine and mine alone.

How dare you exploit that poor girl, reduce her to a narrative object, a symbol, a foil. Yes, oh yes, you have the right to your truth, to tell your story, but let's not shit ourselves here. You've treated her like an object since the day she was born — first as a symbol of your father's selfishness and your own rotten luck, then as a lightning rod for your own bitterness. Now you can't leave her out of it, let her be an innocent kid? You didn't bring her into the world, we all know that. But do you have to bring her into this world? Do you have to be such a piece of shit about it?

When I light up outside the newsroom on a cold fall day, I catch my reflection in a window. For a moment, I see Al's face in mine. No matter how hard I try myself not to notice, I can't not see it.

I take a drag and stare into my own eyes. *How dare you.* I blow the smoke in my face. I'm left unsatisfied. I want to kick in my own teeth.

I'll spend my life waiting for that other shoe to drop, if it ever does: One day Andie will come searching for me. I will tell her what I know. I will tell her what I've done. I will be honest. This is her right, and I will never refuse her.

I return to the same question when I think about my father. *What happens when you outlive your own myth?*

Is that what Al has done, by managing to stick around for his daughter this time? Is that what he has done by reclaiming his former glory and rebuilding his gym — only now he's old?

I turn the question over in my mind. I wonder if it applies to me. What happens when you outlive your own myth? What happens when your cycle ends and you have to keep on living?

I've determined that it does, in fact, apply. Because I showed you where I wish I could've cut the film, the ending I would have preferred. It was an ending that made sense, that would let

me leave you on a high note. I had broken out of so many familial cycles: I'd found someone I loved, whom I could take care of.
I was married; we owned an apartment; I had a good job in New
York City. We could all see where it was going: children, grand-
children, a long happy marriage, a long prosperous career. It'd
all play out for you up on that stage, on the big screen, whatever
you want it to be. The credits roll, or the cast takes their bows.
The theater goes dark for a while, and then we're back where I
first met you: *Autumn in Oregon was hopeless . . .*

Again and again, around and around, performance after
performance, night after night. That's what I could've had, if
only I had a stronger stomach for deception. Every word I told
you would have been true, but I would have been telling you a
lie.

Now I feel like I've burst through some barrier to some
unknown other side. That cycle is going on without me, without the actor, and I'm somewhere else. I'm watching from the
wings or standing in the aisle, or smoking in the back. I'm not
on the stage.

Some cycles seem to be an infinite loop, a road we don't know
we're traveling along, one that takes us down the same path
time and again. I'll try to show you what I mean. During one of
my last visits to Portland, I was going through my childhood
notebooks when I found two letters I'd written to Al while he
was in prison, when I was eleven. Obviously, I never sent them.
The ruled paper I'd printed them out on wasn't even folded. I
must've just forgotten. Judging by how the letter started, I had
a lot of other stuff going on:

> Dear Dad,
> How are you? I'm good. The house still isn't finished yet
> and my baby brother's sick. He has an ear infection, a
> fever, and diareah. And he hasn't eaten a lot and he keeps

on throwing up after he does. We're taking him to the doctor again.

Anyway, school is fine, too. On Friday we're having a Martin Luther King, Jr. assembly. We had to memorize an excerpt from the Constitution and a part of the "I Have a Dream" speech. It was pretty easy to do.

It was the rest of the letter that knocked me back:

It's been raining a lot here, too. But rain here is different: It doesn't pour, like in Chicago. It sort of drizzles, but long enough to make everything muddy. And when it's raining, it's not FREEZING cold, but warm enough so I can go outside with only a sweatshirt.

That was the same phenomenon that had gnawed at me during my college years in Eugene. I had watched it from a window in my mind; if I sat in a certain spot just so, keeping very still, I could see it floating in full view. I had struggled for a long time to find the words to capture it, to put it down. *Hopeless. That's what it was.*

I'd sat there at that window for so long, and kept so still, and yet — not once did I have an inkling that I'd ever been there before. As hard as I've searched, I've never come up with the memory. Where could it have gone?

How could I not remember? That all those years ago, when I was still a kid, I had found that same spot. I'd sat there, perched just so. And I had been moved in the same way. I had to find the words, put it down.

It seemed miraculous. If I hadn't found the letter, I wouldn't be able to believe it.

And yet, there was the proof.

_____

29

She and I

When I tell people about this story, and my writing it down, they're surprised that Al is alive. Then they're surprised that Al and I are estranged. Then they become deeply, visibly uncomfortable when I tell them that he did not love me, that I will never see him again in my life, and that I'm sure of it.

I try to explain. If I have my way — and I intend to — we will both continue to live in our respective realms, keeping to our own sides of the street, then he will die. I might be given advance notice that the time is approaching, that I might want to fly in, to say my piece, to see him one more time. A misguided kindness. An offer I will refuse. Then once he is dead, there will be a funeral and a burial and the Family will gather. I won't be there. _Her own father's funeral_, someone will say. _How could she miss her own father's funeral?_

All of that is to say that our final encounter has come and gone. I will never speak to him again. I've seen him alive for the last time. This is simply a matter of fact. I've done my grieving. No more Al. Not for me.

My voice isn't cold when I explain this, but people look as though I've confessed to killing him myself. Or they look at me pityingly, as if I were a mother keeping watch over a hospital bed, looking at a flat line and swearing I still feel a pulse. They see that I am being honest, that I believe what I'm saying is true, but they know that the illusion will not hold, that I'm not in my right mind, that this is a temporary truth I need to get through in this moment in time, and they need to tread lightly.

When they do speak, it pisses me off.

They say: *You feel that way now, but you'll never really know until that day comes. And by then, you might not feel this way. Who knows?*

I say: "Who knows? *I* do. *I* know. Right now."

Of course. (Again, the pity.) But when it actually happens . . . just saying, you shouldn't feel bad if you change your mind.

"It's not about feeling bad. I just know that I won't feel any differently *then* than I do *now*."

This insufferable dialogue I go through with well-meaning friends, people I respect, people I love — it makes me want to bite their heads off. I want to scream. And then there is a shift. I want nothing more than to be silent. The rage appears extinguished; it has only amplified. My interlocutor fills the new empty space with more of their shit ideas. I remain sociable. I nod along in the barest form of conversational response. But I do not speak.

The only person I've given a bye to on this was Ryan. We'd been married nearly a year when he lost his loving and beloved dad — a sudden end to a long illness. I bore witness to his pain and his sorrow, and the new forms his love took in the face of grief. We watched the ceiling lights flicker, knowing his father was still with us, on some plane. Such profound loss is never a temporary burden to carry; it's not a dark cloud that looms heavy before it lifts. You are changed, and you can never go back. Can you *imagine*, then, if I'd spouted off my own righteous feelings? If I'd told him that Al's eventual death sure will be a relief for me, that the prospect of time lived without my dad was a gift I couldn't wait for? It'd be quicker if I just spat in his face and got it over with. I could never do that to him. Anyone else, though, they were not spared. They got my silence.

I did find some cynical humor in all the pushback. *Really?* I thought. *Do we really have to do this? Don't you know me? That I feel crippling doubt about everything I've ever thought or believed or heard or known, and yet* this — *the* one *thing I am certain of, in my entire fucking life* — this *is the thing you can't accept?*

Yes, I find this infuriating. But I'm still willing to break it down for those who want to understand it: When I survey my life, when I take it all in and tally it all up, I find that Al has only ever made my life worse. Really. He's never made it better. Sure, he bought me an ice cream cone here and there. Once I got a PlayStation. That momentary jolt of childish glee, that shit doesn't count. And even if it did, it wouldn't even tip the scales.

I don't have fond memories of Al — not genuine fondness. Yes, there is warmth. Yes, I did love my father. But the overarching sentiment that remains, across all of our time together, is one of seeking — always one-sided, never fulfilled. I remember how he made me feel stupid, invisible, guilty, ashamed. I remember how deeply I sank into a depressive episode that I thought would last forever. I remember how sick I made myself, all in pursuit of him.

And do I remember how I felt, when I chose to cut our lives together short? When I evaluated the toll of cutting my dad off forever, compared with the damage he could do if I left the lines open? I do remember — I suppose you could call it a feeling, whatever it was. Or a reflex, untethered by any conscious thought, like a primal survival instinct. If I had to put it into words?

Only one of us gets to live. It's either you or me.

My mother isn't a huge fan of hearing me say these thoughts out loud. I believe we share that disease of doubt, the worry that our thoughts have power beyond our understanding. So it's understandable that it's not her favorite thing to talk about. But she's the only person who understands me when I tell her what I told the others: That I know this will be an enduring truth. That no-more-Al is a dependent condition of my life now. That I know I will never go back.

Sometimes she apologizes to me, for not giving me a better father in Al or in Keith. I reject her apologies. I refuse to entertain them; she has nothing to apologize for.

Missing my mom was a near-constant state when I was a kid. It didn't matter where I was or who I was with. There was a timer in my chest that started the moment I hugged her goodbye, marking the minutes we were apart. I never knew when it would go off, though it was usually at night. My chest and throat would tighten and grow hot and I would cry, gulping air between silent sobs. My hands would grow numb and cramp up, curling into stiff fists I couldn't break.

The fear didn't have a name. I wasn't haunted by *what if*s like car accidents or break-ins or heart attacks. It just echoed back the obvious: *She isn't here.* My mom was what kept a small, comfortable warmth burning somewhere between my ribs. Once that timer went off, it snuffed out the flame and flooded my lungs with something cold and dark. *This is what dying will feel like,* I thought.

It's not quite right to say my mother, Mia, was — is — everything to me. She was part of the machine that kept me running, as essential as brain or blood. The problem was that she existed outside of my body. Without her, I didn't know what I was, or whether I was. All I knew was the need.

My fear of death was what set off the panic attacks I started having when I was in middle school. Mia believed in reincarnation, and at first it was a comfort. But my mind eventually found the concept's vulnerability and turned me against it. *If you're reborn, you'll still lose Mia. And — even worse — you won't remember her.*

But maybe I will, I'd argue. Maybe it's a special case.

Or maybe you won't. You don't remember your life before this one, if you even had one. Why would it be any different? But hey — at least you don't have to die for real, forever.

Reincarnation had stretched out its hand to me, a way out of my existential terror. But I couldn't pay that price. I refused politely: *I'll stick with the panic attacks, but thanks anyway.*

If Al was the cosmic price I had to pay to be born to Mia, I'd pay it happily. Are you kidding? I'd ask the world to try a little harder. Go find some greater suffering for me to take on — and put your best men on it. Even then, I doubt they would find any punishment that could come close to the weight and worth of my reward. Every beautiful moment of my life has had her in it. All I want to do is be in her presence. It's simple. I have always been happiest when I'm looking at her.

If myth is the condensation of our human experience, stories that elevate human meaning to its most extreme, boil it down to its most concentrated form, then we are our own myth, Mia and I, together. I claim authority I don't have — I don't need it, either. I know it. She is the only mother the world has ever seen. I am her only daughter. We went through the cycles, what we thought we could not bear. We came through the other side.

I was always amazed that Mia managed to hold on to so many artifacts of my childhood, my brother's childhood, and the life we three share. Not too long ago, during a springtime visit of mine to Portland, we brought up the boxes from the basement and exhumed our past.

I happened to be alone in Mia's living room when I pulled out a blue hardcover book with a sweet illustration on the cover: a stuffed bear looking up at the night sky, at the crescent moon. I let the book fall open, and on the page was a translucent dried flower. It fluttered for a moment. I'd recognize the handwriting anywhere:

I love you with all my heart. You picked a pink flower for
me today — I'll keep it forever. I love you, Mommy.

Weeks later, back in New York, I sent her two large arrangements of flowers for Mother's Day. I had spent hours comparing bouquets, despondent. Every offering from every florist
each failed to capture her vitality in one way or another. Eventually I found a match that I could live with, that I thought
she would enjoy. The shop's website wanted to know: What
message did I want the accompanying card to bear?

The cursor blinked; the text box remained empty for some
time. There I sat, at my desk in the Study, as I confronted the
vastness of *she and I*.

Mia and I both share an understanding that our love is too
great to be contained by language. It is too vast to hold in one
metaphysical space. It has its own atmosphere, its own gravi-
tational pull; it expands; it permeates veils seen and unseen.
It contains quantum properties, like entanglement: an inextri-
cable link between particles, transcending vast distances, not
needing any kind of communication.

The analogy works. It gives an idea. And still the gap remains
as wide as when you began, the lacuna between what it is and
the rough outline that language forms around it.

I knew better than to waste time on a lasso to try to catch it.
I knew better than to cut down a piece of the vastness, some
small part within reach, to examine under a lens. So I left my
tools alone. I reached for my phone. I reread a message from
Mia that I'd nearly memorized. She'd sent it days after my last
birthday, out of the blue in the middle of the afternoon:

> My thoughts every day:
>   I would have picked you if I had the chance.
>   It would have been my best decision.
>   You would have been the friend I talked about to other
> people with pride.

I would have been better just for knowing you.

I like to believe we chose each other in a different realm, consciously. It keeps me entertained and either way I win.

love always,

mom

I wiped my eyes, turned back to the florist's note, and I wrote what was true:

You are the greatest love of my life, and I am so lucky.

———

30

The Man, the Myth

Estrangement is an end, but it's not absolute. It makes strange ghosts of the ones who choose to leave and the ones who are left behind. There can never be a clean break; it's one of the troubles of burying the living.

I was familiar with this state of being, this ghostliness. When I had a stepfather, I also had a stepfamily — aunts, uncles, grandparents. The entire clan ended up moving to Portland from Chicago. As I grew up, we all spent the holidays together; we took trips as a unit to the coast or Mount Hood; they came to my school plays. Most of them vanished as soon as Keith decided we should *call this what it is*. Who knows how much they know about any of it. But they're left with the remains of me all the same. I sit, frozen in time, in their wedding albums and the Christmas photos that can't be cropped. Newcomers will flip through them, and my unfamiliar face will give them pause.

Who's this? the innocent offender will ask. Someone will clear their throat. Someone will try to explain, in their own way, who I was to them and why I am not there now. The offender will think what they think, and wonder what they wonder. They might wish they'd kept their mouth shut.

So now I am a ghost to my father, and he to me. But the veil is permeable, and he finds ways to reach through.

Before I blocked him, I used to get texts and calls regularly from beyond the grave. My radio silence didn't seem to deter him from liking each of my Instagram stories. I wanted him to stop, but I managed to live with the ghost that blew up my phone for a while. It became easier to tune out the notifications, to dampen my anxiety. *He can ring the bell all he wants*, I thought at the time. *There's no way in hell I'm digging him back up.*

Once he had no way to get to me digitally, he put in minimal effort to reach me through the grapevine — primarily through Mia's sister, Jackie, who saw through him immediately. She did show me a photo of his car completely wrecked. I didn't get the details on the cause of the accident, but I remember how the front was completely crushed in. Apparently, he'd had to be saved by the Jaws of Life.

There were other minor miracles. He survived some kind bacterial infection in his arm. And not too long ago, he made a Facebook post about having an aneurysm burst — but I can't tell you if it's true. I had nothing to verify it.

Let's pretend all three are true. How was Al, of all people, managing to cheat death so brazenly? I couldn't believe it.

While I was searching his Facebook to find any proof of the aneurysm, I saw a photo collage of four mugshots. I recognized two faces: One was Al's, the other was Rick's. *Once upon a time in Chicago*, the caption read.

Should've shot Rick, my ass, I thought.

I didn't know I had it in me to still be surprised by Al, but the posts' comments proved otherwise. Someone asked to hear about some of Al's criminal lore, his greatest hits, and he delivered. I gathered that he was referencing the Hicks case. (I cleaned up his social-media-speak, which is borderline unreadable.)

Got a 30-minute crime show made about me — Untrue. He probably meant the *America's Most Wanted* spot that aired about Hicks. I doubt Al was even mentioned. He was just a guy who knew a guy.

And when I got sentenced to four years, literally five minutes later the prosecuting attorney asked me out and gave me her number — The prosecutor, Sonny Pascual, was a nice guy! But he was not, in fact, a woman, and he certainly never hit on my dad.

And later two head cops on the case killed themselves after getting busted — Never happened.

God, I forgot how exhausting this was. Who's buying any of this shit?

It doesn't matter. I see that now. Al only cares that his name is on the marquee and that he's the one who gets to take the final bow. The standing ovations, the roars and applause — even in a silent theater, he'll hear it in his head.

So go ahead, everybody — give it up for my dad, Al Fontana. The man . . . the myth . . . It's all the same to him.

31

_____

Christmas Time Is Here

Chicago, December 2000

In the truck, Al turned on the heat and the window wipers to clear away the light snow that had gathered on the glass while they were in the mall. Frankie reached for the radio dial.

Christmas time is here . . .

Al snuck a glance at Frankie as he pulled out of the parking lot for the Chicago Ridge Mall and onto Ridgeland Avenue. He started singing along in an earnest falsetto. She giggled as Al's voice cracked and strained for the high notes. By the time the second bridge came around, they had settled down. Frankie felt the warmth of the laughter linger in her chest. Something else tugged there, too.

> *Sleigh bells in the air*
> *Beauty everywhere*
> *Yuletide by the fireside*
> *And joyful memories there.*

The light was low by the time Al pulled up outside Mia's house in the suburbs. In the passenger seat, Frankie carried old grocery bags full of all the paper planes they folded back at the Gym. He helped Frankie out of the truck.

"Careful, baby, there's ice." Al hugged Frankie tight as her mother appeared in the doorway. "Love you, baby girl." Mia waved; he waved back.

His phone rang out as his daughter ran up the porch steps. It was Larry Knitter, calling about that job he might be interested in — whether Al would want to go on a ride with his crew. He silenced the call; he'd deal with it later. Al watched Frankie stomp the snow from her shoes. She turned back and smiled. She waved; he waved back. Then she was gone.

32

———

False Starts

I've been a bit blue so far this autumn. The long dark nights probably aren't helping. Neither is the separation heartbreak. And when I sleep, I've been having those dreams again, the ones where I've killed my father and I wake up sweating. So I'm not sleeping too much at the moment. I put off going to bed instead. I find small, quiet things to do with the time. I put out fresh candlesticks, reorganize my library, iron my pajamas.

When I do sleep, it's not for long. I emerge from some somnambulistic reverie to find that I'm standing in my kitchen, or sitting on the couch. I'm impressed by my sleepwalking self, who never forgets to put on our indoor shoes. Jiji doesn't seem to mind my wanderings. He follows me like a shadow and curls up next to me wherever I end up in the night. I listen to his sleeping breath, soft and slow, while I wait for daybreak.

I recognize this feeling. I remember pulling up the corners of my mouth to trick my brain into happiness all those years ago. The hopelessness comes and it goes. I think it always will. Just as the shame comes and it goes, and the remembering. I can live with it. I will live with it.

Christmas is still my favorite time of year. I don't understand how my love for the holiday can endure all of the layered, painful complications. We left Al on Christmas Day. The day my life began, according to my memory. Ryan and I eloped on

Christmas Eve. I still have our handwritten vows from that day. All that love still lives in me. It hurts more this way, more than it would if I had let it all rot first. But I never want to let it die.

I think of the love I had for my father. I loved my father for a long time. Until I didn't. That love doesn't live in me anymore. I packed it gently into the ground.

I'd be lying if I said there wasn't anything else left inside me, in the aftermath of all the loss. But there it was — something like happiness or hope, only feral. Territorial. It bares its teeth, guarding the feeling of freedom within it. It won't let you get too close, and yet it wants to see you try — it dares anyone to try to take it away. It's a clawing, spitting, wild-eyed resolve to live.

To feel like some good has come from the hurt I've caused — all the collateral damage — it's shameful. I want to hide it from you. That's why I'm telling you.

Each Christmas, at some quiet moment, I find myself making the same trip. I can't help it. I wander all the way back to the start of my memory. I stand in all of the dark that came before, the curtain before it rises.

There, in the dark, I wonder what my life would be like if I had a different first memory — instead of the leaving. I wonder who I would be. Then I wonder if my brain could ever, if only for a minute, just shut the fuck up.

When I hear that song, "Christmas Time Is Here," I think of my father. There were years I'd skip past the song on holiday playlists, turn off the radio once I recognized the melody. Now I let it play.

ACKNOWLEDGMENTS

The Family Snitch is my first book. It would not exist outside of myself without the love, support, encouragement, and generosity of so many. I will try to name all of the individuals and institutions to whom I owe my gratitude.

Brent Walth, whose guidance and support put me on the path, whose encouragement gave me strength when I needed it most.

My agent Elias Altman, whose belief in the book never wavered; my wonderful editor Chip Fleischer and the whole team at Steerforth Press; and the phenomenal Aileen Boyle.

Everyone at *The Wall Street Journal* who supported and shepherded my 2019 story, including Mike Miller, Gary Rosen, Matt Murray, Matthew Rose, Lisa Kalis, Emily Gitter, Karen and Jim Pensiero. Special thanks to photographer Lucy Hewett.

Ryan, who gave me his grace, showed me how to be an artist, and taught me how to see.

My dear friends: Emon, Michael, Dave, Charlotte, Emil. And thank you to my two early readers: to Allison, for turning on the light; to Ben, for shooting straight.

I would not have had the means to start my journey without the support of the University of Oregon, the School of Journalism and Communication, the Robert D. Clark Honors College, and the UO's Humanities Undergraduate Research Fellowship.

My family: Mia and Omri — and Jiji, my sweetest friend.

Mams. I wish you were here to hold the book in your hands. I wish I could hold you here, too.

Frankie — for being such a cool kid, a real fighter, and letting me visit sometimes.